The New Local Government Series
No. 17

A HISTORY OF LOCAL GOVERNMENT
IN THE TWENTIETH CENTURY

The New Local Government Series
Series Editor: Professor Peter G. Richards

A HISTORY OF
LOCAL GOVERNMENT IN THE
TWENTIETH CENTURY

BY

BRYAN KEITH-LUCAS

*Emeritus Professor of Government
University of Kent at Canterbury*

AND

PETER G. RICHARDS

*Professor of British Government
University of Southampton*

London
GEORGE ALLEN & UNWIN
Boston   Sydney

First published in 1978

© George Allen & Unwin (Publishers) Ltd, 1978

British Library Cataloguing in Publication Data

Keith-Lucas, Bryan
    A history of local government in the twentieth
century. – (The new local government series;
no. 17).
    1. Local government – England – History
    I. Title · II. Richards, Peter Godfrey
    III. Series
352.042   JS3091   77–30536

ISBN 0 04 352070 7 hardback
      0 04 352071 5 paperback

Printed in Great Britain by Biddles Ltd, Guildford, Surrey

PREFACE

In writing this book we have had generous help from many people. A number have given us the benefit of their recollections of events in the history of local government, including Sir Harold Banwell and Sir James Swaffield, former secretaries of the AMC, Mr S. Rhodes, secretary of the District Councils Association, Mr C. Arnold-Baker, secretary of the National Association of Local Councils, Mr L. W. V. Brown, of the Association of County Councils, and Mr Wentworth Pritchard, of Sharpe Pritchard & Co., all of whom granted us interviews. Many others helped us by correspondence, including Sir Rupert Speir, Mr C. J. Pearce of the Department of the Environment, Mr A. C. Hetherington, secretary of the Association of County Councils, Mr R. G. Puffitt, of Inlogov, Professor Ivor Gowan of Aberystwyth, Mr Derek Senior, Lord Alexander of Potterhill, Mr Dillwyn Miles of Haverfordwest, Mr E. J. O. Gardiner and Mr K. Poole. Mr David Peschek, the editor of *The Municipal Review*, who is also a Leverhulme Research Fellow undertaking a study of the politics of local government reform in England, has made valuable comments on Chapters IX, X and XI. Mr Stuart Millar has commented on Chapter III; similarly Mr Noel Hepworth on Chapter VII.

We are also grateful to Mr L. J. Slocombe and Mr C. A. Cross, former town clerk of Prestwich, who allowed us to use their theses, and to Messrs Sweet & Maxwell for agreeing to our using an article from their journal, *Public Law*, which forms the substance of Chapter III.

We also acknowledge with gratitude the help given to us by Miss Diana Marshallsay in preparing the bibliography and the index, and by our two secretaries, Mrs Joan Denning and Mrs Elizabeth Hampson.

CONTENTS

Chapter I

INTRODUCTION

The choice of the year 1901 as the starting point for this history of local government may seem arbitrary, or facile. In fact, it is a suitable date to choose for it did mark a turning point in history.

Queen Victoria died in January 1901. There were few of her subjects who had, even in infancy, lived under any other monarch. Gladstone had just died, in 1898. The Boer War (1899–1902) was shattering the public complacency about the power of British arms. Fears of the dissolution of the Empire were beginning to stir in men's minds. The Liberal Party was about to blossom in its magnificent reforming splendour, before its slow decay set in, while in 1900 there was established the Labour Representation Committee, which led to the rise of the Parliamentary Labour Party.

In the field of government the turn of the century was significant. The nineteenth century had seen a dramatic revolution in British administration. Parliament had been transformed so that it bore little resemblance to the assembly of gentlemen of the unreformed House of Commons. The Reform Acts of 1832 and 1867 had made it, more or less, a popularly elected body; party organisation had changed the very nature of politics. So too in local government. The strange administration of eighteenth-century England had been totally replaced. The reform of the Poor Law in 1834, and of the municipal corporations in 1835, started a long succession of legislation changing the whole shape of local administration. By the end of the century there had been established that pattern of counties, boroughs, county boroughs, urban districts, rural districts and parishes which was to survive, scarcely changed, until 1974. All were elected by a broad popular franchise, from which women were not excluded; property qualifications for councillors had been abolished, and Dr Redlich, the historian of English local government, was able to proclaim that

'the grand principle of representative democracy has been fully applied to local government, and securely established by the series of measures which culminated in the Act of 1894. In

England at least, de Tocqueville's prophecy of the triumph of democratic ideas was substantially fulfilled before the close of the nineteenth century.'[1]

It was in 1901 that Redlich and Hirst's great work was first published, in German, as *Englische Lokalverwaltung*. There had been, until then, no general history of English local government, and Redlich wrote partly to confound the views of the Prussian jurisprudent, Rudolf von Gneist.[2] There has been, since then, no history of the subject which supersedes Redlich and Hirst. And so it is appropriate, for this reason too, that, with due modesty, we aim to carry on where they left off.

The institutions of local government, which Dr Redlich observed with such respect and awe, were not the outcome of any planned concept, such as Bentham had expounded, or such as Napoleon had introduced in France. They had grown, haphazard, out of the institutions of the previous centuries, adapted, adjusted and democratised. The boundaries of the counties owed more to the Anglo-Saxons and the Conqueror than they did to contemporary political scientists; the boroughs had their roots deep in the municipal institutions of the Middle Ages, in the guilds merchant and the courts leet; the poor law was still basically that of the Poor Law Act of 1601.

The county councils had been established by a somewhat reluctant Conservative administration under Lord Salisbury in 1888. They had taken over the administrative duties of Quarter Sessions, but not the judicial functions. The control of the police had, out of caution, been vested in a joint body, half county councillors, half magistrates; for the Conservative Party had feared that, as had happened after the reform of the boroughs in 1835, the new, elected, county councils would prove to be dangerously radical bodies. The revolution they feared never occurred, for the new county councils looked remarkably like the old Quarter Sessions. The county gentlemen remained in power; about half the elected councillors were already magistrates; in twenty-two counties the Chairman of Quarter Sessions was chosen as chairman of the county council; in six, the lord lieutenant was chosen; 131 peers and 87 members of the House of Commons sat on the county councils.[3]

The areas of the county councils had been taken over in detail from those of the Quarter Sessions, except in so far as the larger boroughs were excluded, as county boroughs. But a number of these had in fact previously enjoyed exemption from county jurisdiction, as counties of cities,[4] and others were not subject to the county rate. Moreover, the acceptance of the existing boundaries of the Quarter Sessions involved the continuation of a number of anomalies, such as the separate existence of the Soke of Peterborough, the Isle of Ely and West Suffolk – all survivals from the great monastic liberties of pre-Reformation days. The powers of the county councils were, however, not wide. Education and Social Services (Poor Law) were administered by other agencies. Planning was not yet conceived; most highways were the responsibility of district councils; the police were in the hands of the Standing Joint Committees. Asylums and bridges, the licensing of theatres, contagious diseases of animals, main roads, technical education, river pollution and a few other responsibilities did not add up to a very heavy burden of work. It is not surprising that, at the beginning of the century, a county council such as Wiltshire could manage with a staff of twenty-six and an annual expenditure of £133,000.[5]

The most active and effective part of local government was, without a doubt, the town councils. After the Municipal Corporations Act of 1835 the activity in the towns increased rapidly. There was much to be done in the great industrial cities, and the powers of the old Improvement Commissioners and other bodies were concentrated into the hands of the municipal corporations. Local Acts of enormous length, such as the Birmingham Act of 1851, extended the powers and duties of the council in many ways, and were copied in many Bills promoted by other councils. The borough councils became the main agents for social and sanitary progress.

The men who drafted the Local Government Bill of 1888 included ten of the largest towns in England as county boroughs, to be exempt from the jurisdiction of the new county councils. But there was pressure from many towns to be included in the list, and the county gentlemen were often quite happy to have the radicals and tradesmen of the manufacturing towns excluded from the county council. So when the Bill reached the Statute Book there were sixty-one county boroughs. What had been intended as an exception became part of the pattern.

Meanwhile many small boroughs survived, with populations and rateable values quite inadequate for their functions, some of them with a bare thousand inhabitants.

In 1894 the Local Government Act had systematised the district councils of England, and produced the patchwork of urban and rural districts which existed until 1974. The urban districts were basically those smaller towns which, though not dignified with the title and trappings of boroughs, had none the less been made responsible for their own sanitary services. Some of these were, for historical reasons, absurdly small. Childwall (Lancashire) and Kirklington-cum-Upsland (Yorkshire) had 219 and 255 inhabitants respectively.

The rural districts were, in essence, the poor law unions of parishes, less any town that had acquired a charter or urban district status. But the poor law unions had as a general rule been formed on a pattern of a 5-mile radius round a market town. That market town was, in most cases, a borough or urban district. So the typical rural district was a 5-mile circle with the centre left out. In East Anglia, however, the unit was usually based on the medieval hundreds, combined by the local act legislation of the eighteenth century into the 'Incorporated Hundreds' of Suffolk and Norfolk.

Within the rural districts were the smallest units – the parishes. These were based on the traditional ecclesiastical areas, but generally coincided with the village community, and in many cases with the old manorial areas. In the towns they had lost their functions. But in the villages the old vestries, which had been slowly stripped of their duties through the previous century, were revived by the 1894 Act as parish councils. Much was expected of them; they were to be a counterweight to the power of the vicar and the squire; they were to be village parliaments, reviving the self government of happier Anglo-Saxon days; they were to establish smallholders and peasant proprietors as a new yeomanry of England. But the powers they were given to enable them to do these things were sadly few.

But there still survived, outside this pattern of local authorities, some special bodies, responsible only for a single function. Most important of these were the Poor Law Guardians, originally established in 1834 as the responsible body for each union of parishes. Since then they had changed to some extent; the boundaries had been adjusted to fit in each case within a single county. The Act of 1894 had ended the system by which the magistrates sat as of right beside the elected guardians, and it had also abolished the property qualifications. Thus control of the Poor Law was no longer in the hands only of the well-to-do.

The provision of schools had been vested in 1870 in the school boards, elected by a system of cumulative voting which was aimed at giving substantial representation to the minorities – particularly non-conformists and Catholics. But already the future of these was in doubt, as controversy raged about their constitutions and allegedly sectarian attitudes. Their powers were transferred to the counties and county boroughs in 1902.

Such were the local authorities at the beginning of the century. It looked to many people as if an entirely satisfactory system had now been evolved – or perhaps would soon be, when the school boards and guardians had been absorbed into the general system. Central control was slight, but strong enough to create a constant resistance. The rates were the mainstay of expenditure, but bolstered by various grants in aid and the revenues assigned in 1888 from central taxation. The franchise was enjoyed by every householder, and the wealthier classes performed their local government functions with generous benevolence. Payment for this service would have seemed improper. In the counties it was normal for the chairman of the county council to be a peer or a member of a major land-owning family; in the county boroughs the manufacturers and major tradesmen played the leading part in local affairs.[6]

Even in the parish councils, there was a similar predominance of the upper and middle classes; the first elections resulted in over 60 per cent of the councillors being in these categories, and only 9 per cent were labourers and other unskilled workers.[7]

The system of local government thus appeared to be firmly established in a pattern of rational authorities, based on a universal franchise, but guided by men (and, in a few cases, women) of experience and substance. There was little to suggest that, half a century later, the whole pattern of administration would come under increasing criticism, culminating in the Royal Commission of 1966-9, and the Local Government Act of 1972. It is this change of attitude that forms the underlying theme of the history of local government from 1900 to 1974.

NOTES

1 Josef Redlich and F. W. Hirst, *Local Government in England* (1903), vol. 1, p. 215.
2 For the controversy between Redlich and von Gneist, see the introduction to the *The History of Local Government in England*, by Redlich and Hirst, ed. B. Keith-Lucas (1958).
3 B. Keith-Lucas, 'Local government in Parliament', *Public Administration*, Summer 1955, pp. 207–10.
4 Canterbury, Bristol, Southampton, Exeter, Gloucester, Worcester, Norwich, Kingston on Hull, Newcastle, Chester, Nottingham, Coventry, York, Oxford, Lincoln, Poole, Lichfield, Haverfordwest, Berwick on Tweed.
5 *Victoria County History, Wiltshire*, vol. V, pp. 267–70.
6 See J. M. Lee, *Social Leaders and Public Persons* (Cheshire), (1963);

R. V. Clements, *Local Notables and the City Council* (Bristol), (1969); G. W. Jones, *Borough Politics* (Wolverhampton), (1969); E. P. Hennock, *Fit and Proper Persons* (Birmingham and Leeds), (1973).

7　Annual Report of the Local Government Board, 1894, C 7473, xxix.

Chapter II

THE CONSTITUTION OF LOCAL AUTHORITIES

The constitutional history of the local authorities of England and Wales in the last 140 years is essentially the history of the pattern adopted in the Municipal Corporations Act of 1835. The pattern has been altered in a number of ways, but its broad outline has survived; still today the constitutions of all our local authorities reflect clearly the thinking of the Radicals of 1835, and the compromises then made with the Tory House of Lords. This framework was extended to county councils by the Local Government Act 1888 to urban district, rural district and parish councils by the Local Government Act 1894, and to London boroughs by the London Government Act 1899 – legislation which swept away the chaos of institutions that formerly dominated local administration. Thereafter each type of local authority was controlled by a series of Acts which adjusted its powers. Each individual council followed the rules of its own category. The only significant variations came from local legislation which permitted particular authorities to exercise closely defined additional powers. The rules governing the constitutional framework of all types of local authority were codified in the Local Government Act 1933.

Councils have been expected to carry out tasks of detail by forming committees. For some functions, notably police and education, the appointment of a committee has been a statutory requirement; otherwise they were optional. But the establishment of a committee system has been a dominant feature of local authorities. The statutes gave no encouragement to dynamic political leadership, as in the 'strong mayor' concept found in the United States, or to strong administrative leadership through a city manager. Nor has there been any power, such as would be allowed under an American 'Home Rule Charter' for an individual authority to change its own constitution to one which it felt would give better results. Of course, some British local authorities have experienced strong leadership, either through the personal prestige of an individual or, in more recent times, because of the power of the leader of a dominant party group.

The basis of such power is non-statutory. It rises and wanes with the fate of individuals and the flux of political opinion.

The constitutional structure which emerged from the struggle over the municipal corporations in 1835, and the subsequent adaptations of a century of experience, has been not only universal in this country, but has been reproduced widely in the Empire and Commonwealth. In India, Canada, Africa, Australia and New Zealand, the same framework has been used. Throughout the Commonwealth the structure was widely copied, even down to such details as the town clerk's wig, the mayor's red robe, and that potent instrument, the mace. When Creech Jones in 1974 saw the approach of self-government in the African territories, it was to this pattern that he turned as an exemplar from which the people could quickly learn the arts of public administration within an elective framework.[1]

This system has, of course, not gone unchanged in the 140 years since the Municipal Corporations Act 1835, but its main features – the committee system, the mayor or chairman without executive power, the sharp division between councillors and officers, the lack of a separate executive and the corporate status of the council – have proved strangely enduring. So it is that a chapter on this topic becomes to some extent a commentary on the development of this system.

The Electoral System

The constitution thus established was one more suitable for a local authority seen as the trustee of the rate fund than for one whose primary duty is the development of major social services. This attitude was reinforced by the nature of the franchise for electing the councillors; this was restricted to the ratepayers on the assumption that they alone had a legitimate interest in the administration of municipal affairs. Indeed, until 1894, some types of local authority were elected by a franchise which gave up to six votes to a man rated at a high figure, none to anyone who did not directly contribute to the rates.[2]

By 1900, the franchise for all forms of local authority was basically the same – the occupier of rateable property. Unmarried women with the necessary qualifications were admitted in 1869, and married women in 1882. It was not until 1918 that a male voter's wife was admitted as such to the register – provided her age was over 30,[3] nor until ten years later that men and women were put on exactly the same footing.[4] But women, though competent to vote, were not enabled to sit as members of a county or a borough council until a private member's Bill[5] in 1907 enabled them to be elected.[6] Even so, the position of a married woman remained in question until the Sex Disqualification Removal Act 1919 left no doubt of their right to be elected.[7]

The other main class that had been excluded from the franchise was the paupers. They had traditionally been disfranchised from all parliamentary and local elections as, in effect, a separate and inferior estate of the realm. This was reversed by the Representation of the People Act 1918, on the grounds that the old definition of a pauper – one in receipt of parochial relief – covered only a small proportion of those receiving services of one kind or another from the state or local authority. So paupers were allowed to vote in local government elections. But though in boroughs and counties anyone entitled to vote was also entitled to be elected, it was not so on the boards of guardians and district councils, where paupers were still specifically excluded from membership by the Local Government Act 1894. This had a certain logic in the case of the guardians, as they had to administer the Poor Law and, if they were at the same time in receipt of poor relief themselves, a conflict of interest could easily arise. So, when in 1929 the Poor Law functions were transferred from the guardians to county and county borough councils, the exclusion was applied to those councils also. Thus only in the non-county boroughs was a pauper eligible for election. This anomaly was avoided by the Local Government Act 1933, which made paupers ineligible for service on any local authority.[8] But in 1948 the concept of pauperism was swept away by the opening words of the National Assistance Act – 'The existing poor law shall cease to have effect.' Paupers as such ceased to exist, and no longer was the man or woman who received relief denied on that account the full rights of citizenship.

The franchise, however, was still based on the conception that it was the ratepayer who should control the local authority – a doctrine that led inevitably to a great emphasis on economy by councillors who saw themselves as essentially trustees of the rate fund. Long after the property qualifications had been abolished for voting for Parliament, the local government vote was denied to all except the occupier of rateable property and his wife (or her husband), and the final abolition of this restriction was due to chance rather than to policy.

During the Second World War, local government elections were suspended, and vacancies on councils were filled by co-option. Both the parliamentary and the local government registers were allowed to lapse, while the staffs were engaged on more immediately urgent business. But there was one register – the

National Register, on which rationing and conscription were based. This was a straightforward list of all citizens, without distinction of ratepaying or occupation of property. In 1944, it was felt that local government elections could reasonably be started again. In default of any other appropriate register, the elections were to be fought on the basis of the National Register, which was also in use for parliamentary by-elections. So the inhabitant who was not an occupier of rateable property at last got the vote for local authorities, which had been denied to him in previous centuries. Meanwhile, the Speaker's Conference had been considering the franchise in general, and recommended that the local government franchise should be assimilated to the parliamentary. So the Representation of the People Act 1945, in making provision for the resumption of local government elections, provided that all parliamentary electors should also have the local government vote. The system which had been introduced by chance thus became permanent. Some 8 million voters were thereby added to the lists, and at last the right to vote in local elections came to be based on the person rather than on the occupation of property. It was a significant change, which implied also a change in the attitude to local councils – no longer primarily trustees of the rate fund. But yet the change was not complete, for still non-resident ratepayers, such as shopkeepers who lived outside the town in which they traded, had a vote for the shop as well as a vote where they lived. Furthermore, they were by implication also qualified to be elected as councillors, even though not residents in the area of the authority. It was generally assumed, no doubt rightly, that most of these non-resident voters were Conservative and, in 1969, the Labour government resolved to exclude them from the registers, despite the protests of the local authority associations, and in conflict with the advice of the Maud Committee. The legislation was duly passed,[9] but soon afterwards the Conservatives returned to office. They did not reinstate the vote for the non-resident occupier, but they did, with a minimum of delay, restore to him the right to stand for election, and extended this to anyone whose principal place of work was in the area of the local authority.[10] These changes and counter-changes were perhaps more a matter of party manoeuvring than of long-term principle.

Another aspect of the electoral system which dated back to the Municipal Corporations Act of 1835 was the system of election by wards. This had its origins in the Middle Ages, but became a political issue in the debates on the Bill in 1835. The Tories were fearful that, if elections were held at large over the whole town, they might fail to win any seats at all. If, however, the towns were divided into wards, some predominantly middle class, others working class, they should win some seats at least in the former. So they pressed for division of the boroughs into wards, and it was finally agreed that towns of over 6,000 inhabitants should be so divided but that, in defining the wards, attention should be paid not only to the number of voters in each ward, but also to the rateable value – a provision that implied that the rich man's vote should count for more than the poor man's. In fact, the Home Office in the twentieth century tacitly ignored this provision, until it was repealed in the reform of 1972. But the system of 'block-voting'[11] in wards continued, and this meant that, in many cases, the results of elections were far from being an accurate reflection of the wishes of the voters. The ward system also meant that the drawing of boundaries could have a deciding influence on the results of elections. There was a tradition in the Home Office, which was responsible for the drawing of boundaries after consultation with the local council and electors, that party political considerations should be ignored. But this was a policy difficult to maintain, as the political consequences could be so significant. The matter came to the public notice in the case of Northampton in 1965. The borough boundaries had been extended, so new wards had to be defined. The Labour Party put up one scheme, the Conservatives another. Both protested that there was no element of party advantage involved. The Labour Home Secretary, Sir Frank Soskice,[12] accepted these assurances, and chose the Conservative Scheme. Immediate vociferous protests from the Labour Party (who controlled the council by a small majority) persuaded him to change his mind. Thereupon, a vote of censure in the House of Commons was only negatived by 299 to 291,[13] amid cries of 'Tammany' and 'caught cheating'.

In fact, the decision had not been made by Sir Frank Soskice, but by Richard Crossman, the Minister of Housing and Local Government, fully aware of the political implications of what he was doing. He was cynically amused at the vote of censure on the wrong minister, and aware that, had the attack been rightly directed at himself, he 'would have been for the high-jump'.[14] But the problem remained whether a minister in such circumstances should pretend to be totally blind to party considerations or should be a realist and recognise, what everyone knew, that drawing ward boundaries affects electoral results.

Not until the Act of 1972 was this power taken out of the hands of the minister and vested in the non-political Local Government Boundary Commission.

In the counties and rural districts and parishes the normal pattern was an election every three years of all the members, whereas in the boroughs elections were held annually of one third of the councillors. On account of this wards in the boroughs normally returned three or six councillors each. In London boroughs after 1963 some returned four. The system of 'block-voting' meant that, whichever party got marginally more votes than the next largest party, normally won all the seats, even though it might have in some cases less than half the total vote. This is illustrated for example by the result in the West Barnes ward of Merton in 1964, which returned four members (see Table 2.1).

Table 2.1 *Voting Figures in the West Barnes Ward of Merton, 1964*

Conservatives	2,223	Independent	1,158
	2,136		1,074
	2,090		989
	2,037		963
Labour	1,502	Liberal	847
	1,477		764
	1,441		703
	1,438		676

The four Conservatives were accordingly declared to be elected, the others defeated. Taking the highest vote for each party, the Conservatives had under 39 per cent of the vote, but won 100 per cent of the seats. It also meant that, in a number of authorities, there was no opposition party on the council, although there was a considerable opposition vote at the election.[15]

The system was widely criticised and, in 1910, the Royal Commission on Electoral Systems[16] had recommended the adoption of proportional representation; this was endorsed by the Speaker's Conference of 1918, and a Bill to allow local authorities to adopt the system if they wanted to was passed three times by the House of Lords before it was defeated in the Commons in 1923 by 169 votes to 157. It had been supported by eighty municipalities and twenty-seven county councils, including the LCC. None the less, interest in the subject waned thereafter; the Maud Committee on Management dismissed the suggestion of Proportional Representation as unsuitable and inappropriate if not adopted for Parliament too.[17] The Redcliffe-Maud Commission made no mention of the subject at all.

Thus, though the franchise had been widened to include

women, and paupers, inhabitants who are not also occupiers, and those between the ages of 18 and 21, the system of block-voting in wards continues, despite criticism and objection.

Aldermen

In other respects also, the pattern of constitutional structure established in 1835 has proved remarkably durable. For example, the institution of aldermen survived until 1974, and even beyond that in vestigial form. The original Bill of 1835 had not included aldermen, and their introduction was part of the compromise made between the Whig government and the Tory House of Lords. It was thought that the system would serve to maintain a degree of continuity, including in the first instance some members of the old, unreformed corporations.[18] When the county councils were created in 1888, the pattern was repeated and in many cases, the system was used to bring the County Members and territorial peers on to the new councils. It was not, however, introduced into the district and parish councils in 1894.

In the boroughs in particular, the system of aldermen came to be used in many cases for party political purposes only. Borough aldermen were elected for six years, half of them retiring in every third year. The electoral body was the councillors together with the continuing aldermen. Thus, it happened in a number of cases that a party which had been defeated at the polls was able to retain control and even to increase its power by electing only aldermen of its own persuasion – in some cases choosing men or women who had just been rejected by the electorate. To some extent, this was remedied by the Municipal Corporations Amendment Act of 1910, which provided that the continuing aldermen should not take part in the election of new aldermen. But still the major objections continued; some councils elected only members of the majority political party; others promoted councillors in strict proportion to the strength of the parties on the council; others elected, and regularly re-elected every six years, their senior councillors, irrespective of party or any other considerations except seniority, until they were long past any likelihood of active participation in public affairs.[19] An extreme example was Lloyd George's brother, William George, who was still an alderman of Carnarvon County Council when he died at the age of 101 years and 11 months. Very rarely was the system used to bring into the councils men or women of outstanding ability or experience, as, for example, was done at Lincoln when Sir Harold Banwell became an alderman after retiring from the post of Secretary of the Association of Municipal Corporations.

The Labour Party tried to win an amendment to the Local Government Bill of 1933 to abolish aldermen, but in vain. In 1949, the LCC elections resulted in a tie between the Labour and Conservative councillors, with one Liberal. But the Labour Party, supported by the continuing aldermen, was able to elect a Labour chairman and, with his casting vote, elected a bench of Labour aldermen, giving themselves a clear working majority. Rather similar tactics, turning on the use of the mayor's casting vote, were used at Slough, and at Wolverhampton in 1961 when, after a long wrangle and action in the law courts, the manoeuvre was held to be illegal.[20]

But questions about the calibre of people in local government were being asked, not least by Dame Evelyn Sharp.[21] At their annual conference at Brighton in 1961, the Conservatives, previously the defenders of the aldermen, resolved that the system should be abolished or drastically changed.[22] Five years later, the Maud Committee on Management heard extensive evidence on the question of whether the system should be retained, amended or abolished. The committee unanimously recommended the total abolition of the aldermanic system.[23] Perhaps the most compelling argument was the age of the aldermen – one third of all aldermen were found to be over 70 years of age.[24]

The Royal Commission, in one brief paragraph, endorsed the view of the Management Committee.[25] Only the Association of Municipal Corporations, on whose committees many aldermen served, was prepared to defend them, and in the debates on the Local Government Bill 1972, all parties agreed that the time had come to abolish the system, and so the Act brought the system to an end, except in the City of London, and elsewhere as an empty honour for retired councillors, involving no duties or authority.[26]

Officers

As a general rule local authorities have been free to employ such officers as they see fit, and a relationship of master and servant has existed between the council and the officer. But this has not by any means been a universal rule. In a number of cases councils have been under a statutory obligation to appoint particular officers; in some cases they have been restricted in their freedom of choice; and in some cases the officers whom they have so appointed have not been merely the servants of the council, but have statutory status and duties of their own, duties which in some cases could come into conflict with the policies or interests of the employing councils.

A number of Acts of Parliament have required local authorities to appoint such officers as clerks, treasurers, surveyors, public health inspectors and medical officers; in some cases, necessary professional qualifications have been laid down, though this has never been done for the most senior of all – the clerk. In some cases, too, such as the education officer and the chief constable, the approval of a central ministry has been necessary. In other cases, such as the medical officers of health and sanitary inspectors, there has been a prohibition of dismissal without the approval of the appropriate minister.

Though in general the officers have been the servants of the council, some of them have enjoyed a different status. The convention of appointing solicitors as part-time clerks gave them a peculiar position; as professional men they tended to regard the councils as clients rather than as employers, and to regard themselves as bound by their professional ethics and conventions rather than by the orders of the local authorities.

Some were employed full time, some part time. In either case, many of them held, in addition to their appointments under the council, statutory offices, such as that of registration officer for parliamentary elections.[27] These were quite distinct from their duties as officers of the council, and they were in no way answerable to the council for how they discharged them.[28]

This tendency towards independence was reinforced in the boroughs by the legal fact that the corporate body there (but not in the county and district councils) was not the council, but the whole body of the burgesses or citizens. Thus the town clerk and treasurer, for example, had a duty not merely to the narrow body of aldermen and councillors, but to the wider community of the town as a whole, much as a company official owes a duty not only to the board of directors, but to the whole body of shareholders.

The principle was clearly laid down in the case of the treasurer of Tenby in 1906, in which the High Court proclaimed that

'the treasurer is not a mere servant of the council; he owes a duty and stands in a fiduciary relation to the burgesses as a body, he is the treasurer of the borough . . . and although he holds office during the pleasure of the council only, this does not enable him to plead the orders of the council as an excuse for an unlawful act'.[29]

The argument was taken a stage further in the case of the Town Clerk of Finsbury who, on the orders of the council leader, refrained from disclosing some very important information to the council. The Lord Chief Justice in his judgement said that 'the office of Town Clerk is an important part of the machinery of local government. He may be said to stand between the borough council and the ratepayers. He is there to assist by his advice and action the conduct of public affairs in the Borough, and if there is a disposition on the part of the Council, still more on the part of any member of the Council, to ride roughshod over his opinions, the question must at once arise as to whether it is not his duty forthwith to resign his office, or, at any rate, to do what he thinks right and await the consequences.'[30]

A few years later, however, the Clerk of Bognor Regis District Council, acting in accordance with this dictum, resisted what he saw as the improper actions of his council, and was dismissed. The Minister, Richard Crossman, asked a Queen's Counsel (J. Ramsay Willis, QC), much versed in local government law, to report on the episode. He disagreed with the dictum of Lord Caldecote in the Finsbury case, and expressed the view that a town clerk or clerk of a UDC 'is the employee of his council and it is to them that his primary loyalty and duty lie, and it is to them that he is answerable for his actions'.[31] This view has been widely supported, but never positively affirmed in the courts.

The position in the counties was somewhat different; the corporate body was the council, not, as in boroughs, the body of burgesses or electors; but on the other hand the office of clerk of the peace existed long before the creation of the county councils, and, until 1931,[32] the clerk of the county council was always also clerk of the peace; since then the two offices have not necessarily been held by the same person. So, too, the other county officers – the county treasurer and the county surveyor – existed long before the county councils, and they had established traditions of their own, based on their relations with the Quarter Sessions.[33]

The most notable case was that of the chief constable, who clearly had duties beyond those of a servant bound to obey the legal orders of his master. The chief constable is first and foremost a constable, and in the leading case on his status[34] Viscount Simonds laid down that his 'authority is original, not delegated, and is exercised at his own discretion by virtue of his office'.

A number of cases arose in which there was some conflict between chief constables and their councils. In 1936 the Home Secretary, Sir John Simon, had to answer allegations in the House of Commons that the Oxford police had shown partiality in handling political riots in Oxford. He said, 'The Oxford Police are subject to the ratepayers of Oxford who elect the City Council out of which the Watch Committtee is formed.'[35]

On the other hand the Home Office generally took the view that 'the enforcement of the criminal law was a matter for the chief officer of police, and that it is a well established principle that he should not be subjected to any interference or control by the police authority in carrying out his duty in that regard'. This principle was enunciated in relation to the case in 1959 when the Watch Committee of Nottingham suspended their chief constable, Athelstan Popkess, because, *inter alia*, he refused to comply with the committee's instruction to inform them about inquiries by Scotland Yard officers into corporation matters in Nottingham. The Home Secretary held that they had no authority to do this, and instructed them to reinstate him.[36]

The matter was further complicated by the fact that in some respects a chief constable of a county had greater discretion than one of a borough; in the county the disciplinary authority was the chief constable, but in a borough, the Watch Committee. Moreover, there had grown up in the counties a much stronger tradition of independence. This may have been partly due to the composition of the county police authority – the Standing Joint Committee – which was composed of equal numbers of magistrates and county councillors, and partly to a difference of background of the chief constables. In the boroughs, chief constables were normally promoted from the ranks of the police force, whereas in the counties they were, before the Second World War, usually retired senior army officers, perhaps more inclined to assert their independence of authority.[37]

Partly as a result of the Nottingham case, a Royal Commission was appointed in 1960, and reported in 1962.[38] Among 111 recommendations they proposed that 'the legal responsibility for the efficient policing of an area be transferred from police authorities to the Secretaries of State', thereby assuming that it was at that time vested in the police authority rather than the chief constable.

In the subsequent Act,[39] the duty of a police authority was defined as being 'to secure the maintenance of an adequate and efficient police force for the area'. It also provides that 'the police force . . . shall be under the direction and control of the chief constable'. Exactly how far this changed the existing law remains obscure.[40]

The Local Government Act 1972 does not clarify the law on chief constables. In regard to other chief officers it does, however, make some changes: many of the restrictions on the appointment of officers are repealed, but ministerial control of the appointment of chief education officers, inspectors of weights and measures,

agricultural analysts and directors of social services is retained.[41]
The treasurer, the town clerk and the clerk of the county council
cease to be statutory officers, and there is no requirement that
such officers be appointed. They are in practice replaced by the
director of finance and the chief executive officer, neither of
whom will probably claim the constitutional status that was
apparently attached to the offices of their predecessors. Important,
responsible and powerful though they are, they cannot be said
to stand on their own constitutional legs, but rather to be the
superior servants of the council.

The Maud Committee on Management[42] found that in every
foreign country at which they looked there was wider power than
in England for councils to delegate their powers to officers, and
they recommended that this should be copied here, to avoid 'the
cumbrous machinery, the multiplication of committees, the
clogged agenda, the long meetings, the neglect of matters of
importance' that existed in many local authorities. This proposal
was accepted in the Local Government Act 1972,[43] but it is, as
yet, too soon to say how successful it has been in avoiding these
evils.

There remains, however, one great principle – that of the
absolute separation between the councillors and the officers. No
councillor can hold any paid office while he remains a councillor,
nor for twelve months thereafter.[44] This constitutional barrier
dates from the Municipal Corporations Act 1835.[45] Before that,
town clerks were commonly members of the corporate bodies; in
a number of other countries no such rigid division exists. But in
England the gulf between the two is absolute.

Charters and Ultra Vires

During the nineteenth century, there grew up a technical and
esoteric distinction between the boroughs, created by royal
charter, and the other local authorities, whose corporate existence
depended on Acts of Parliament. Based on a series of ancient
decisions of the Courts,[46] it had the sanction of no statutory
provisions.

The essence of these decisions was that all local authorities,
other than boroughs, were subject to the legal rule of *ultra vires*
– the rule that a statutory authority can only perform such
functions as are conferred on it by Act of Parliament[47]. But
borough councils (not including the metropolitan boroughs of
London and their successors, the London boroughs, which have
no charters) were in a fundamentally different position. They
were creatures of the Royal Prerogative and, as such, had all

the powers of a natural person, except in so far as statutes might impose specific restrictions on their actions. In the words of Mr Justice Luxmoore in a case concerning Leeds Corporation . . .

'The corporation was incorporated by royal charter in the year 1627 in the reign of King Charles I. The fact that it is incorporated by royal charter is of importance because a corporation so constituted stands on a different footing from a statutory corporation, the difference being that the latter species of corporation can only do such Acts as are authorised directly or indirectly by the statute creating it; whereas the former can, speaking generally, do anything that an ordinary individual can do. If, however, the corporation by charter be, as the corporation is in the present case, a municipal corporation, then it is subject to the restriction imposed by the Municipal Corporations Act, 1882, and can be restrained from applying its funds to purposes not authorised by that Act'.[48]

The restrictions referred to were reproduced from the Act of 1835, and prevented a borough council from spending money out of the borough fund except under the authority of an Act of Parliament, or by order of the council or by the authority of a court. The words 'by order of the council' had been judicially held to mean an order of the council itself authorised by an Act of Parliament.[49]

The effect of this was not to make borough councils subject to the rule of *ultra vires*, but, as there is little that a local authority can do without spending money, the restriction on spending money added up to much the same thing.

But in 1933, the Local Government Act consolidated the accumulated mass of municipal law, repealing the old statutes and re-enacting them in a less complicated form.[50] In doing so, the relevant words were omitted, not with any intention of changing the law, but solely in order to simplify it.

Unexpectedly, some years later, it was held in a case concerning the bus undertaking at Leicester[51] that the repeal of the 1882 Act re-established the common law position, and borough councils were again free to do whatever they saw fit to do, and to embark on whatever enterprises they thought desirable in the interests of their inhabitants – though still with an over-riding limitation that, as trustees, they must act in the interest of the area and its inhabitants.

The case did not go to appeal, and was not tested in other cases. Many lawyers were doubtful of its validity, but yet its logic was hard to challenge. But the result was absurd; every little borough of one or two thousand people apparently enjoyed a freedom of action far beyond that of the London County Council or the great provincial county councils.

This uncertainty ceased with the passing of the Local Government Act 1972.[52] All the existing borough corporations came to an end; the Crown could still grant charters conferring privileges and titles on local authorities, but these are not charters of incorporation, and all the new authorities are the creatures of statute, not of the Royal Prerogative, and so are subject to the principle of *ultra vires.* The rather shadowy freedom of the old prerogative corporation has passed away, except perhaps in the case of the City of London and a few half-forgotten unreformed municipal corporations.[53]

Towns Meetings and County Meetings

A traditional part of the British Constitution is the right of the people to assemble to discuss matters of common interest. In the eighteenth and early nineteenth century, county meetings of the freeholders of the county, assembled in the open air under the sheriff, were common events. They would debate matters of local or national interest, and would often send petitions to Parliament. In the towns, the mayors would call similar public meetings, which also were exempt from the restrictions of the Seditious Meetings Acts,[54] and enjoyed a clear but undefined constitutional status. So, too, at the parish level, the open vestries, though sometimes riotous and usually inefficient, provided a form of direct democracy.

The age of Victoria was an age of boards, committees and councils. The old county meetings died out. The towns meetings became almost, but not completely extinct; they were occasionally called, particularly in the smaller towns, and the Borough Funds Act of 1872 included a provision that a borough council could not promote a Bill in Parliament unless this was first approved by a meeting of ratepayers and, if demanded, by a poll of the ratepayers, conducted much like a municipal election, but with plural voting for the larger ratepayers, including companies. This was intended to make it more difficult to promote local Bills, and was particularly aimed at those establishing municipal gas and water undertakings. It did, however, only formalise a principle which had existed before – that the consent of the ratepayers should be obtained to a private Bill in Parliament.

The system was simplified in 1903;[55] the poll was no longer to be of the ratepayers, but of the local government electors, and plural voting was abolished. The system was proving inconvenient and time-consuming,[56] but yet it was defended as a safeguard against rash and ill-considered legislation. The Onslow Commission on Local Government in 1925 heard evidence on the working of these Acts, and all the representatives of local government condemned them severely, but they found a champion in Lord Donoughmore, Chairman of Committees in the House of Lords, who supported the view of a Select Committee of the House of Commons five years before, that some form of referendum was desirable as it enabled Parliament to gauge the strength of public opinion.[57]

The Royal Commission of 1925 reported that the statutory towns meetings should be abolished, as did also the Chelmsford Committee in 1933, but yet no action was taken to change the law. Opposition continued to grow to a system which was proving absurd. Many statutory meetings of the electors were attended only by a dozen people in addition to the councillors and their staff; when more did attend, it was usually at the instance of an energetic opponent of the Bill, who persuaded supporters or employees to attend and object. In 1954, Cardiff Corporation promoted a Bill, and, out of an electorate of 172,000, thirteen people attended the towns meeting, of whom three were not members or employees of the council. In the same year, a towns meeting at Bristol (with an electorate of 316,000) was attended by seventeen, of whom seven were the representatives of the general public. In the following year, the Joint Committee on Private Bill Procedure[58] reported that the towns meetings should be discontinued. Sir Eric Bullus introduced a Bill for that purpose, which had been drafted by the AMC. Though it received a favourable second reading, it was blocked in committee and never reached the statute book.[59] Not until the general reorganisation of the 1972 Act was this procedure abolished.

Apart from these towns meetings, the only remaining statutory open assemblies in the whole of English local government were the parish meetings, the direct successors of the open vestry. Some of these were sparsely attended, with only a few people other than the councillors present; others attracted large crowds: for example, in its evidence to the Royal Commission on Local Government, the Parish Councils Association referred to a meeting in 1955 at Capel-le-Ferne in Kent at which the public 'not only filled all the 250 seats in the hall but jammed the stage and leant in from outside through the windows'.[60] But, apart from these parish meetings, direct democracy had died out. No county meeting has been called for perhaps a century; towns meetings may still be called to discuss matters of public interest, but this is rarely, if ever, done. And yet, at the same time, there has been a growing demand for 'participation' and the Skeffington Committee[61] in 1969 recommended the establishment of 'community forums' for the discussion of planning matters.

The electoral franchise has been extended to all inhabitants over 18 years of age; aldermen have been abolished; statutory towns meetings have gone; charters have lost their significance. None the less, the constitution of local authorities in England and Wales retains the essential features that were established in the Municipal Corporations Act 1835: a mayor or chairman with virtually no power except to preside over meetings; a clear and almost unbridgeable gulf between the elected members and the appointed salaried staff; no provision for referenda or public participation in discussion; a standard constitution decreed by Parliament with almost no local variety or choice; and a system of committees in which the great majority of the decisions are made.

This pattern is not inevitable; other countries have other methods; none of these elements is to be found universally, and some of them, such as the powerless mayor or chairman, would be unacceptable in many countries. The research done for the Maud Committee on Management shows that the British pattern cannot fairly claim to be the most democratic, or the most efficient[62]. But it does demonstrate a most remarkable degree of resistance to change.

NOTES

1 See B. Keith-Lucas, 'The dilemma of local government in Africa', in *Essays in Imperial Government*, ed. K. Robinson and F. Madden (1963); R. Wraith, *Local Government in West Africa* (1964).
2 See B. Keith-Lucas, *The English Local Government Franchise* (1952).
3 Representation of the People Act 1918.
4 Representation of the People (Equal Franchise) Act 1928.
5 Qualification of Women (County and Borough Councils) Act 1907.
6 They were entitled to sit on vestries and boards of guardians, and after 1894, on urban and rural district and parish councils.
7 See Chitty's *Annual Statutes*, vol. 8, p. 181n., and Arnold's *Municipal Corporations*, p. 30.
8 Following the recommendation of the *Local Government and Public Health Consolidation Committee* (chairman, Lord Chelmsford) Interim

minor change in the law and demonstrates that the Local Government Act 1933 was not, as is sometimes supposed, a purely consolidation measure.

9 Representation of the People Act 1969.

10 Local Authorities (Qualification of Members) Act 1971.

11 'Block-voting' is the system by which each elector has as many votes as there are seats to be filled, but can give only one vote to any one candidate.

12 Created Lord Stow Hill in 1966.

13 706 HC Deb., 17 February 1965, cols. 1283–321; vol. 707, 25 February, cols. 628–94.

14 R. H. S. Crossman, *The Diaries of a Cabinet Minister* (1975), vol. 1, pp. 160, 170.

15 e.g. in 1922, in London, Chelsea, Fulham, Lewisham, Holborn, Paddington, Wandsworth and Westminster; in 1960, Harrow, Hillingdon and Richmond; in 1964, Hackney, Islington and Tower Hamlets.

16 1910, Cd 5163, 5352, xxvi.

17 *Management of Local Government*, Committee Report, para. 335 (HMSO, 1967).

18 Parl. Deb., 17 August 1835, vol. XXX, col. 596. Lord Wharncliffe argued that, 'if it were determined that a body of aldermen or life members were unnecessary to a corporation, hereditary members in the House of Lords would be deemed equally unnecessary'.

19 See G. W. Jones, *Borough Politics* (1969), p. 265.

20 See Jones, op. cit., ch. 16; and *Re Wolverhampton Borough Council's Aldermanic Election* [1961], 3 All ER 446.

21 See *Municipal Review*, August 1961, p. 508; *Municipal Review*, November 1972, p. 731; J. L. Blake in *New Society*, 11 July 1963; B. Keith-Lucas, *The Councils, the Press and the People* (1962); *The Mayor, Aldermen and Councillors* (1961).

22 *Daily Mail*, 11 October 1961.

23 Para. 353.

24 *Management of Local Government*, vol. 5, p. 96.

25 Para. 460; 1968–9, Cmnd 4040, xxxviii.

26 Aldermen also still exist in the unreformed borough of Newport, Dyfed, with some minor functions.

27 During the Second World War, many town clerks were appointed also as civil defence controllers and air raid precautions controllers, directly responsible to the Home Office. See T. E. Headrick, *The Town Clerk* (1962), pp. 145–6.

28 See Representation of the People Act 1949, sec. 6.

29 *Attorney-General v. De Winton* [1906], 2 Ch. 106.

30 For accounts of this case, see C. R. H. Hurle-Hobbs, *The Law Relating to District Audit* (1955); T. E. Headrick, *The Town Clerk* (1962), pp. 45–8. It is not reported in the Law Reports.

31 Report of the Bognor Regis Inquiry (HMSO, 1965), p. 66.

32 Local Government (Clerks) Act 1931.

33 The office of county surveyor dates back to the Bridges Act 1530.

34 *A. G. v. New South Wales Perpetual Trustee Co.* [1955], AC 457.

35 314 HC Deb., col. 1625.

36 The question of the status of chief constables has been discussed *inter alia* in the Report of the Royal Commission on *Police Powers and Procedure*, 1928–9, Cmd 3297, ix; B. Keith-Lucas, 'The independence of chief constables', *Public Administration*, Spring 1960, pp. 1–15;

Geoffrey Marshall, *Police and Government* (1965); the Report of the Royal Commission on the Police, 1961–2, Cmd 1728, xx.

37 *Whitaker's Almanack*, 1934, shows thirty-two out of forty-two county chief constables as having army or naval rank – mostly lieutenant-colonels.

38 Cmnd 1728.

39 Police Act 1964.

40 Geoffrey Marshall, op. cit., pp. 96–9.

41 Sec. 112.

42 pp. 16, 17, 18.

43 Sec. 101.

44 Local Government Act 1972, sec. 116.

45 Secs. 28, 58.

46 Particularly Sutton's Hospital Case (1912), 10 Co. Rep. 1.

47 See *Baroness Wenlock* v. *River Dee Co.* (1885), 10 C 354. See also A. C. Cross, *Principles of Local Government Law*, 2nd edn (1961), ch. 1.

48 *A. G.* v. *Leeds Corporation* [1929], 2 Ch. 295.

49 *Tynemouth Corporation* v. *A. G.* [1899], AC 293.

50 This was part of a process of consolidation, based on the reports of the Addington and the Chelmsford Committees.

51 *A. G.* v. *Leicester Corporation* [1943], Ch. 86.

52 Sec. 1 (11).

53 e.g. Winchelsea in Sussex; Newport, Dyfed; Fordwich in Kent; and the Corporation of Romney Marsh.

54 B. Keith-Lucas, 'County meetings', *Law Quarterly Review*, January 1954, pp. 109–14; H. Jephson, *The Platform* (1892), *passim*.

55 Borough Funds Act 1903.

56 Redlich and Hirst, vol. I, p. 365.

57 Select Committee on Procedure governing Bills which involve charges (1920), (257), viii.

58 1954–5 (139–I), iii.

59 564 HC Deb., 15 February 1957, col. 1633, *et seq.*

60 Memorandum of Evidence of the National Association of Parish Councils to the Royal Commission on Local Government (HMSO, 1967), p. 13.

61 *People and Planning* (Report of the Committee on Public Participation in Planning), (HMSO, 1969).

62 *Management of Local Government*, vol. 4, *Local Administration Abroad* (HMSO, 1967).

Chapter III

FUNCTIONS

The Pattern in 1900

At no stage of English history has any government held a consistent and logical policy on the range and limits of municipal services. Local government was not evolved to provide a co-ordinated system of administration for a logically defined range of services; it emerged, piecemeal, in answer to a succession of separate needs and demands. The nineteenth century showed no recognisable pattern of evolution in this respect.

The boroughs were the creatures of the Municipal Corporations Act of 1835, which treated the corporations as trustees of public property, rather than as providers of social services; the county councils in 1888 took over from the Quarter Sessions a motley collection of functions, including licensing, asylums, bridges, contagious diseases of animals, wild birds, main roads, river pollution and (through the Standing Joint Committee) police.

For other functions there was, until 1894, a bewildering array of special bodies, called into being as need became apparent; burial boards, local boards of health, lighting inspectors, commissioners of baths and washhouses, and highway boards, all of which were in that year consolidated into the more inclusive urban and rural districts and parish councils. Other such bodies – particularly the school boards and boards of guardians – survived into the twentieth century as separate local authorities.

The greater part of the functions of the major authorities had originated not in the initiative and policy of central governments, but rather in the enterprise of individual local authorities through the cumbersome and ancient procedure of local, or private, Acts of Parliament. Since the late seventeenth century this had been the main field of growth in English local government. The mass of local Acts of the period 1750 to 1850 is so vast that no man has ever read it all; there is no comprehensive study of the subject.[1] It was from this source that there developed the sanitary laws, the social legislation, the early experiments in smoke abatement, town planning and building regulations. Many of these initiatives were later incorporated into public general Acts, such as the

Public Health Act of 1848 and the Highways Act of 1864;[2] others were made generally available through the system of Clauses Acts, started in the 1840s by Joseph Hume.[3] So, by the beginning of the twentieth century, the powers of the major local authorities were a strange mixture; some granted by public general Acts; some included in adoptive and clauses Acts, and some, individual to each corporation, granted by local Acts. Thus by 1900 local authorities generally provided sanitary services, police and highway maintenance, according to their classification and status; a number of local authorities were providing such services as water, gas, electricity, trams, buses, libraries, cemeteries and docks. In addition, seaside and other towns were providing municipal entertainments; Doncaster had a racecourse, Wolverhampton a cold store, Glasgow and Tunbridge Wells had telephone services; a few years later, Birmingham was to get powers to establish its 'penny bank'.[4] In the same way, a number of authorities had acquired regulative functions, not connected with municipal trading or the prospect of profit. Birmingham, for example, had acquired powers to deal with receiving stolen property, blackmail, gambling houses, cruelty to animals, and the powers of arrest by constables;[5] Bolton had got powers to regulate the sale of poison;[6] Bath to regulate coffee and tea houses;[7] Leeds had power to control brothels;[8] and Liverpool prohibited pawnbrokers from accepting pledges from children;[9] and Newcastle had got power to provide technical schools;[10] Rochdale controlled the trade in ice cream;[11] Halifax had power to regulate dairies and to establish reading rooms and restaurants in the parks.[12] So this process of gaining new powers through local Acts continued through the nineteenth and into the twentieth century. In 1900 no fewer than 291 local Acts were passed, the majority of which were promoted by individual local authorities in order to extend their powers in one way or another, but thereafter the number of such Acts began to diminish.

Thus, in relation to the major urban authorities, local Acts were more important than the public general Acts of Parliament. County councils had no power to promote Bills until 1903,[13] and the urban and rural districts were primarily sanitary authorities, with highway duties and other cognate responsibilities. The development of new services was not within their normal range, as it was for the great county boroughs and county councils; the districts were more work-a-day authorities. So, too, the parish councils did not themselves promote local Acts, but relied on public general statutes for their powers. They had been called into being by the Local Government Act of 1894, and had inherited the civil functions of the old vestries. There was a clear policy in the minds of the Liberals who promoted and supported their creation; the new councils were to be the instrument for bringing the peasants back to the land, through smallholdings and allotments, re-establishing the idyllic state in which every peasant was the owner of three acres and a cow. The parish councils were to unseat the squire and the vicar from their seats of power, and to flourish as village parliaments, in a new golden age of rural England.[14]

The smallholdings movement had a great hold on men's minds. It had been expounded by the younger Pitt in his Bill of 1796; it was later to win the support of Lloyd George. In the late nineteenth and early twentieth centuries it attracted wide support, from Gladstone, Fowler, Jesse Collings and others.[15] A series of Acts gave powers to local authorities[16] for this purpose and Labouchere declared that this policy of land settlement had been 'the aim and object of the Parish Council Bill, which slowly and quietly nationalise the land by throwing the property little by little, and very quickly, I think, into the hands of the parish councils, who will let it to the villagers'.[17]

But events took a different turn; the interest in land settlement waned, and other, urban, problems seemed more urgent. The parish councils did not achieve a rural revolution and, with very limited financial means and restricted powers, they failed, in their early days, to live up to the high hopes of their creators. They continued to serve a useful, unexciting purpose, and it was not until after the second war that they began again to catch the popular imagination.

Meanwhile other functions of the local authorities widened. New responsibilities were given to them; in 1902 the school boards were abolished and the duty of providing schools came to be shared between counties and the larger boroughs and urban districts while secondary education passed to the counties and county boroughs; maternity and child welfare and supervision of midwives were added to the existing health services; housing and town planning, public libraries, school meals and other new functions were given to the major authorities, but still there was no clear pattern of services, and no general concept of the proper role of local authorities in the nation's life. The functions of local authorities were a heterogeneous collection of statutory powers, each one dependent on a specific Act of Parliament.

Ultra Vires *and Municipal Enterprise*

Some of the major political issues of our society first emerge in a local context. The arguments about the respective merits of public ownership and private enterprise arose out of the trading activities of local authorities. During the nineteenth century the urban authorities had developed four services operated on a commercial basis – water, gas, electricity and passenger transport. The earliest of these services, water and gas, were the least controversial. A pure water supply was necessary for public health: a properly maintained gas supply was essential for public safety. But the appearance of municipal trams and municipal electricity in the 1870s and 1880s was challenged as an assault on the concept of private property. The Liberty and Property Defence League was formed to resist further advances of municipal trading. The Fabian Society was prominent on the other side of the argument: it urged that a steady expansion of public ownership was desirable and that this could best be achieved through widening the range of enterprise undertaken by local councils. Bernard Shaw's work, *The Commonsense of Municipal Trading*, appeared in 1904. In *The Constitution for a Socialist Commonwealth of Great Britain* (1920), Sidney and Beatrice Webb advocated that many services should be municipalised rather than nationalised because a local community had a common interest in the quality of a service everyone must use. In a local unit, producer and consumer lived close together and were aware of each other. So the incentive to efficiency would come not from private profit but from community feeling.

The ideological conflict over municipal trading in the early years of the century was fought out at national rather than local level. At this period the party political element in local government was of limited importance. The number of socialist councillors was negligible. Municipal electricity and transport had been supported by both Conservatives and Liberals who felt that their local authority should press ahead with these services as a contribution to progress and prosperity. Such extensions of municipal trading were regarded as a practical necessity rather than as a contribution to a long-term socialist agenda. The other reason why the debate was national rather than local arose from legal requirements. Local councils had to go to Parliament whenever they wanted extra trading powers. So Parliament was faced with a growing stream of local Bills and provisional orders. This flow of additional parliamentary business and also pressure from the guardians of private enterprise led in 1900 to the appointment of a Joint Committee of Lords and Commons to inquire into municipal trading.

The report of this committee[18] records that it was appointed too late in the session to be able to reach conclusions. However, the evidence presented to it illustrates the contemporary objections to municipal enterprise. Local debts would increase. Councils would not have enough time to devote to other pressing municipal problems. Alternatively, if local authorities made too heavy a demand on the time of their members, busy men would be debarred from serving the community. It was undesirable for local councils to be involved in labour questions. If they accepted union demands for a fair wage this could affect labour costs elsewhere in a town. Trading activity offered wider scope for local corruption. Local councils with a gas supply were prejudiced against the introduction of electricity.

Parliament was little influenced by these views. The committee was not reappointed until 1903, when it restricted itself to the narrower question of local accounts.[19] It reported that the government system of district audit had no experience of commercial accounting and recommended that it be replaced by professional auditors. Again, no action was taken on this proposal and the controversy continued to expand,[20] but attempts to open up new spheres of activity were effectively blocked by the alarm-calls on behalf of private enterprise. Some local initiatives were frustrated by the courts through the application of the *ultra vires* principle. In *Attorney-General* v. *Manchester Corporation*[21] it was laid down that the power to carry parcels on trams did not permit a local authority to act as a general carrier. Fulham failed to convince a court that their powers under the Baths and Washhouses Acts entitled them to run a municipal laundry.[22] The cost of obtaining the necessary legal powers from Parliament may well have deterred smaller local authorities from entering the accepted fields of municipal enterprise. When the Ramsbottom Urban District (population 17,000) applied for powers to operate a fleet of eleven buses, the legal costs were nearly 20 per cent of the cost of the buses.[23] A further deterrent was the uncertainty of the result of an approach to Parliament, especially as objection might be encountered in the Lords as well as the Commons, where defenders of private enterprise might well be even more vigorous. Thus, in 1938, the Lords refused to allow the City of Oxford to take over the local electricity company, preferring the rival claim of the Wessex Power Corporation.[24] In the Commons the Local Legislation Committee, under the chairmanship of Sir Thomas Robinson, used its influence

during the 1920s to secure that the profits of municipal undertakings should be used to improve services or reduce charges,
rather than provide a subsidy for the local rates.[25]

Hull is famous for its municipal telephones and Birmingham
acquired powers to start its municipal savings bank in 1915.
Otherwise political opposition in Parliament made it unlikely
that local legislation could open up new vistas for local enterprise. Throughout the inter-war period Labour backbenchers
introduced private member's Bills which sought to give wide
powers to local councils to engage in commercial ventures and so
to achieve at least part of the vision of the Webbs. The proposals included coal, bread, milk, meat and savings banks. Such
trading would have been in direct competition with established
interests – which most of the original municipal trading undertakings were not – and were certain to arouse objection. It was
claimed that council competition would be unfair competition
since a local authority was under no compulsion to make a profit.
Losses would be borne automatically by the ratepayers. Private
enterprise offering the same services as a council would be forced,
through paying rates, to subsidise its competitors. Not surprisingly, these Local Authority Enabling Bills failed to obtain a
second reading, except in 1930, when the Bill failed at a later
stage of the parliamentary process.

The election in 1945 of a Labour Government with a secure
majority might have been expected to revive the issue. By this
time, however, the Labour movement was interested in nationalisation rather than municipalisation. Municipal enterprise failed
to expand. On the contrary, it declined as local authority gas and
electricity undertakings were taken over in 1948 by the regional
boards forming part of a nationalised industry. A year later the
Civil Aviation Act created the possibility that local authorities
would develop aerodromes, but this has proved to be an unhappy
field of local endeavour.

The extension and development of the local government
services in the period between the wars did not arise out of either
of these two idealistic movements – land settlement and municipal
trading. Both of them proved to be to some extent will-o'-the-
wisps, which led their followers on, and then disappeared. The
real growth came from the extension of existing services, expanding and developing to meet changing needs.

For example, before the First World War some local authorities were building a few houses under the Artisans and Labourers'
Dwellings Act 1868, and the Housing Act 1890. At this period
local authority housing was thought of as an aspect of public

health responsibilities. Families living in property unfit for human habitation had to be provided with alternative accommodation. No houses, private or municipal, were built during the war. After the armistice, housing became a major social priority. The government followed the policy of 'homes fit for heroes' and gave a subsidy to local authorities building houses; through the next twenty years the policy on subsidies varied widely, but in all, 1,136,457 houses were built, and 273,000 slum houses were demolished or closed.[26] For the second-tier authorities and the industrial cities, this became the most important service. But others, too, were expanding.

Education, which had been in most areas a matter only of elementary schools in the nineteenth century, blossomed into the new structure of primary and secondary education; school meals and school medical services developed; technical colleges were built; between the beginning of the century and the outbreak of the Second World War, the revenue expenditure on education increased six-fold.[27] The work of the sanitary inspectors increased similarly, as the attack on the slums developed; the public library system grew rapidly after the Public Libraries Act of 1919 enabled county councils to enter this field, and removed the limit on expenditure of a penny rate.

Delegation
The picture of the powers of local authorities has throughout the century been somewhat confused by the system of delegation, which has made it difficult to determine who is responsible for what. The Local Government Bill 1888, introduced by the Salisbury government, was intended to be a great decentralisation Bill; provision was made for extensive devolution of functions from the central government to the new county councils,[28] and also for delegation by the county councils to other authorities. The devolution from the central government never took place, greatly because of the reluctance of the civil servants to relinquish their authority. The devolution to smaller authorities could not become generally effective until the Act of 1894 had consolidated the numerous district boards and committees into the urban and rural district councils; then the power of delegation was extended, and this process was continued by the Education Act of 1906, and a succession of other statutes.[29] But meanwhile the county councils were growing increasingly apprehensive of the incursion of new or expanding county boroughs into their territory. So the whole question of the relation between counties and other authorities came under review by the Onslow Commission

on Local Government.[30] The County Councils Association saw
the system of delegation as a means of appeasing the demands of
the county districts for independence, at the same time as enabling the county councils to keep down the size of their own
bureaucracies.[31] The association therefore pressed for a scheme
of statutory delegation from counties to county districts. The
Association of Municipal Corporations on the other hand argued
that all functions should be clearly assigned by statute to the
authorities that were to carry them out.

The Royal Commission was not prepared to endorse the
county councils' proposals for extending the system of delegation
and issued a negative report on these suggestions.[32] But yet, in the
years that followed, powers of delegation were included in a succession of statutes, and became increasingly a normal feature of
local government. Most important, perhaps, was the education
Bill 1944, which proposed to replace the old 'Part III Authorities'
and concentrate the responsibilities for primary education in the
hands of county and county borough councils. The old authorities
(boroughs with a population of 10,000 or more, and urban districts with a population of 20,000 or more) were reluctant to lose
their schools. A deputation of back-bench MPs led by Lord
Winterton, 'Father of the House', persuaded the minister, R. A.
Butler, to allow a system of delegation to divisional executives
and excepted districts. Some 200 such bodies came into being
and survived until the 1972 Act.

The system was in fact considerably extended by the Local
Government Act 1958, which enabled the larger boroughs and
urban districts to claim delegated powers in health, welfare and
education, as of right. Again, the purpose of this seems to have
been less the need to improve the services than a desire to placate
the second tier authorities, which had been complaining of the
loss of many of their powers, while at the same time acceding to
the County Councils Association's preference for a system of
delegation.[33]

Poor Law and the Social Services
The period between the wars was predominantly one of the
expansion of existing services, rather than of the introduction of
new ones. There was, however, one major change in the functions
of local government; the transfer from the guardians of the poor
to the county councils and the county borough councils of the
responsibility for the poor. The Act of 1601 had made this the duty
of the parish; the unit had proved to be too small and ineffectual,
and too closely involved with the poor themselves, so the unit had

been widened in 1834 to the union of parishes. Now the same process was taking place again, moving from the union to the county.

Guardians of the poor had been appointed for a number of unions of parishes under local Acts in the eighteenth century; the system had been made general under the Poor Law Amendment Act of 1834. It had been linked with the policy of the segregation of the paupers in union workhouses, their children educated in separate workhouse schools, and the paupers themselves treated both in law and in practice as a distinct and inferior estate of the realm. When the county councils were created in 1888, Joseph Chamberlain had argued for the Poor Law being handed over to them, but the Prime Minister, Salisbury, fearful of the consequences if the county councils, responsible for the Poor Law, were to be dominated by the poor themselves, had dismissed the idea on the grounds that it was, 'look at it how you will, rather like leaving the cat in charge of the cream jug'.[34] But events of the early twentieth century gave a great impetus to this proposal.

In 1905, the Conservative Government appointed a Royal Commission to inquire into and make recommendations on the existing Poor Law. This was still the Elizabethan code, amended and extended by the Act of 1834, which implicitly made general the principles of the workhouse test and of 'less eligibility'. The harshness of the system, as it was at first enforced, had been somewhat softened, and the workhouses were now filled not with the able-bodied labourers, but with the sick, the aged, orphans and the disabled. To them the principle of 'less eligibility' was scarcely relevant, and it was not rigidly applied, though still the doctrine influenced men's minds.

The members of the Royal Commission included politicians, civil servants and social reformers, such as Beatrice Webb and George Lansbury. They made a very detailed and exhaustive inquiry, and Mrs Webb harried them with endless memoranda. Finally, they reported in 1909 with a Majority Report,[35] signed by fourteen members. This recommended the transfer of the functions of the guardians to the county councils, who would work in close touch with voluntary aid committees. It also condemned the idea of a deterrent Poor Law, and the application of the principle of 'less eligibility' to anyone other than the able-bodied paupers, and an extension of old age pensions and medical services.

The Minority Report was written by Sidney Webb, from information provided by Beatrice Webb, and was signed by four members. It went much further than the Majority Report in recommending a preventive system, treating the individual, and based on disciplinary supervision. The general Poor Law should be broken up into its component parts; the county council would take over from the guardians, and the sick poor would thereafter be looked after by the Public Health Committee; children would be taught in the ordinary schools, not in Poor Law schools; others would become the responsibility of appropriate committees such as the asylums and pensions committees.[36] Thus the Poor Law would be effectively broken up.

The Mental Deficiency Act of 1913 transferred the responsibility for the mental defectives to the county councils, but apart from this no legislation resulted directly from the two reports, partly perhaps because of the outbreak of war in 1914. But another factor came to affect the situation – the growth of unemployment after the war, and the development of militant Poplarism.[37] It became clear that the old Poor Law was quite inappropriate to large-scale industrial unemployment, and that, in some parts of the country, the guardians were too closely involved with the recipients of relief to be a completely impartial administrative body. Furthermore, the introduction of national insurance had undermined one of the fundamental principles of the Poor Law – the need for each union to support its own poor, applying the workhouse test to the unemployed.

It was not until Neville Chamberlain's reign at the Ministry of Health that the reform of the Poor Law was undertaken. He was shaken by his experience of conflict with George Lansbury over Poplarism; he was convinced of the need for larger units of local administration and firmer central control; and he was determined to bring the Poor Law into the general pattern of local government.[38] He had to face opposition both inside and outside the Cabinet, but set about converting public opinion in preparation for a Bill transferring the duties of the guardians to the county councils.[39] He had also to convert his colleagues in the Cabinet, and they were reluctant to do anything precipitate.[40]

However, after much internal conflict with the Chancellor, Winston Churchill, over the financial provisions, Chamberlain introduced the Local Government Bill which abolished the guardians, transferring their duties to the counties and county boroughs. It enabled these authorities to break up the Poor Law by passing the hospitals over to the health committees, and other parts to their appropriate committees. The name 'Poor Law', with all its unpleasant associations with Chadwick and the 'workhouse test', was replaced by 'public assistance', although, legally, the Poor Law Act of 1601 remained the foundation of the system.

The old workhouse infirmaries had in fact by this time grown in many cases to be the greater part of the workhouses; they had become general hospitals, not only for the paupers, but for the major part of the population. Transferred to the health committees, they now expanded, and developed specialised branches for maternity, tuberculosis and other purposes. The infirmary buildings inherited from the guardians continued in most cases as the main hospital; the name might be changed to 'The Pines' or 'The Laurels', but they remained in law a branch of the Poor Law.

In 1934 another large part of the old Poor Law functions passed completely out of the hands of local authorities; the Unemployment Assistance Board took over the responsibility for the outdoor relief of the able-bodied unemployed,[41] who had previously been provided for by the Poor Law authority, once their period of insurance ran out. There remained, however, the sick, the aged and infirm, the crippled, homeless children, mothers with babies, and the casual poor, or vagrants; these categories remained under the care of the county and county borough councils, as Poor Law authorities. To them, the Elizabethan law of settlement still applied, together with the principle of the first duty to maintain them lying on the shoulders of their families. But they were in general no longer provided for in the old workhouses; 'cottage homes' for children and old people's homes for the aged had already been developed by the guardians. But yet there remained in the workhouses not only the sick, but many old people unable to look after themselves, and the temporarily homeless, the unfortunate and the vagrants.

The Second World War

The approach of the Second World War inevitably had its impact on local authorities; there had been plans for civil defence in the minds of the ministries since the end of the First World War; a preliminary scheme of regional organisation had been used at the time of the General Strike but had little time to take effect. In 1935 the government took steps to organise civil defence on a national scale, working through the local authorities; the Air Raid Precautions Act of 1937 and the Civil Defence Act of 1939 gave the local authorities full responsibility for civil defence, including the provision for shelters, housing the homeless, first aid, repair of houses and practically every other aspect of emergency action. In the pre-war period the local authority associations appear to have been mainly concerned with arguing about the cost of civil defence, trying to get the central government to accept at least 80 per cent of the cost, if not the whole. The central government felt some impatience with the reluctance of local government to recognise the urgency of positive action, and the refusal of a few local authorities to take any action at all.

With the Munich crisis, and then the outbreak of the war, the various provisional schemes came into force. Regional commissioners were appointed for each of the twelve civil defence regions; in 'normal war conditions' they were to co-ordinate the work of local authorities through persuasion and personal contact. But, in the event of London being captured or destroyed, they were to take over executive control and exercise 'full powers of civil government'.[42] The details of this plan were published in February 1939, and the government did what it could to forestall any criticism of a scheme which might be compared with the Cromwellian rule of the major-generals, or Hitler's *Gauleiters*. With a few exceptions, such objections were avoided.

Meanwhile the Home Office had arranged for the appointment in each local authority of an air raid precautions controller to take over responsibility for local services if war broke out; nearly half of these were town clerks, about a quarter were chief constables, and the rest were aldermen or councillors. They were to work with emergency committees, usually of three councillors or aldermen, to whom the local council would delegate all their executive functions. But local politics and personalities resulted in a wide variety of patterns in practice;[43] some authorities refused to delegate power to so small a body; others were reluctant to accept the idea that their town clerk, as ARP controller, had powers vested in him personally, as distinct from the traditional pattern of his being, in theory at least, no more than their servant and adviser.

It was in London that the impact on local government was strongest, greatly because the bombing was heavier there than in all but a few of the provincial cities, such as Dover, Southampton, Coventry and Canterbury. Before the war, London boroughs had had but few functions – mainly housing, libraries and sanitary inspection. But now, with the full brunt of bombing falling on them, with all its attendant physical and social problems, they became suddenly very important. On the shoulders of their town clerks there rested a great responsibility, and their town halls became centres of a new and vital activity. The scale of the problem with which the London local authorities had to cope is illustrated by the fact that in London in the four months from 7 September to 31 December 1940, 13,339 people were killed by enemy action, and 17,937 were admitted to hospital, most of them seriously injured. So too, at a later stage, when the flying bombs were being used in 1944, after three weeks of such attacks, there was a backlog of 194,000 houses awaiting repairs; over 20,000 were being damaged each day, and, in spite of a labour force of 33,000 men, arrears were mounting at the rate of 6,000 houses a day. It was with such problems as these that the London boroughs had to cope.

Because the country escaped invasion, the regional commissioners never assumed their wider powers. The local ARP controllers remained responsible for mitigating the distress and damage caused by enemy action. Civil defence, the evacuation and reception of schoolchildren and repair of buildings was organised from local council offices. Meanwhile, the regional commissioners steadily accumulated staff and they came to be used more and more as outposts of central ministries concerned to maintain communication with local authorities. Although accepted as necessary for war-time purposes, the regional headquarters were resented by local councillors as a threat of ever more central control. After the end of hostilities the regional commissioners' offices were disbanded.[44]

Beveridge and Reform

As the war advanced, more thought was given to the shape and nature of the post-war world; the social services, education, the control of land use, planning and the structure of local government came under review in a series of reports from commissions and committees.

The most significant of these was the Beveridge Report on Social Insurance and Allied Services,[45] which laid the foundation for the pattern of the 'Welfare State'. Out of this report and the subsequent discussions emerged a series of statutes. First came the National Insurance Act 1946, the National Insurance (Industrial Injuries) Act 1946 and the National Health Service Act 1946. It was this last measure which made most difference to the role of the local authorities; on the one hand it took away from them all the hospitals, maternity homes, sanatoria and mental hospitals, vesting them in the Minister of Health, to be administered through regional hospital boards. On the other hand, it expanded the lesser functions of local authorities in such fields as ambulances, prevention of sickness and after-care, midwifery, and the provision of health centres.[46] This Act in effect removed from the purview of the Poor Law one of the largest groups of what were technically paupers. No longer would they be treated as such, but rather as sick people, in need of medical help.

So, too, the unemployed, the aged, widows and those in need because of sickness were now covered by insurance schemes under the National Insurance Act and the National Insurance (Industrial Injuries) Act of 1946. Thus, they too were brought outside the scope of the Poor Law.

Another statute in the same category was the Children Act of 1948, springing from the recommendations of the Curtis Committee.[47] Previously, the responsibility of the local authorities had rested mainly on the Poor Law, with its provision that pauper children should be set to work or put out to be apprentices.[48] Much had changed since the beginning of the Elizabethan Poor Law and since the days of the Victorian workhouses depicted in *Oliver Twist*. Many children were looked after by voluntary societies; some were in children's homes provided by county or county borough councils; others were boarded out; but conditions were in many cases very unsatisfactory. The inadequacies of the law and of the provision made by local authorities were shown in the Curtis Report, which recommended that all responsibility for the care and maintenance of deprived children should be vested in one committee of each major authority, under the supervision of a single minister. Furthermore, the responsibility should extend to all children who, from any cause whatever, are deprived of a normal home life, not only those who were technically paupers. The Children Act followed these recommendations closely, making county and county borough councils responsible, through their children's committees, for all such children, who were thus taken out of the purview of the Poor Law, as others had been by the National Health Service Act, and the National Insurance Act.

Despite those provisions, there would still be some people in need, and financial help to them was now, under the National Assistance Act 1948, to be provided by the National Assistance Board, envisaged as a sort of safety net for those whose financial needs were not met by the other provisions. So, too, there remained some groups in need of help of other sorts – the blind, the deaf, cripples, the aged too infirm to look after themselves, and those who found themselves temporarily and unexpectedly homeless. For these, the counties and county boroughs were to make provision.

So, it appeared, the whole field of the old Poor Law was covered by the new legislation, and the Act of 1601, with all its innumerable amending statutes, could be repealed, and the ghosts of Edwin Chadwick, Oliver Twist, and the doctrine of the 'workhouse test' could be laid.[49] This was achieved by the portentous opening words of the Act – 'The existing Poor Law shall cease to have effect.' The word 'pauper' thereby ceased to have any meaning in English law.

Another statute of the same period which had a great effect on the duties of local authorities was the Education Act of 1944, a product of the Coalition Government, and commonly called after its sponsor, R. A. Butler, then Minister of Education. It repealed the previous legislation, and transferred the whole responsibility for public education to the county and county borough councils, making them responsible for reorganising their secondary schools to provide education appropriate to the pupils' age, aptitude and ability. At the time, this was generally interpreted as meaning grammar schools for the academically inclined, technical schools for the practically minded, and modern schools for those of general abilities, all to be of equal esteem and importance. But out of this developed a ferment of experimenting in new forms; multi-lateral schools, bi-lateral schools, sixth-form colleges and comprehensive schools.

The Education Act also raised the school-leaving age to 15, with provision for a later rise to 16. It provided for local education authorities paying grants to students at universities and colleges, and it established the principle of part-time education in 'county colleges' for youths over school age. It abolished all fees in schools outside the private and 'direct grant' field. But it also provided for a general oversight of the whole system by the Secretary of State, with power to give orders if he thought that local education authorities were behaving, or proposing to act, unreasonably.[50]

One direct effect of the war was the destruction of very large numbers of houses in London and a number of other cities and towns.[51] No new houses were built and, when the war finished, there was an immediate demand, from returning soldiers and others, for somewhere to live. After the First World War, Lloyd George had demanded 'homes for heroes'. After the second, Churchill demanded 'work, food and homes'. and immediate action was taken to meet the demand; 180,000 prefabricated metal houses were erected; councils were helped to get house-building started again, and a start was made on the building of new towns.

The idea of creating completely new towns had a long history, including such early examples as Winchelsea, New Lanark and Charterville. More recently, there had been successful experiments at Bournville, Letchworth and Welwyn Garden City. The Barlow Commission had advocated the same policy in 1940,[52] and in 1945 a committee under Lord Reith[53] had worked out in detail how such a policy could be implemented, with a primary purpose of relieving the great pressure in war-damaged London. In 1946 the New Towns Act was passed, and the first steps taken towards the actual building of the houses; but the responsibility for building and managing the towns was given not to the local authorities, but to special development corporations appointed by the minister – a proposal much criticised in the parliamentary debates.[54]

Meanwhile, the local authorities themselves were building year by year an increasing number of houses, reaching a pinnacle of over 200,000 in 1952–3.[55] Such activity in building, added to the reorganisation of industry and development of all sorts, had been foreseen, and the whole problem of land use, control of development, and the problem of who should receive the increased value of land for development, had been considered by two major inquiries – the Uthwatt Committee[56] on Compensation and Betterment, and the Scott Committee on Land Utilisation.[57] The pre-war planning, based on the Town and Country Planning Act of 1932, had proved quite inadequate, for two principal reasons: first, the controls only applied to those areas for which the local authority had made a scheme, when this had been approved by the minister; by 1 April 1939, only about 2 per cent of the land in the United Kingdom was covered by such approved schemes. Secondly, the cost of good planning was proving to be prohibitive; owners prevented from development were entitled to compensation, and the provisions in the Act for payments from the adjoining owners for betterment were of little practical value. The planning authorities – county boroughs and county districts – found that they could not afford good planning, even if they wanted it.

The Act of 1932 had, however, accepted an enlarged view of the role of planning; it was no longer seen as merely a matter of the layout of new urban areas, but rather as a means of making the best use of all the land in the country, planning for the future of both urban and rural areas.[58] Out of these experiences and arguments, there emerged the Town and Country Planning Bill of 1947. It brought the whole of the country within the ambit of the planning law; it transferred responsibility from the district councils to the county councils; it regulated all forms of development, which was comprehensively defined as 'the carrying out of building, engineering, mining or other operations in, on, over or under land, or the making of any material change in the use of any buildings or . . . land'.[59]

The most controversial aspect of the Bill was the provision

relating to compensation and betterment. The old approach was abandoned. Instead, from the date of the Act, all owners of land were to be regarded as if they held their land subject to restrictive covenants, prohibiting its use for any purpose other than its present use. If, then, they applied for, and got, permission to develop, they had to buy the right to do so, at a price equal to the increase in the value of the land arising out of the permission to develop – the 'development charge'. Thus, tne increase in value of the land, which arose out of the demand for development, flowed not to the private owner but to the community, in the shape of the local authority. If permission to develop was refused, there was no compensation to the owner or occupier.

But many people, including charities and trustees, had legitimately and properly bought land at a value above its present use value, hoping to realise that extra value when they developed, or sold for development. They would be heavily penalised by these provisions, and so the Bill provided for their being compensated out of a national fund of £300 million, to be distributed among those who, on 1 July 1948, owned land then 'ripe for development' – that is to say, land which had a substantially higher value if it were used for development than it had for its existing user.

The financial provisions, though ingenious, did not work as they were meant to; there was no longer any financial benefit to be reaped from developing land, because it all went in the development charge. The new system, therefore, inhibited development and angered landowners, who saw the development charges as a tax. So, when the Conservatives were back in office, these provisions were repealed and a much modified system of compensation in case of refusal of permission to develop was substituted.[60] The development charges which had already been paid were returned (sometimes to the wrong person) and the grand share-out of £300 million was abandoned.

One effect of this change of policy was unfortunate. Under the Act of 1947, the owner of land who applied for permission to develop was in much the same position financially whether he was refused permission (and so restricted to the present user) or whether he was granted permission (and had to pay a development charge equal to the added value). But after the repeal of the Act, this was no longer so. If he got permission to develop, he received thereby, as a general rule, a great financial bonus in the added value of his land. Permission to develop thereby became a valuable commodity, worth perhaps tens or hundreds of thousands of pounds. It was, therefore, worth buying, and many of the criminal prosecutions of recent years, in which corruption has been proved in local government, have been founded on the advantage that a man may get from permission to develop his land, and the great profit to be made thereby.

The repeal of these provisions relating to the 'development charge' had another indirect effect on local authorities. Under the 1947 Act, they enjoyed a favoured position, being able to buy land at only the 'present use value'. After its repeal, they had to pay a sum corresponding much more nearly to the current market price, and so they came to be in much the same position as ordinary purchasers.

More important, however, from the local government point of view, was the development of the machinery and procedure of planning control. What had before the war been a very minor part of the local authorities' duties was now becoming one of the most important, and the most complicated. Inevitably, the content of planning expanded beyond the initial concept of the layout of roads and land use; it came, step by step, to encompass social problems of housing and recreation, industrial problems of the location of industry and commercial development, cultural problems such as the conservation of buildings and their environment; almost every aspect of human life was within the consideration of the planner, and might affect the decisions of the planning committees. To some people, this seemed to be an intolerable growth of paternalism; to others, a desirable extension of social control.

Retreat from Municipal Activities

While functions of local authorities were expanding in these fields of planning, education and housing, they were contracting in other ways. Their hospitals were taken away by the National Health Service Act 1946. At the same period they began to lose trading undertakings which had been built up over previous decades. The Labour Party was now more interested in nationalisation than municipalisation and the technical developments of the twentieth century were demanding larger areas for gas, electricity and water. So these services were taken from local authorities and private enterprise and vested in regional bodies appointed by a minister. Each had its own, technically convenient, area of supply. The Electricity Act 1947, and the Gas Act 1948, provide the leading examples. The procedure under the Water Act 1945, for *ad hoc* piecemeal amalgamations of local undertakings aroused considerable local protest and failed in its objective of rationalising distribution. Ultimately, the Water Act 1973 transferred the water supply and the main sewerage system to regional water authorities. Thus the local authorities were forced to surrender, under the impetus of nationalisation, many of their trading activities. Also, having lost their hospitals in 1948 they parted with their remaining responsibilities for personal health under the National Health Service Reorganisation Act 1973.

It seemed in 1968 as if municipal bus undertakings were about to follow the same path as gas and electricity. The Transport Act of that year provided for the creation of passenger transport executives appointed by the government in the major provincial conurbations. These took over municipal and other road passenger transport services. However, almost immediately a reaction took place and the pendulum began to swing back. In 1969 the Greater London Council accepted responsibility for London buses which had been controlled by an independent public corporation since 1934. Then the Local Government Act 1972 nominated metropolitan counties as passenger transport authorities and the four passenger transport executives nominated under the 1968 Act passed back into local authority control. Transport has been treated differently from the other traditional municipal services because it raises issues not simply of technical efficiency but of social policy. The problem about public transport has become: which services should be maintained by subsidy and which should be abandoned?

The transfer of functions from the elected local authorities allowed, indeed required, a new tangle of nominated boards and councils. In the nineteenth century this had happened at the parish or district level – highway boards, local boards of health, Poor Law guardians, burial boards, drainage boards, inspectors of lighting and watching, commissioners of baths and washhouses, and so on. Now the process was being repeated at a higher level. There was now a similar confusion of boards, with varying boundaries for a variety of purposes, and with no co-ordinating authority or organised co-ordination.

Among these were

> Regional Economic Planning Councils
> Regional Sports Councils
> Regional Electricity Boards
> Regional Gas Boards
> Regional Water Authorities
> Regional Arts Councils
> Regional Tourist Boards
> Regional Health Authorities.

The police had been slowly reorganised on the basis of larger forces, covering in some cases several county boroughs and counties; the control of colleges of advanced technology had passed from local authorities when they were promoted to university status in 1966, and, in a number of other ways, the powers of local authorities were being reduced, and responsibility was passing out of the hands of elected councillors.

Similar action was widely advocated for a number of other municipal services – for example, evidence given before the Royal Commission on the Police by the Law Society and the Police Federation urged the creation of regional police authorities[61] divorced from local government; the Crowther Report[62] recommended the creation of regional planning authorities, and professional planners argued for the planning functions to be taken right out of local politics. Similar pleas were heard from educationists and social workers, all arguing that their own service was so important that it should be entrusted to experts, not to amateur local politicians. This attitude was reinforced by two further influences; the demand for suitable areas and boundaries for each service, and the problem of inadequate financial resources which led critics to propose the transfer of functions from local to central government.[63] Thus there grew up a strong pressure from several quarters to strip local authorities of even more of their functions.

Ultra Vires *and Local Bills*

This actual and threatened erosion of the powers of local authorities made them look the more carefully at the restrictions on their activities, which kept them within narrow statutory limits; the restraining effect of the doctrine of *ultra vires* was a serious limitation of the powers of local authorities. The doctrine had been evolved in relation to 'statutory authorities', and in particular to limited liability companies. Strictly, it never applied to boroughs created by royal charter,[64] but, in effect, the law for these authorities was much the same – that they must not spend money out of the Rate Fund on anything not specifically authorised by Act of Parliament – as the law for statutory authorities, that they legally were incapable of acting outside the authority of Acts of Parliament.[65]

The restrictive effect of this had long given rise to complaint and had led to much unnecessary expenditure in promoting local Bills to obtain even the most trivial powers – the Abingdon Corporation Bill 1951, for example, contained powers to put small fish into the river Thames, to provide mooring places for the boats of anglers who wanted to pull them out again, and to provide footbridges over the streams and ditches on the riverside. The Newquay UDC Act of 1967 authorised the district council to plant trees and shrubs on their own land and, by a later subsection, to cut them down again. Such activities would otherwise have been *ultra vires*.

But, in 1963, Rupert Speir, a Conservative member, introduced a private member's Bill, in which he was supported and encouraged by the Ministry of Housing and Local Government. It was a modest measure in comparison with some of those introduced in the 1920s by the Labour Party, but yet it made a substantial inroad into the *ultra vires* doctrine. A clause in the Bill, originally suggested by the Association of Municipal Corporations, allowed local authorities to spend a rate of one penny in the pound on anything which, in their opinion, is in the interests of their area or its inhabitants, other than their existing statutory functions.[66] The Bill, unlike the enabling Bills of the 1920s, was passed. To the major authorities it did not mean very much, because they already had very wide powers; it did, however, save trouble about minor services which were desirable but were *ultra vires*. But it was of very great importance to the parish councils. They, however, had not originally been included in the draft Bill, and when their National Association pressed their claim, they were only included on the basis of being allowed to spend the absurdly low figure of a fifth of a penny rate – in many villages only a few pounds a year. None the less, there was a great outburst of enterprise among the parish councils up and down the country, able at last, within these narrow limits, to provide a variety of useful services – car parks, village surgeries, preservation of old buildings, disposal of abandoned cars, etc., lifebelts at bathing places, parish guides and histories, and many other services for which they had previously lacked statutory power.[67]

The value of this provision was established by this extensive use by parish councils, and the Local Government Act of 1972 raised the limit from one fifth of an old penny rate to two new pence – an increase of twenty-four-fold; at the same time, it removed the previous ceiling of a 4d rate on the total expenditure of a parish council, thus setting them free to spend whatever they judged necessary.

The Redcliffe-Maud Commission, in considering the functions of local authorities, recommended that this power should be made general, without any statutory limit: 'We suggest that the only limit on the use of the new power should be the wishes of the electors and such restrictions as have to be placed on local government expenditure in the interests of national economic and financial policy.'[68] The Local Government Act 1972, however, included no such provision for a general competence for local authorities.

The 'free twopence' of the Local Government Act 1972 did not remove the need for local act powers, and it did not in any way affect those powers which dealt not with the provision of new services but with the control or supervision of other people's activities. But since the Second World War the volume of local Acts had been somewhat reduced, partly because of the cost of the procedure, and partly because of a growing tendency on the part of the ministries to oppose any clauses that could be dealt with by public general Acts, even though the introduction of such Bills was not included in the legislative programme. So the number of local Bills promoted by local authorities fell to about twenty a year by 1965-7, and these bills contained generally fewer pioneering provisions – though some were still included, such as the 1965 'Manchester Clause' aimed at establishing closer control over dealing in drugs in the evening clubs of the town, extended by the Brighton Act of 1966 to coffee bars, and copied by a number of other authorities;[69] and the proposal in the West Midlands County Council Bill of 1976 for motor racing in the streets, which was sternly rejected by the House of Commons.[70]

The departments also attempted to stop the well-established procedure by which county councils promoted Bills to give powers not only to themselves, but also to the district councils in their areas. The Kent County Council Bill of 1958 was drastically curtailed by the exclusion of all such clauses, but the outcry from the local authorities was such that a Joint Select Committee of both Houses was appointed to consider the matter, and reported in favour of the resumption of this practice.[71] County council Bills thereafter continued to include clauses for the benefit of district councils, and also, in many cases of parish councils.[72]

Perhaps the most controversial case of private Bill legislation in this period was that of the Brighton Marina. A development company persuaded Brighton Corporation to support its scheme for building a 'marina' or yachting harbour out into the sea, with hotels, flats, a casino, an ice-rink, cross-channel ferry and shops, at a total cost then estimated at £10 million (but later estimated at £50–100 million). The company promoted a Bill, supported by the corporation, to get authority to build on the foreshore, about half a mile of which would have to be closed to the public. Objection was taken to this, and to the grant of compulsory purchase powers for what was essentially a private commercial, rather than a public, purpose. In the Commons, contrary to normal practice in private Bills, a number of amendments were moved at Third Reading, and in the Lords a procedural precedent was created; though the Bill was technically 'unopposed', the Select Committee was authorised to hear evidence other than that tendered by the promoters, because of the controversial nature of the Bill. None the less, the Bill was passed, with some hesitation, in both Houses.[73]

A subsequent Bill, presented by Brighton Corporation, to enable it to provide the necessary access roads and car parks, was rejected in 1969, but passed, after further opposition, in 1970.[74] There was much reluctance to use the procedure of local Bills and compulsory legislation for the support of large-scale commercial enterprise of this sort.

There had, however, accumulated over the centuries a vast jungle of local Act provisions; much of this was obsolete, and much of it had been superseded by subsequent public general statutes. But yet there remained a great quantity of relevant provisions in the local Acts. But the redrawing of boundaries under the 1972 Act made the matter yet more complicated, for, as authorities were amalgamated, different provisions applied in different parts of the new areas. The Act therefore provided, in order to disentangle the matter, that all existing local Acts were to be automatically repealed, in the case of metropolitan counties by the end of 1979, and elsewhere by the end of 1984. Meanwhile, the local authorities were to comb through their local Act powers and promote new Bills to continue such powers as they still needed.

Social Services and Participation

The Redcliffe-Maud Commission also gave its mind to the relation between the various types of social service provided by local authorities. Since 1948, there had been a series of inquiries into different aspects of the local authority services.[75] The variety of these reports showed the extent to which the social services had come to be broken down into distinct and sometimes overlapping provision for families or individuals in trouble. The Ingleby Committee on Children and Young Persons had drawn attention to this, and had suggested that 'it may be that the long-term solution will be in a reorganisation of the various services concerned with the family and their combination into a unified family service . . .'[76]

In other countries, and particularly the United States, there was a move to bring the various social services into closer relation to each other. In England and Wales, most of the services had their origins in the old Poor Law. It now seemed as if the 'break-up of the Poor Law' had gone too far in separating the different agencies which existed to help those in trouble or need. So, in 1965, a committee was appointed, under the chairmanship of Frederic Seebohm 'to review the organisations and responsibilities of the local authority personal social services in England and Wales, and to consider what changes are desirable to secure an effective family service'.

The committee made a clear and unanimous recommendation that the various social services should be brought together in a unified social service department within each major local authority, including the existing children's and welfare departments, with elements from the education, health and housing departments, and additional responsibilities designed to ensure an effective family service.[77]

The principles involved in this report were widely accepted and were written into the Local Authority Social Services Act 1970, passed just before the Labour Party went out of office. It did not achieve all the objects of the Seebohm Report; housing was left out, as the district councils were still responsible for this, and the introduction of Redcliffe-Maud's 'unitary authorities' had not been achieved;[78] the health services were omitted because the government proposed to reorganise the whole National Health Service; and school welfare was not mentioned. None the less, the Act did achieve the greater part of its purpose in creating an integrated social service in each county.

This reorganisation of the social services was in accordance with a changing attitude to the functions of local authorities. These were, by many people, coming to be seen less as a collection of diverse duties and powers under a variety of statutes, more as an all-embracing range of responsibility for the well-being of the people of an area. The emphasis, developing in the early 1970s, on 'corporate management' stressed this view of local government, rather than the traditional attitude of separate departments, each under its appropriate chief officer and committee anxious to get on with its job, without interference by other departments. The Maud Committee on Management in Local Government had proclaimed that 'in the wider context, individual services however disparate are provided for the community as a whole. Planning for the development of the community, the allocation of priorities for finance or for space on the drawing board, the timing of the various schemes all demand a co-ordinated approach.'[79]

Professor Stewart, in his advocacy of 'corporate management' went further, and claimed that

'the philosophy of general management in local government rests on the view that the local authority is the "primary" organ of government within the areas for which it is responsible. Within the area that it administers, individuals, families and organisations have developed a pattern of life. That pattern has been deeply influenced by the environment – both the natural, physical environment and the social, economic, political and technical environment, and has itself moulded that environment. In a very real sense, the general management of a local authority is the management of that environment, for the individuals, groups and organisations that live within that environment.'[80]

This increasingly paternalistic view of the role of local authorities advanced a stage further in the report of the Bains Committee in 1972, which stated that[81]

'Local government is not, in our view, limited to the narrow provision of a series of services to the local community, though we do not intend in any way to suggest that these services are not important. It has within its purview the overall economic, cultural and physical wellbeing of that community and, for this reason, its decisions impinge with increasing frequency upon the individual lives of its citizens.'[82]

Such a grandiloquent claim is far removed from the exact legalistic attitude to functions of local authorities which was usual in the text books of the earlier part of the century.

Perhaps as an antidote to paternalism there also developed a growing concern about the relationship – or rather the lack of relationship – between the government and the governed. Both the Maud Committee on Management and the Redcliffe-Maud Commission[83] had remarked on 'the indefinable gulf between local authorities and the communities which they serve'. The recognition of this gulf stimulated a desire to bridge it both through greater participation in local affairs and by the provision of better means to deal with grievances. In 1966 a parliamentary commissioner had been established to review complaints against the Civil Service: quite inevitably, the issue was then raised of extending this type of arrangement to local authorities. Harold Wilson, in a statement to the House of Commons in July 1969, accepted the principle of using similar checks against maladministration in local government. Such a system was initiated by the Local Government Act 1974.

The increasing interest in the preservation of the environment was demonstrated both by letters to local papers and by the extraordinary growth of residents' associations and amenity societies[84] demanding a voice in the planning of their towns and villages. Other national bodies, some with vigorous local branches, sought to bring pressure to bear on local councils; notable examples were the Campaign for the advancement of State Education, Shelter, and the Neighbourhood Councils Association. Out of this last organisation there developed a demand for something in the nature of parish councils, in the wards and communities of London and other large cities.

The government took notice of this growing demand for 'participation' in two ways. First in 1968 a committee was appointed under Mr Arthur Skeffington, MP, to consider how the public could be given a larger voice in the formulation of development plans of the towns and villages in which they live; and they thought not only of those who join amenity societies and other such groups, but also the 'non-joiners', perhaps less articulate but just as much concerned.[85]

Secondly, in 1974 the Department of the Environment consulted the Local Authority Associations and the political parties on how best to create neighbourhood councils in the big cities, building on the experience of those authorities such as Kensington, Hornsey and Lambeth, which had already sponsored the birth of such bodies in parts of their areas.[86] This movement sprang in part at least from the fact that local authorities had come to be so much more important in the lives of their people. As landlords of nearly a third of the houses in the country, as arbiters of planning, education and much else besides they had become so significant that the man in the street could not ignore them. But yet the official processes of election coupled with the party systems did not seem to give him an adequate voice in shaping his own destiny. There was something lacking in our democratic system – an adequate link between rulers and the ruled. And so there grew up, side by side with the statutory local authorities, a complicated network of unofficial bodies, aiming at exercising influence on the working of local authorities, without actually taking part in the formal procedures.

NOTES

1 But see S. and B. Webb, *Statutory Authorities for Special Purposes* (1927), and F. H. Spencer, *Municipal Origins* (1911), both of which deal with the first part of this period.

2 On the incorporation of Local Act provisions in Public General Acts, see Ministry of Health Annual Report, 1937–8, p. 141; Dame Evelyn Sharp, *The Ministry of Housing and Local Government* (1969), pp. 52–4.

3 Lands Clauses Consolidation Act 1845; Town Police Clauses Act 1847; Towns Improvement Clauses Act 1847; Cemeteries Clauses Act 1847; Commissioners Clauses Act 1847; Waterworks Clauses Acts 1847; etc.

4 See Herman Finer, *Municipal Trading* (1941); Lord Avebury, *On Municipal and National Trading* (1906); Leonard Darwin, *Municipal Trade* (1903).

5 Birmingham Improvement Act 1851.

6 Bolton Corporation Act 1850.

7 City of Bath Act 1851.

8 Leeds Improvement Act 1866.

9 Liverpool Improvement Act 1865.

10 Newcastle Improvement Act 1865.

11 Rochdale Corporation Act 1900.

12 Halifax Corporation Act 1900.

13 County Councils (Bills in Parliament) Act 1903.

14 See J. Collings and J. L. Green, *Life of Jesse Collings* (1920), p. 192; A. L. Thorold, *Life of Henry Labouchere* (1913), p. 433; Corrie Grant, *The Parish Councillor's Handbook* (1894), pp. 1–6.

15 Gladstone in Parl. Deb., 8 February 1893, vol. XXII, p. 225. See also Parl. Deb., 2 November 1893, vol. XXVI, pp. 1–82; Jesse Collings, *Land Reform* (1908), pp. 184–5.

16 Allotments Acts 1887, 1890, 1922, 1925; Smallholdings Act 1892; Smallholdings and Allotments Acts 1907, 1908, 1926; Allotments Extension Act 1882; etc.

17 A. L. Thorold, op. cit., p. 533.

18 1900, (305), vii.

19 1903, (270), vii.

20 For a full description covering the period up to 1939, see H. Finer, *Municipal Trading*.

21 [1906], 1 Ch. 643.

22 *Attorney General* v. *Fulham Corporation* [1921], 1 Ch. 440.

23 Royal Commission on *Transport*, Minutes of Evidence, vol. 1, p. 253 (HMSO, 1929).

24 The provisions of the Parliament Act 1911 did not apply to local legislation, so the Lords had an absolute veto.

25 Finer, op. cit., p. 147.

26 J. B. Cullingworth, *Housing and Local Government* (1966), pp. 24, 28.

27 *Statistics of Education 1971* (HMSO), vol. 5, p. 3.

28 See Peter G. Richards, *Delegation in Local Government* (1956), chs. I and II. Redlich and Hirst, *The History of Local Government in England* (1901), pp. 202 *et seq.*

29 Midwives Act 1902; Smallholdings and Allotments Act 1907; Education (Choice of Employment) Act 1910; Shops Act 1912; Rats and Mice Destruction Act 1919; Advertisements Regulation Act 1925.
30 See pp. 201–3.
31 Royal Commission on *Local Government*, Minutes of Evidence, Part X, (HMSO, 1928). See also Peter G. Richards, op. cit., ch. II.
32 Royal Commission on *Local Government*, 2nd Report, p. 49; 1928–9, Cmd 3213, viii.
33 White Paper, *Functions of County Councils and County District Councils in England and Wales*, paras. 8–24; 1956–7, Cmnd 161, xxvi.
34 Lady Gwendoline Cecil, *Life of Lord Salisbury* (1931), vol. III, p. 327. George Brodrick had advocated the same policy in the Cobden Club Essays, *Local Government and Taxation* (1875), p. 85.
35 1909, Cd 4499, xxxvii.
36 See Beatrice Webb, *Our Partnership* (1948), chs. VII and VIII; S. and B. Webb, *English Poor Law Policy* (1910), chs. V, VI and VII.
37 See ch. IV.
38 Keith Feiling, *Life of Neville Chamberlain* (1947), ch. XI.
39 Letter to his sister Hilda, 4 December 1927, Chamberlain Papers, Birmingham University Library. 'I wonder if you have noticed the constant reports in the press of extravagance on the part of various Boards of Guardians and of observations by M/H Inspectors brought to their notice. This is part of a deliberate plan of campaign designed to awaken public opinion.'
40 Letter to his sister Ida, 5 February 1927, Chamberlain Papers, Birmingham University Library. 'Cabinet decides to postpone Poor Law legislation until the Autumn. The fact is the Cabinet has got cold feet in view of the General Election, although we hope to put that off till 1929.' See also Keith Feiling, op. cit., pp. 142–8.
41 Unemployment Act 1934.
42 For the war-time organisation, see T. H. O'Brien, *History of the Second World War, Civil Defence* (HMSO, 1955).
43 See T. H. O'Brien, op. cit., pp. 313–15.
44 See Regionaliter, 'The regional commissioners', in *Political Quarterly*, 1941, vol. 12, No. 2, pp. 148–53, reprinted in W. Thornhill, *The Case for Regional Reform* (1972), pp. 87–93.
45 1942–3, Cmd 6402, vi.
46 The original proposal of building health centres in which all services, including doctors, dentists and pharmacists, would be available, was slowly dropped, because of the cost.
47 Report of the Interdepartmental Committee on the *Care of Children*, 1945–6, Cmd 6922, x.
48 43 Eliz. cap. 2, sec. 1.
49 In fact, schedule 7 of the Act repealed eighty previous Acts in whole or in part.
50 Sec. 68.
51 280,000 houses were destroyed, 250,000 made uninhabitable, and 250,000 seriously damaged. M. Foot, *Aneurin Bevan* (1973), p. 67.
52 Royal Commission on the *Distribution of the Industrial Population*, 1939–40, Cmd 6153, iv.
53 Reports of Committee on *New Towns*, 1945–6, Cmd 6759, Cmd 6794, Cmd 6876, xiv.
54 422 H.C. Deb., 8 May 1946, col. 1072 *et seq.*
55 For the details of the Conservative Government's housing drive, and

the creation of Regional Housing Production Boards, see Harold Macmillan, *Tides of Fortune* (1969), pp. 39 *et seq.*
56 Report, 1941–2, Cmd 6386, iv.
57 Report, 1941–2, Cmd 6378, iv.
58 The Surrey County Council Act 1931 had first extended the control to rural areas. The demand for control in the rural areas had, to a great extent, been expressed through the Council for the Preservation of Rural England, and in writings by G. M. Trevelyan, Patrick Abercrombie and Thomas Sharp.
59 Town and County Planning Act 1947, sec. 12(2).
60 Town and Country Planning Act 1954. See also Harold Macmillan, *Tides of Fortune* (1969), pp. 427 *et seq.*, and Evelyn Sharp, *The Ministry of Housing and Local Government* (1969), ch. VI.
61 Final Report of the Royal Commission on the *Police*, paras. 119–27; 1961–2, Cmnd 1728, xx.
62 *Traffic in Towns*, a Report of the Steering Group appointed by the Minister of Transport (HMSO, 1963).
63 e.g. A. R. Ilersic, *Local Government at the Crossroads* (1975).
64 See C. A. Cross, *Principles of Local Government Law*, 2nd edn (1962), pp. 6–16, and B. Keith-Lucas, *Public Administration* (1949), vol. XXVII, pp. 87 *et seq.*
65 See pp. 28–30.
66 Local Government (Financial Provisions) Act 1963, sec. 6.
67 See Memorandum of Evidence from the National Association of Parish Councils to the Royal Commission on Local Government, Appendix 6 (HMSO, 1967).
68 Report of the Royal Commission on *Local Government in England*, para. 323; 1968–9, Cmnd 4040, xxxviii.
69 Manchester Corporation Act 1965, sec. 18, extended to coffee bars in the Brighton Corporation Act 1966, sec. 7, and copied in the Kingston-upon-Hull Corporation Act 1967, sec. 47, the Guildford Corporation Act 1967, sec. 78, and the Torbay Corporation Act 1971, secs. 90–6.
70 906. H.C. Deb., 11 February 1976, col. 527 *et seq.*
71 E. Melling, *History of the Kent County Council 1888–1974* (1974), p. 107.
72 e.g. Somerset County Council Act 1967, secs. 15, 25, 40 and 41.
73 749 H.C. Deb., 26 June 1967, col. 173 *et seq*; 286 H.L. Deb., 23 November 1967, cols. 1144–50.
74 796 H.C. Deb., 23 February 1970, col. 925 *et seq.*
75 Guillebaud Committee on the *Cost of the National Health Service* (1956), Cmd 9663; Jameson Report, *An Inquiry into Health Visiting* (1956); the Royal Commission on the *Law Relating to Mental Illness and Mental Deficiency* (1957), Cmnd 169; Albemarle Committee on the *Youth Service* (1960), Cmnd 929; Younghusband Report on *Social Workers in the Local Authority* (1959); and the Ingleby Committee on *Children and Young Persons* (1960), Cmnd 1191.
76 Para. 47.
77 Report of the Committee on Local Authority and Allied Personal Social Services, p. 43; 1967–8, Cmnd 3703, xxxii.
78 Circular DoE, 18/74, DHSS, 4/74, encouraged county councils to delegate the function of housing the homeless to district councils.
79 Vol. 1, para 98 (HMSO, 1967).
80 J. D. Stewart, *Management in Local Government* (1971), p. 17.

81 *The New Local Authorities: Management and Structure*, Report of a Study Group on Local Authority Management Structures (HMSO, 1972), p. 6.

82 Ch. 2.

83 Paras. 95–9.

84 The Kent Federation of Amenity Societies, for example, in 1975 had sixty-two constituent societies; this figure did not include all the small societies, of which, in Canterbury alone, there were eight outside the Federation. Dr Kenneth Newton identified at least 4,250 pressure groups of one sort or another in Birmingham, *Second City Politics* (1976). See also Anthony Barker, *The Local Amenity Movement* (1976).

85 *People and Planning*. Report of the Committee on Public Participation in Planning (HMSO, 1969).

86 Consultation Paper LG4/743/45 of 1974. See also Michael Young, *The Hornsey Plan: A Role for Neighbourhood Councils in the New Local Government* (1970).

Chapter IV

POPLARISM

In the history of English local government there have been few dramatic events which have changed the course of affairs, as Waterloo or Lepanto did in continental history. But there is one outstanding case of a series of events which did play a very significant and somewhat dramatic part in the history of English local government – that long-drawn episode which is commonly referred to as 'Poplarism'.[1] This is the outstanding example of conflict between central and local government, which illustrates the thesis that when such conflicts do arise, the strictly legal relationship is soon submerged in the political. It illustrates also the degree to which party ideology may influence local administration, and belies the argument that there is no real difference between a Labour and a Conservative way of running local government. Furthermore, this chronicle shows how the action of individual local authorities may influence not only the politics of the day, but the whole climate of opinion within which legislation takes place. Poplarism indeed is one of the most important events in the history of English Poor Law, as well as in the history of local government. It, therefore, deserves special treatment, in considerably more detail than can be given to other parts of the history of local government.[2]

The parish of Poplar lies in East London, in the poorest part of the dock area, between Stepney and West Ham. This single parish coincided both with the Poor Law Union and, after 1899, with the metropolitan borough of the same name.

In the latter part of the nineteenth century the union workhouse was run by the guardians in a rather easy-going way. An unsuccessful experiment had been tried in 1871 to make it a 'test-house' for the whole of London, where the able-bodied unemployed were treated with the full rigour of 'less eligibility' and the 'workhouse test', but this had been abandoned seven years later.

The law as it then stood excluded poor men from playing a part in administering the Poor Law. All Justices of the Peace were *ex officio* guardians, and the other members were elected by a system of plural voting, which gave as many as six votes to the larger ratepayers, and completely disfranchised those who, for themselves or their families, received Poor Relief. Moreover, no one was eligible for election who was not the occupier of land worth £40 a year. When, in 1892, this was reduced to £10, two Labour guardians were returned at the election in Poplar – Will Crooks and George Lansbury. Two years later plural voting and *ex officio* members were abolished by the Local Government Act 1894. Actual paupers were still disqualified, but the main barriers which had kept poor men off the Boards of Guardians had gone.

The number of Labour guardians in Poplar quickly rose to five, and Crooks became chairman of the board. From then on, although the Labour members remained in a minority until 1919, in effect they controlled the administration. The old guardians had been on the whole well-meaning, but easy-going tradesmen and shopkeepers, who left things very much in the hands of their officers. Now they were shocked to realise some of the abuses that had grown up, and were apparently easily led by the more enterprising and enthusiastic socialists. Some, however, were determined to continue the existing system without change. Others recognised that abuses must be remedied, but feared the ultimate results of too drastic a change.

So the forces were arrayed for conflict. On the one side stood the socialists, led by Crooks and Lansbury. They were in revolt against the inhumanity of the workhouse system, against the low standard of food and clothing for the paupers, and against the whole spirit of 'less eligibility'. Not least, they demanded more generous treatment of the 'outdoor' paupers in their own homes. In his autobiography Lansbury wrote: 'From the first moment I determined to fight for one policy only and that was decent treatment for the poor outside the workhouse, and hang the rates!'[3]

The official policy of the Poor Law Board was still based on the principle of less eligibility – the doctrine that the lot of the unemployed pauper on poor relief must be less eligible than that of a man in employment. This doctrine had been much modified in practice by the beginning of the century, but it still applied in theory.

The Labour guardians of Poplar, however, rejected the doctrine completely. They saw their duty as that of relieving the sufferings of the poor, without reference to any such limit. They did much to improve the conditions in their workhouse; with the aid of Joseph Fels, a rich American soap manufacturer, they established farm colonies for the unemployed at Laindon in Essex and Hollesley Bay. They abandoned the rule, also established in 1834, that no relief should be given to the able-bodied except in the workhouse, and they justified their giving outdoor relief to the unemployed by reference to an order of 1852, which allowed such relief in cases of sudden and urgent necessity.

It is not surprising that in these circumstances their expenses should rise and the number of paupers increase. And as the scale of the problem grew bigger, so it became more difficult for the guardians to supervise the administration. Rumours were heard (as they had been for many years before) of jobbery in the granting of contracts, and of guardians eating and drinking copiously at the public expense. Indignant ratepayers united to form a Poplar Municipal Alliance, determined to prevent extravagance and waste.

In 1906, at the request of the Municipal Alliance, an inquiry was instituted by the Local Government Board. The chief inspector of the board, Mr (later Sir James) Davy, was instructed to investigate the complaints against the guardians. The Municipal Alliance, represented by counsel, acted in effect as prosecutors. Basically there were two charges – that the guardians gave assistance to the poor with too generous a hand, both inside and outside the workhouse, and that individual guardians had regulated the workhouse rations and contracts to their own advantage. Much of the evidence was about a room in the workhouse, commonly called 'the Horn of Plenty', where, it was alleged, officers and guardians drank freely. The accounts of this were probably exaggerated; but the plea that the rolling gait of two of the guardians was due to their sea-faring past was unconvincing.[4] Mr Davy found that most of the personal charges against individual guardians were not proved, but that 'some have been guilty of misconduct in relation to the management of the workhouse, and that, to say the least of it, there has been a great want of business capacity in dealing with the contracts'. On the charge of adopting an unwise policy he found the guardians guilty; this generosity in giving relief was, he held, encouraging pauperism. Moreover, the giving of outdoor relief to the unemployed was subsidising and encouraging the system of casual labour. 'It seems clear that the giving of [outdoor] relief not only perpetuates the system of casual labour, but tends to keep wages down.' In other words, they were guilty of abandoning the 'principles of 1834'; they rejected the policy of less eligibility, and did not apply the 'workhouse test' to able-bodied applicants for relief. This they openly admitted, and argued that the 'principles of 1834' were inhuman and cruel. They were proud of having set a higher standard.

Crooks and Lansbury were exonerated from all suspicion of dishonesty or corruption, but Crooks felt that the evidence showed that, as a Member of Parliament, he was too busy a man to keep a proper control over the workhouse and the granting of relief, and so he resigned from the chairmanship, but not from the board of guardians.

Despite this hostile report, no direct action was taken by the government to interfere in Poplar. The policy of the guardians there was disapproved by the Local Government Board, but a direct intervention to reduce the scale of outdoor relief or to make the workhouse less comfortable would have been politically difficult, and possibly ineffectual. So the guardians continued to manage affairs much as they had done before, though probably with more scrupulous attention to detail.

Up till now the Labour members on the board of guardians had been a minority, although they had, in fact, made the policy of that body. They were at a disadvantage electorally, because every recipient of relief (other than medical) was, as a pauper, automatically disfranchised. Their policy of generous relief therefore disfranchised many who were no doubt among their keenest supporters. The more widespread the relief they gave, the more of their supporters were disfranchised. But in 1918 this pauper disfranchisement was abolished by the Representation of the People Act. From then on the recipients of relief had a vote equal to that of the ratepayer who provided the relief. Indeed, the ratepayers were very much at a disadvantage in Poplar, for over half the rates were paid by companies which had no votes, or by businessmen who lived outside the borough. This was presumably one of the reasons why in the first elections after the passing of the Representation of the People Act, the Labour Party won eighteen out of the twenty-four seats on the board of guardians, and thirty-nine out of the forty-two seats on the borough council. Lansbury was the moving spirit on both authorities, and, out of the twenty-four guardians, thirteen were also members of the borough council.

Meanwhile, the decline in trade was causing increased unemployment in the docks of East London. In 1921 there were 15,000 unemployed in Poplar, out of a total population of 160,000, but the need for assistance was not matched by proportionate wealth. The average rateable value per head in the rich city of Westminster was £42. In Poplar it was only £5. In Westminster, with very few unemployed, the rate for Poor Law purposes was 4¾d in the pound. In Poplar it was 7s 2½d in the pound.

Some little assistance was given by the wealthy West End

boroughs, but it was quite inadequate. In 1867 the infirmaries of all the London unions had been put under the common management of the Metropolitan Asylums Board. The Metropolitan Poor Act, which established the board, also provided for the establishment of a Common Poor Fund, maintained by subscription from all the metropolitan unions, and out of which was paid to each union 5d a day for each pauper maintained in the workhouse. Since that time costs had risen greatly, but the grants from the Poor Fund remained stabilised at the 1914 level. More important, however, was the fact that the grants were only paid for paupers receiving indoor relief. Now, in 1921, these indoor paupers were of very little significance beside the army of unemployed, on outdoor relief.

There were thus two problems arising out of the unemployment in the docks. First, should the guardians continue their policy of helping the unemployed by relief more generous than was given by other boards? To this their answer was definite – they should. Second, could they contrive to win financial help from the rich West End? Without this, it was probably impossible for the Poplar guardians to maintain their unemployed, whether they adopted generous or economical scales of relief.

Behind these two questions, however, there lay a deeper problem; the guardians were socialists; in the words of George Lansbury, 'We are all clear class-conscious Socialists working together, using the whole machinery of local government and Parliament for the transformation of Capitalist Society into Socialism. We are under no delusions about our day by day work. We are only patching up and making good some of the evils of Capitalism.'

Even before their electoral victories, the Labour members had dominated the board of guardians, but now, with scarcely an opponent left on the board, they had a free hand.

Unemployment in the docks was increasing, and the problem of destitution was becoming more urgent. As trade decreased, wages fell, and the state of Poplar became increasingly desperate. The guardians fixed a scale of relief which for the smaller families differed but little from the Ministry of Health scale, but for the larger families was considerably more generous.

At the same time the workhouse continued to be run, as it had been for some years, 'more as an almshouse than a workhouse'; the conditions were easier, and the food was better, than in most other such institutions in the country.[5]

The Poor Law guardians did not themselves levy a rate for their expenditure, but sent a precept to the local council (in this case the Poplar Borough Council), who levied a general rate to cover the expenditure of themselves, the guardians, the London County Council, the Metropolitan Water Board, the Metropolitan Asylums Board and the Metropolitan Police. The rate for the year 1920–1 had risen to 22s 10d in the pound, compared with 11s 2d which was levied in the rich City of Westminster, and 11s 10d which had been levied in Poplar only three years before. The increasing cost of the Poor Law threatened to force this rate up yet higher.

But at the same time the expenditure of the borough council was also rising. Aided by loans authorised by the Minister of Health, the new Labour council set to work energetically to improve the libraries of the borough, to build new baths and washhouses, and to provide relief work for the unemployed. Streets were widened and improved, two swimming baths and several new playing fields were provided.

The estimates for 1921–2 showed increased expenditure not only by the guardians and the borough council, but also by the other precepting authorities. More than half the increase, however, was due to the rising cost of Poor Relief. To raise the necessary money would have entailed a rate of at least 27s 3d in the pound.

For years the borough council, like the guardians, had been demanding that the cost of outdoor relief should be spread over the whole of London. It was clear that only if something of this sort were done could the policy of the guardians be continued without resulting in something like bankruptcy. It was thought to be necessary to make a dramatic gesture, emphasising again the injustice of leaving the poor alone to help the poor. Accordingly, despite the clear legal duty of the council to collect the money to pay the precepts, Charles Key (on the suggestion, apparently, of Lansbury) moved in the borough council 'that the precepts for the London County Council, the Metropolitan Police, the Metropolitan Water Board, and the Metropolitan Asylums Board be deleted, and that the estimates as amended be referred to the Valuation and Rating Committee to ascertain the rate in the pound necessary to be levied'.[6] This resolution was accepted with but one dissentient. The council would collect the money for themselves and the guardians only; on the rest they would default.

On 31 March 1921, the council formally resolved to levy a rate of 4s 4d in the pound for the first quarter – enough to meet the requirements of the council and the guardians only. This decision, apparently, was reached without consultation with the other Labour councils of London or with the London Labour Party

Within a month, the county council had applied to the High Court, and an order had been issued fixing a date (20 June) for the council to show cause why a writ of mandamus should not issue commanding them to pay the precept and, if necessary, to make and levy a rate for the purpose.

An affidavit was filed on behalf of the Poplar Council, contending that it was useless to levy so high a rate in a borough where 15,574 were unemployed out of a total population of about 160,000. The court proceeded to issue the writ of mandamus addressed both to the council and to the individual councillors and aldermen.

On 29 July, the councillors were summoned to appear in the High Court. They marched together, led by the macebearer and the deputy mayor wearing the chain of office. Before them was carried a banner inscribed 'Poplar Borough Council marching to the High Court and possibly to prison to secure equalisation of rates for poor boroughs'.[7] They appeared before a Divisional Court, composed of the Lord Chief Justice, Sankey J., and Branson J. Here they exasperated the court by making political speeches, but nothing could alter the legal fact of their liability, and so writs of attachment were issued against the councillors concerned, but were ordered to lie in the office for fourteen days.[8] After an unsuccessful appeal, the writs became effective on 31 August.[9]

The writs of attachment were issued against the council and the individual recalcitrant members. They were held to be void against the council, as it had no personality which could be committed to prison for contempt. But they were valid against the councillors themselves. In the early days of September, the mayor and twenty-nine of the council were arrested, and taken to prison – the men to Brixton, the women to Holloway. A few Conservatives, who had voted in favour of paying the precepts, and one alderman who had changed his mind, were left at liberty, with Councillor Key, the deputy mayor.

Public opinion, in Poplar at least, was strongly in favour of the imprisoned councillors. The women had been escorted on their way to prison by a band and a procession with banners. On the next day, a crowd, estimated to number 15,000 assembled outside Holloway prison to cheer them.[10] In the street beside Brixton prison large crowds collected, and Lansbury was able to address them from the window of his cell.

The councillors refused to submit to all the indignities of prison life; they continued to wear their own clothes, and would do no work. They demanded – and got – newspapers and footballs, and better cooked food. Naturally, the ordinary prisoners observed these privileges and demanded that they, too, should enjoy them.

Incidents such as this made them unwelcome guests for the prison governor. The government also found their imprisonment embarrassing. Throughout the country there was growing unrest among the unemployed; there were riots in Dundee, Bristol and Liverpool. In some of the East End unions the unemployed were attempting to intimidate the guardians into paying more generous relief. The Woolwich guardians were besieged all night in their office by 10,000 unemployed.[11] In this dangerous situation the imprisoned councillors appeared as martyrs; they themselves, in an open letter to school children, emphasised the precedents of John Hampden and George Washington. Moreover, there were signs that other councils might follow the same course, unless the government gave them the help which they demanded; Bethnal Green had resolved to levy no rates for the precepting authorities until the Poplar councillors were released. Stepney and Battersea were ready to follow. A Tenants' Defence League was formed in Poplar, with over 10,000 members pledged to pay no rent to their landlords until their councillors were released.[12]

The Prime Minister, meanwhile, was having a holiday at Gairloch, near Inverness. Thither the Labour mayors of London, led by Herbert Morrison, who was Mayor of Hackney, pursued him. But he refused to see them, pleading sickness. So they waited in Inverness for him to recover.[13] After four days he saw them, but could offer no solution to their problems. Back in London, they had a series of conferences with the Minister of Health, Sir Alfred Mond. The Poplar Council, however, refused to take part in any conferences unless the councillors were first released unconditionally from prison.

The government would obviously have preferred that the councillors should be at liberty, but there were serious difficulties in their way. These the Home Secretary pointed out in reply to petitions for their release. Had they been imprisoned for committing a crime the Home Secretary could have advised the Crown to exercise the Prerogative and release them. But they were detained, not for crime, but for contempt of court. Before the prisoners could be released, they must purge their contempt. This the councillors could only do in one way – by obeying the order of the court, and paying the precepts. This they would not do. Moreover, the power to release them lay with the court which had committed them, and with no one else. Never had a minister interfered with this power of the judges.

The councillors were allowed to meet in Brixton gaol, and were joined there by those from Holloway and those who were still at liberty and by the town clerk. Here, too, they met representatives from the Labour mayors and from the LCC. Out of these discussions there grew an agreement; the imprisoned councillors would apply for their release, and apologise for their conduct. They would not undertake to pay the precepts on which they had defaulted, but would undertake to join in a conference; the county council and the Asylums Board would raise no objection to their release; and the minister would convene a conference with the object of achieving some degree of equalisation of rates.[14]

In this programme there was one major difficulty. The High Court was not, and could not be, a party to such an agreement. Nor was it probable that the court would release the prisoners unless they purged their contempt. And yet the internal peace of England depended greatly on this agreement being carried out. The Minister of Health therefore decided to send a personal message to the Lord Chancellor, urging him to ask the judges concerned to release the prisoners, even though they did not purge their contempt. Civil servants might protest at what seemed to be an unconstitutional meddling with the Judiciary, but the message was sent.

On 12 October, application was made to a Divisional Court for the release of the prisoners. The affidavit, sworn on behalf of the imprisoned councillors, explained their desire to take part in the conference and apologised for any personal disrespect to the court, but gave no offer to pay the precepts. The county council and Metropolitan Asylums Board told the court that they would 'welcome any action on the part of the Borough Council which would enable them freely to participate in such a conference'. In these circumstances, the court came to the conclusion, with considerable difficulty, that the prisoners could be discharged. So they marched triumphantly out of Brixton gaol, singing 'The Red Flag', and returned to Poplar, where they were greeted with bands and banners.[15] In fact, their victory was very far from complete. The precepts were still payable, and the rich West End still contributed nothing to the cost of outdoor relief in the East End. But a week after their release, the conference opened at the Ministry of Health. There were representatives of all the metropolitan boroughs, of the City, and the county council, and of the ministry. The representatives of the Labour councils came fully armed with facts and figures, which gave them a great advantage in discussion over the Conservative boroughs. It was agreed that the existing machinery of the Common Poor

Fund should be used to achieve more equal contributions to the cost of poor relief.

As soon as possible, the minister introduced the Local Authorities (Financial Provisions) Bill, based on the decisions of the conference. The Common Poor Fund was henceforth to pay not 5d a day for indoor paupers, but 1s 3d a day for all paupers, whether on indoor or outdoor relief. The guardians were also to be allowed to borrow money, to an extent and at a rate of interest to be sanctioned by the minister, the interest payable being allowed as a charge against the Common Poor Fund. But no charge on the fund was to be allowed in respect of any relief granted in excess of a scale to be laid down by the Minister of Health. Provision was also made for dealing with any subsequent case of a council defaulting on its precepts, by allowing the precepting authority to appoint a receiver – a simpler and less spectacular procedure than committal for contempt.

This was a real victory for Poplarism. It meant that Poplar received from the richer boroughs a contribution equivalent to about a 10s rate. In the first three and a half years it received more than £1,300,000.

On the other hand, a victory in this battle did not mean complete triumph in the whole campaign. Poplar had won on the point of rate equalisation. To some extent that was only a means to an end. It was a means to afford the more generous treatment of the poor and the unemployed; a means to help in the overthrow of the old Poor Law and 'the principles of 1834'. The government was still as rigidly opposed as ever to the policies of Lansbury, Key and Scurr. It had, moreover, new weapons in its hands; the Local Authorities (Financial Provisions) Act 1921 could only help the ratepayers of Poplar in so far as their guardians complied with a scale and conditions of relief which were to be prescribed by the minister. So also their new powers of borrowing depended on ministerial consent.

Within a few days, the minister, Sir Alfred Mond, issued the necessary regulations defining the scale of relief. This was based on 15s a week for a person living alone, 25s for a married couple, and 5s for each child, together with a fuel allowance of up to 3s a week. But in any case the relief was not to exceed a sum of 10s below the standard rate of wages of an unskilled manual worker in London.

This scale had been accepted by the London boards of guardians, including the Poplar Board. It did not imply that the boards were debarred from paying any more, but only that no claims would lie against the Common Poor Fund in respect of any payment in excess of this scale. Some boards decided to pay less, some, including Poplar, to pay more, finding the excess entirely out of their own funds.

Meanwhile, until the grants from the Common Poor Fund came in, the guardians of Poplar had to borrow for their current expenditure. In December of that year they borrowed, with the minister's consent, £146,250. In February 1922, they reported to the minister that this sum was nearly exhausted, and asked for consent to a further loan. Meanwhile, on 18 January, a very large body of the unemployed went to the guardians' office to demonstrate their dislike of the scale proposed by the minister. A deputation from this assembly was seen by the Guardians, and they determined to support the demand of the unemployed.

The scale demanded by the unemployed was based on £1 7s 6d for a man and wife, 6s 6d for the first child, and 6s for other children. The guardians met on 25 January. As a result of the pressure of the unemployed and the unyielding attitude of the minister, they were in a defiant mood; they decided not merely to pay what the unemployed demanded, but more; their scale was based on £2 for a man and wife, 6s for each child, rent up to 15s a week, and one hundredweight of coal a week (or the equivalent in gas). They also decided to give all old-age pensioners 10s a week in addition to their pensions.

At their next meeting the clerk reported a letter from the ministry about the new scales of relief. This stated that:

'The Minister understands that this scale is in excess even of the revised scale, submitted at the Guardians' meeting by the deputations to which you refer. It is in excess of any scale in force either in the metropolis or in the provinces, and it appears to be admitted by the Guardians themselves that it is in excess of what is required for the relief of destitution.

'Inasmuch as the legal powers and duties of the Guardians are limited to the relief of destitution, the grant of allowances in accordance with the scale will be unlawful'.

A letter from one of the large employers of the borough – George Armstrong & Co., Ltd – was also read, stating that

'Our employees who live in Poplar have pointed out to us that they can get more money by being unemployed than working for us, and as we have no wish to prevent them from getting as much as possible, we propose to dismiss them so that they can take advantage of your relief.'

The clerk also reported that if the new scales were applied, the guardians would be insolvent by the beginning of March. A reluctant board decided not to enforce their new scale, to apply for a further loan from the ministry, and to instruct the clerk, meanwhile, to hold up every possible cheque except those required for salaries and wages.

So, in March 1922, Sir Alfred Mond appointed Mr H. I. Cooper to conduct an inquiry into the administration of the Poplar guardians 'with a view to securing, without delay, such economies as are consistent with efficient administration'. Mr Cooper, the clerk to the Bolton guardians, had been chosen for this task by the minister, after consultation with the President of the Association of Poor Law Guardians, but it was alleged by the Poplar guardians that he was chosen because he could be relied upon to produce a hostile report.

After two interviews with the Secretary of the Municipal Alliance, Mr Cooper started his investigation of the books and records of the guardians. He did not, however, interrogate or formally discuss matters with the board of guardians or any member of the board – an omission for which he was severely criticised by Lansbury, who had taken a personal dislike to him.

The report was issued to the Press before the guardians themselves had seen it. It was highly critical of their administration. The general conclusions were summarised at the end:

'The administration of the Poor Law in this parish is dictated by a policy adopted by the Guardians which is in many instances foreign to the spirit and intention of the Poor Law statutes.

'The principles which influence the Guardians in the excessive expenditure referred to in this Report are as bad as, if not worse than, those existing prior to the present Poor Law system.

'There is no justification for the expenditure in out-relief so much in excess of the scale prescribed by the Metropolitan Common Poor Fund (Outdoor Relief) Regulations, 1922. Based on the present number of cases, these excess payments represent additional expenditure – which cannot be charged on the Metropolitan Common Poor Fund, and therefore fall on the Poplar ratepayers – at the rate of over £93,000 per annum.

'The lavish allowances of Outdoor Relief encourage persons to apply who would not otherwise do so, and it is made altogether too easy for persons to obtain assistance from the Guardians. The Guardians' policy has a tendency to demoralise the recipients and is calculated to destroy incentive to thrift, self-reliance and industry . . .

'I consider that, on the present rate of expenditure, by careful administration, a saving of at least £100,000 per annum would result.'

The report in fact produced little in the way of new information or unexpected disclosures, but it emphasised clearly the main point of conflict between the ministry and the guardians. The socialists of Poplar had abandoned the 'principles of 1834'; they did not follow the rule of 'less eligibility'; they made their paupers as comfortable as they could, and they applied no labour test to the able-bodied.[16]

The guardians published their reply to the Cooper Report, and appropriately called their pamphlet *Guilty and Proud of It*. 'That', they wrote, 'is the charge against Poplar – that it refuses to treat poverty as a crime, and paupers as criminals. Worse, it has succeeded in its campaign to compel the richer boroughs to take up a portion of their fair share in the work of relief. To that double charge and all that it involves, Poplar, we repeat, is proud to plead guilty.'[17]

So far, the minister had tried to regulate the amount of relief given in Poplar and other East End boroughs by exercising his powers under the Local Authorities (Financial Provisions) Act of 1921. It was under this Act that he had made the Metropolitan Common Poor Fund (Outdoor Relief) Regulations in January 1922. These had established the scale which was commonly known as the Mond Scale. There was, however, no effective means under that Act of compelling the guardians to comply with the regulations; the minister could withhold assistance out of the Common Poor Fund for any expenditure beyond the authorised scale, but the Poplar guardians merely paid the difference out of the rates, or, when they could not do that, they borrowed it.

There was, however, a more effective power of control in the Poor Law Amendment Act of 1834.[18] That Act gave the minister (as successor of the Poor Law Commissioners) power to order to what extent outdoor relief might be given in individual unions. Any outdoor relief given contrary to such orders was declared to be illegal, except in certain circumstances, such as cases of emergency (provided that the facts of such cases were reported to the minister within fifteen days).

After receiving the report from Mr Cooper, the minister decided to issue an order under the Act of 1834. Accordingly, he made the Relief Regulations (Poplar) Order 1922, which is commonly known as the 'Poplar Order'. This made no change in the authorised scale for outdoor relief; it merely declared that any outdoor relief granted by the Poplar guardians above the Mond Scale was illegal. The minister also announced that if the guardians would agree to comply strictly with this order, he would allow them to borrow a further sum to cover their existing overdraft.

The guardians at once protested and, in an interview with the minister, declared their inability and unwillingness to enforce this scale of relief. They agreed, however, that all cases contravening the order should be reported, as 'cases of emergency', for the minister's approval. Sir Alfred Mond then promised that advances would be sanctioned to the extent necessary to enable relief to be given in accordance with the order.[19]

From the first, the number of such 'emergency' cases justifying a departure from the authorised scale, and so reported to the minister, was large; in the first week after the issuing of the Poplar Order, the guardians reported 1,829 such cases. It thus became incumbent on the staff of the ministry to check each case in detail.

So matters continued for eighteen months, during which the coalition under Lloyd George was brought to an end; the Conservatives under Bonar Law came into power; Lansbury again won the election in Poplar; Griffith Boscawen and then Neville Chamberlain replaced Sir Alfred Mond at the Ministry of Health.

Neville Chamberlain saw that his predecessors had made a tactical blunder in getting into this position, and he determined to argue only on principle, avoiding individual cases. He decided that the London County Council must be asked to take over the duties of poor relief in Poplar, if the guardians refused to change their policy. The county council was apparently willing to do this, and a Bill was prepared, authorising the minister to make such transfers of responsibility by Statutory Orders. But there was not time to introduce the Bill before the General Election of 1923.

When the election results were known, the Conservative Government resigned and Neville Chamberlain left the Ministry of Health, to be succeeded by the most ardent socialist in the new cabinet, John Wheatley. He found that the finances of Poplar guardians and Poplar Borough Council called for his immediate attention.

The guardians had continued their policy of giving outdoor relief on a scale exceeding that authorised by the minister, and reporting as emergencies between 1,000 and 2,000 cases a week. Successive ministers appear to have acquiesced in what they could not stop. The Poplar guardians had been allowed to borrow £506,500 through the Goschen Committee to meet their current expenditure; the borough council had been allowed to borrow £300,000 in order to pay the precepts on which they had defaulted. Meanwhile the number receiving relief in Poplar was alarmingly high; 1,919 out of every 10,000 compared with an average for London as a whole of 533 per 10,000. This, claimed the guardians, was the reason why they had to follow the policy they did. This, argued their opponents, was the natural and disastrous outcome of their policy.

As soon as Wheatley took office as Minister of Health, a deputation waited on him, asking him to repeal the Poplar Order.

His civil servants advised him that there was no objection to such a course, as the order had been so effectively ignored. He also discussed the question privately with Lansbury in the House of Commons, and agreed to repeal the order if the guardians would undertake to prevent the cost of relief in Poplar rising beyond the figure which it had then reached.

Accordingly, on 20 February, 1924, the Minister revoked the Poplar Order, and made no new order in its place.[20]

At the same time, he promised to remit any surcharges that might be made for expenditure on relief which was illegal under the Poplar Order. Since the order was made the guardians had regularly spent about £2,000 a week beyond the scale which it allowed. This expenditure was perhaps illegal, but the auditor still omitted to close his audit, and the successive ministers had acquiesced in this omission. Had the audit been closed it might have resulted in a surcharge of about £150,000. It was manifestly absurd to imagine that Lansbury and his colleagues on the Poplar board could find such a sum.

The Conservative and Liberal Parties immediately attacked Mr Wheatley's decision, and obtained a debate on 26 February, 1924. They complained not so much of the rescission of the Poplar Order – that had proved a failure – as of the fact that the minister had put nothing in its place. He had apparently given the Poplar guardians permission to continue their policy of relief. This might be regarded by other unions as an invitation to do the same. They also complained that the minister had acted improperly in promising to remit the surcharges; his power to remit them was a judicial duty, only to be performed after a careful and impartial weighing of the evidence. He had not acted in any way judicially.

Their criticisms were no doubt justified to some extent, but yet the revocation of the order was probably inevitable. John Wheatley's rule was, however, a short one, as the first Labour Government only survived from January to November 1924.

During this period the district auditors were faced with problems of exceptional difficulty. They had until 1922 generally avoided conflict with the borough council, surcharging only £10, the cost of the band which serenaded the councillors in prison. But the ambitious schemes of the borough council were being carried out with but little regard for economy. In all their work the council felt that they, as a public authority, should behave not merely as ordinary, but as model, employers. In March 1920, the metropolitan borough councils had, after negotiations with the trade unions, decided to accept a scale of wages for municipal employees, with six grades, ranging from £3 10s 6d to £4 14s per week. Poplar Council accepted this decision in principle. It then however carried on further discussions with local trade union officials, and decided to merge the lower grades into one, at £4 a week. It was further decided that any fall in the cost of living should not entail a reduction of wages below this level. This decision was never approved by the other Labour councils of London, nor by the responsible trade union officers, many of whom (including Ernest Bevin) were annoyed at the 'politicians' going over the heads of the unions and fixing such a minimum wage.

In the next two years prices and wages were falling all over England. But the council would not reduce their minimum, for they regarded it as the least that any man or woman should be offered. In 1921 and 1922 the district auditor made no comment on the wages, but in 1923 the auditor, Mr Carson Roberts, considered them to be unreasonably high, compared with the current trade union rates for such work. Accordingly, he certified that 'I found that the total of the wage payments made by the Council in the year 1921–22 exceeded by about £17,000 the total amount of the wages that would have been paid by them if the agreed wages of the awards referred to (i.e. the JIC and the Trade Union rates) had been adopted.'

At first sight the auditor had no authority to intervene. His power was based on section 247 of the Public Health Act 1875: 'Any auditor acting in pursuance of this section shall disallow every item of account contrary to law, and surcharge the same on the person making or authorising the making of the illegal payment.' This meant, it was argued, that the auditor could only surcharge payments for which there was no legal authority; but in this case there was such authority, for the borough council, as successor to the old Poplar Vestry, was authorised by section 62 of the Metropolis Management Act 1855 to pay to its 'clerks, treasurers, surveyors, officers and servants respectively such

salaries and wages as it may think fit'. All that the councillors
had done was to pay wages on a more generous scale than the
auditor thought was prudent. But that, it appeared, was not
illegal.

The auditor, however, took the opposite view. He gave notice
to the councillors of his opinion that the excessive wages should
be surcharged, and so gave them an opportunity to state their
case. A number of them did so, and explained that they regarded
themselves as bound to make these payments by the 'mandate of
the electors', expressed in by-elections, when candidates supporting the payments were returned unopposed. He then, in the
words of his affidavit,

'took the view that the Council, in the exercise of their statutory
powers, had not paid due regard to the interests of the ratepayers
whose funds they administered, had imposed unreasonable charges
upon those funds, and had made payments which were far in
excess of those necessary to obtain the service required and to
maintain a high standard of efficiency, and which were thus in
reality gifts to their employees in addition to remuneration for
their services, and that the persons responsible had thus incurred
an unjustifiable waste of the rate fund and had acted arbitrarily
and contrary to law'.

Accordingly, he made a surcharge, not for the full sum of
£17,000 but for £5,000, on the councillors concerned.

The councillors appealed against the surcharge on the ground
that the auditor had no power to act in such a way, as they had a
legal authority to pay such wages as they saw fit. The appeal
came before a Divisional Court, which upheld the auditor, on
the grounds that 'a payment to a servant entitled to be paid by
the Council may be of so excessive a character as to go beyond
the limits of legality and become an illegal or *ultra vires*
payment'.[21]

An appeal was promptly lodged against this decision, and came
on for hearing on 14 May before Lords Justice Bankes, Scrutton
and Atkin.[22]

Lord Justice Banks agreed with the decision of the inferior
court, but Scrutton and Atkin did not. They held that the auditor
had no power to interfere in such a case, so long as the council
had acted in good faith. Lord Justice Scrutton declared: 'The
question is not whether I should have sanctioned these wages; I
probably should not; nor whether the Auditor or the Whitley
Council would have sanctioned these wages; it is for the Poplar

borough council to fix these wages which are not to be interfered with unless they are so excessive as to pass the reasonable limits of discretion in a representative body.'

Thus, by a majority vote in the Court of Appeal, the auditor had lost his case; but he could still appeal to the House of Lords, and this he did. Already, six judges had considered the case; now five Lords of Appeal were to give a final decision. They found unanimously in favour of the district auditors.[23] They argued that the discretion conferred upon the council by the statute must be exercised reasonably, and that the fixing by the council of an arbitrary sum for wages without regard to existing labour conditions was not an exercise of that discretion. Further, they argued that, though expenditure of the rate fund on wages was authorised by statute, this particular expenditure was so excessive as to be unlawful. From this it followed that the auditor was right to make the surcharge. Lord Sumner seemed to take the case further than his colleagues when he said of the auditor: 'I do not find any words limiting his functions merely to the case of bad faith, or obliging him to leave the ratepayers unprotected from the effects on their pockets of honest stupidity or unpractical idealism.'

This judgement caused considerable controversy at the time, and has been much criticised since.[24] It has been said that it resulted in the auditor being endowed with a general power to over-ride the decision of the elected councillors, where he considers that their conduct has been 'unreasonable'.

This judgement had originated in the application of the councillors to the King's Bench, asking for a writ of certiorari. But although this application had failed, there remained, apparently, an alternative course. The Poor Law Amendment Act of 1844 permitted in lieu of such an application an appeal to the Minister of Health (as successor to the Poor Law Commissioners). The minister was authorised to remit the surcharge if he found that it was fair and equitable to do so.

At first sight, it might appear that the two forms of appeal – to the court and to the minister – were alternatives. But it had been stated by Wills J. in the case of *R.* v. *Cockerton*[25] that the appeal to the minister was still open after an appeal had been made to the court. Accordingly, within a week of the judgement in the House of Lords, the council, acting on behalf of the individual councillors, appealed to the minister to remit the charges.

Meanwhile, as these legal arguments were being pursued, the wages scale remained in force in Poplar, and surcharge was piled upon surcharge; the original sum had been £5,000, but in subsequent years the auditor disallowed sums of £11,500, £22,500, £24,600 and £23,000. These five surcharges against the borough councillors were matched by nine against the Poplar guardians, also for paying too generous a scale of wages.

The minister by this time was Neville Chamberlain. He had little sympathy himself for the rulers of Poplar, but he had wisdom enough to see that he must remit the surcharges. Had he failed to do so, the councillors and guardians would clearly have been unable to pay the very large sums for which they would be legally liable, and would probably have been imprisoned. He certainly did not want to have them in prison for a second time. So, after he had obtained from the council and the guardians a pledge that they would bring their wages down to a scale negotiated with the trade unions, he issued the necessary orders for the remission of the surcharges. At this stage, the Municipal Alliance intervened. It had been determined throughout to protect the interests of the ratepayers, and to force the borough council to reduce the wages. At a meeting in October 1923, attended by representatives of most of the large commercial ratepayers, it had decided in favour of a general refusal to pay rates. The Minister of Health, however, had no desire to have the difficulties of the situation increased in this way, and persuaded the Alliance to change its mind.[26] It continued nevertheless to agitate for a number of statutory reforms to the local government franchise, which, it was hoped, might re-establish responsible administration. It asked for the reintroduction of pauper disqualification, for it regarded voting by paupers as the main cause of the socialist victories. It also wanted votes for companies and corporations, and a return to the old system of plural voting, which gave more votes to the larger than to the lesser ratepayers.

In May 1925, the Alliance had heard that the borough council was appealing to the Minister of Health for remission of the surcharges. The chairman hastened to see Mr Chamberlain to protest against any such remissions being granted. The Alliance urged the minister to use his authority to fix a scale of wages for the employees of Poplar Council, and felt aggrieved when he replied rather curtly that he could not do so. It sought counsel's opinion from Mr Joshua Scholefield KC, and, after discussion on policy with the district auditor,[27] resolved to seek an injunction against the payment of excessive wages by the borough council, and a writ of certiorari to quash the minister's remission of the surcharges.[28] A guarantee fund of over £5,000 was raised from the commercial firms of Poplar to cover the expenses.

The action for an injunction was dropped when the council, by agreement with the minister, reduced its rates of wages, but the application to quash the remission of the surcharges went on. It was argued that the two remedies which were open to the councillors when they were surcharged – appeal to the court and appeal to the minister – were alternatives, and that, having lost their appeal to the court, they could not then turn for relief to the minister.

The court accepted this argument, dismissing the remark of Wills J. in *R.* v. *Cockerton* as a mere *obiter dictum*.[29]

Chamberlain now found himself in a curious predicament. He had come to the rescue of his enemies, but in doing so had acted illegally. The surcharges for £86,600, therefore, revived, and his gesture was in vain. Nor was it only in Poplar that such surcharges were outstanding – the council of Bethnal Green had followed a similar policy in wages and incurred the same penalties. But legislation which merely reversed the decision in *R.* v. *Minister of Health, ex p. Dore* was not enough; to cure the technical fault in his attempted remission of the surcharges was no solution to his problems. His main difficulty was that his existing weapons were inadequate for his purpose. It was futile for the auditor to go on adding surcharge to surcharge when the councillors could obviously never pay them, and the minister would have to remit them. Public inquiries had been tried, and had failed. Control through the regulation of loans had proved to be little more effective. So he determined that the Bill which altered the law of remissions of surcharges should also provide more powerful sanctions against the councillors who incurred the surcharges.

Accordingly, on 9 May, 1927, Mr Chamberlain introduced the Audit (Local Authorities) Bill, with the object of extending his powers of remitting surcharges, and providing that anyone surcharged for £500 or more should be disqualified from membership of any local authority for five years. This last provision, however, was not to apply to surcharges already incurred.

To the Municipal Alliance the Bill seemed quite inadequate. They urged that

'the penalties were not sufficient, and also vacancies were likely to occur on the Borough Council when persons were surcharged, and there was nothing to prevent another candidate with a like policy being elected. It was suggested that, in the event of disqualification taking place under clause 1, the Government should take steps to fill the vacancies.'[30]

To such representations from the Alliance, Sir Kingsley Wood (who was Chamberlain's parliamentary secretary) replied that the government wanted to keep the Bill on democratic lines, and not institute bureaucratic arrangements if democratic ones could be made successful.

However Mr Chamberlain and his colleagues might justify the Bill, the Opposition regarded it as a direct attack on the Poplar borough councillors, and also as a clear threat to the liberty of all local authorities. The resentment which he aroused was increased by his unfortunate manner. At the end of the week in which the second reading took place, he recorded in his diary that 'Stanley begged me to remember that I was addressing a meeting of gentlemen. I always gave him the impression, he said, when I spoke in the House of Commons, that I looked on the Labour Party as dirt.'[31]

It is not surprising that, in these circumstances, the Bill was hotly opposed and damned by the Labour Opposition as a 'Political Opponents (Suppression) Bill'; it is not surprising that it was fought at length and in detail at every stage.

In the course of the debates the Opposition complained constantly of the increased power of the auditors, and alleged that they acted on instructions from the minister. This roused Mr Chamberlain to make an oft-quoted declaration: 'They are not my Auditors. They are entirely independent of me. I have never attempted to give a District Auditor instructions as to what he should do; I have never sought to influence a District Auditor in carrying out his duties. It would not have been any use if I had.'[32] This statement was made in the heat of debate when the speaker was being interrupted by his opponents. It has been much discussed and sometimes doubted. In fact, the minister had probably never even spoken to an auditor, nor in this case would it have had much effect if he had, for Carson Roberts was a man of determination, who placed a high value on the independence of his office; he had, however, apparently gone beyond the normal bounds of judicial conduct in discussing matters with the Municipal Alliance, and he lived in the climate of the ministry where he worked, and no doubt would have discussed the problem of Poplarism with the Chief Inspector of Audit. The Chief Inspector himself would have been consulted by the senior officials of the Ministry on how to deal with the problems which arose, but he would not have been given orders or instructions, nor would he in his turn seek to give instructions to the district auditors.

The Labour Party regarded this point as of some importance, arguing that, if the auditor was, in fact, a subordinate of the minister, it followed that the minister could influence him to make a surcharge against councillors whose policy he disapproved. They would then have either to accept their own exclusion from local government, or incur the expenses and uncertainties of an appeal. This would be either to the minister himself, which would presumably be in vain; or to the High Court. This latter course was not only expensive, but seemed little more hopeful than the first, for the socialists had come, after the series of judgements against them, to regard the High Court as an unsympathetic body.

Despite the protests of the Labour Party and the uneasiness of local councillors throughout the country, the Bill was passed and became law. The Minister of Health was also contemplating the reintroduction of the rule that paupers should be disfranchised in local government elections – a rule which had been of general application until its repeal in 1918.

The decision to alter the system of Poor Law Administration was reinforced by events outside Poplar. The General Strike took place in May 1926 and, after it was finished, the coal strike continued and was supported by some of the Poor Law authorities. In a number of unions in the mining districts the guardians paid relief not only to the families of the strikers, but also to unmarried strikers with no dependants. Apart from this, the long strike led to unemployment and need in many other industries, and so to increasing demands for relief.

One of the most difficult districts was West Ham. Lying in the East End of London, just beside Poplar, it was outside the boundaries of the County of London, and so did not qualify to receive any help from the Metropolitan Common Poor Fund. Its guardians had generally followed the same policy as those of Poplar, but the minister had never made for West Ham a specific order such as the Poplar Order of 1922. When John Wheatley, as Minister of Health, had repealed that order, he had obtained a promise from the Poplar guardians that they would not allow the cost of relief in Poplar to rise any higher. But no such situation had arisen in West Ham, nor had any such promise been given.

So in West Ham the cost of relief increased, and much of the expenditure came, not from the rates, but from loans obtained from the government. By the middle of 1925, these loans had reached a total of £1,975,000, and still the guardians had to come back and ask for more – another £350,000. The Goschen Committee, which regulated the amount of these loans, attached conditions – that the rate of relief should be reduced. The guardians refused.[33]

By the end of September 1925, the guardians had no money left with which to pay relief to the poor, or salaries to their officers. The minister was not prepared either to give way to the guardians or to allow the poor of West Ham to starve. He therefore took a step which had no precedent: he guaranteed the payment of the accounts of tradesmen who had supplied food and fuel as outdoor relief, provided that the accounts were marked with a distinguishing stamp, and that the value of this relief in any case did not exceed three quarters of the amount which would have been paid under the guardians' scale.[34]

This system continued for four weeks, during which the unemployed and other paupers were preserved from starvation, but were getting no money with which to pay their rent and other expenses. The guardians had no money to give them, and the ministry would give them none. The guardians refused to abate their claims, and the minister let them know that he intended to take over the administration of relief himself, with the aid of an advisory committee of guardians. For this action he would seek a subsequent indemnity from Parliament. When the guardians realised that this was his intention, they gave way and accepted the conditions which he proposed. They were then allowed to borrow the £350,000 for which they were asking and, later, another £300,000.

During 1926, the financial position of the union grew worse. During the General Strike one out of every five of the population was receiving Poor Relief, and the guardians had to apply for a further loan of £425,000.

Relief was granted with a generous hand, and in many cases, but little inquiry was made into the needs of the applicants. Meanwhile, the poverty of the borough and the extent to which its people depended upon relief were affecting the moral standards of the officers; in eighteen months there were eight cases of fraud or misconduct on the part of relieving officers; remunerative positions under the board of guardians were given too freely to the friends and relations of guardians. It was becoming clear to Mr Chamberlain that he must take direct control of the Poor Law in West Ham. On 20 June 1926, he wrote to his sister:

'West Ham is boiling up again but I am determined to stand no nonsense from them. They would really love to give way but they are desperately afraid of the "people outside" and they have so often bragged of what they would do with "the Minister" that they simply daren't accept my conditions. I should myself like really to take over the relief and work it for at least 6 months. I believe I could show a saving of something like £300,000 or £400,000 a year without inflicting any hardship upon the deserving cases. The undeserving would no doubt speedily make tracks for one of the neighbouring Bolshie Paradises and it would be a glorious lesson for the country. The difficulty is to find time for the legislation, but I have taken the precaution to arm myself with Cabinet authority.'

And, reverting to the topic six days later, he added:

'I shall go in and stop in now till I get some results. I expect I shall be properly abused but I am not much moved by abuse nowadays so long as it comes from the enemy'.[35]

On 29 June 1926, he introduced the Boards of Guardians (Default) Bill.

The Bill provided that if it appeared to the minister that a board of guardians had ceased to discharge any of its functions, or was acting in such a way as to be unable to discharge those functions, the minister might nominate a new board to take over from the existing guardians. The justification for the Bill, Chamberlain explained, was to be found simply in the extravagance and corruption of West Ham. He intended to supersede the guardians there, but hoped that he would not have to do so in any other unions. He was, however, deeply disturbed at the trend of the times. Paupers now enjoyed the same political power as those who had wealth and property at stake. Political power was passing from the responsible to the irresponsible. The new electorate was open to corruption by offers of more lavish relief and more generous pensions. The Labour Party, he feared, would strive to capture local government by a policy of bribes. Would he have to 'West Ham' municipalities?[36]

The introduction of such a Bill caused deep alarm in the Opposition. Chamberlain's attitude to socialism and Poplarism was well known. He now appeared to be arming himself with the oppressive powers of a dictator. At the same time, it was impossible to deny the existence of mismanagement and corruption among the guardians of the threatened union. Even Mr Killip, vice-chairman of the West Ham Board of Guardians, admitted that some of his fellow socialists on the board were abusing their position in a scandalous way.

Lansbury's Labour Weekly threatened a campaign to stop the payment of rent and rates wherever the Act was brought into force; but the threatened resistance was never organised, and

the opposition inside Parliament was no more effective. So the
Bill received the Royal Assent, and in August Mr Chamberlain
replaced the elected guardians of West Ham by two serving and
one retired civil servant.

He had said that he hoped that the Act would only be used in
that one union. But there were other boards of guardians which
refused to obey his orders. In Chester-le-Street, the guardians
were using their position and their rates to support the coal strike.
They were paying generous allowances to the strikers, irrespective
of whether they had families to support. The money was paid out
in a number of buildings in the area; in Birtley it was paid out in
the building of the Co-operative Society. A collecting box stood
near the exit, and those who received relief were asked to 'remember the Guardians'. In defence of this action, it was pleaded that
the guardians, like most of the population, were unemployed. To
have accepted Poor Relief would have disqualified them as
guardians, and left their seats open to their opponents. So, in
order to maintain socialist control of the board, they had to get
money from some source other than Poor Relief. Moreover, this
board was getting further and further into debt. So, late in August
Mr Chamberlain dismissed them also, and substituted his own
nominees. In February 1927, he superseded the elected guardians
of Bedwellty, where circumstances were similar to those in West
Ham. The total debt of the board had risen to £1,071,425.

The Municipal Alliance was anxious that such action should
also be taken in Poplar. They employed accountants to collect
evidence which, it was hoped, would justify the minister in taking
over the duties of the Poplar guardians. They did not, however,
persuade him to do so.[37]

As long ago as 1888, Joseph Chamberlain had pleaded for the
Poor Law to be handed over to the county councils. Both the
Majority and the Minority reports of the Royal Commission on
the Poor Law had advocated such a change in 1909, and the
Maclean Committee had urged it in 1918. The idea of enlarging
the areas of Poor Law administration was in line with the reforms
of 1834, when parishes had been superseded by unions of parishes,
and it was now generally advocated by all parties; the Webbs and
the Poplar Municipal Alliance alike argued that such a reform
was needed. The government had accepted the policy in 1926, but
had not as yet carried it out. For some years, Chamberlain had
been planning extensive reforms to the local government system
and Poplar provided a major stimulus for the sections of the Local
Government Act 1929, which abolished the guardians and handed
over their duties to the counties and the county boroughs.

These important reforms, and a number of minor ones, were included in the Local Government Bill of 1928, though the financial provisions differed somewhat from what Chamberlain himself wanted. There was little opposition to the proposal to abolish the guardians and hand over their functions to the county councils and county borough councils. This was partly because the Labour Party and many others had for nearly twenty years been in favour of such a change. It was also partly due to the fact that, in the last few years, the reputation of the guardians had sunk low. There had been many rumours of corruption and nepotism among the guardians, particularly in the poorer unions, where they had to handle large sums of money – very large when compared with the poverty of the people and of the guardians themselves.

Accordingly, the Bill was passed, and on the appointed day, 1 April 1930, the Poplar guardians, together with all the other guardians in England and Wales, ceased to exist.

NOTES

1 Another such conflict, which lies mainly outside the time limits of this book, is that of the Clay Cross councillors, in the years 1970–6.
2 This chapter is based on an article in *Public Law*, Spring 1962, pp. 52–80, by permission of the publishers, Sweet & Maxwell Ltd.
3 George Lansbury, *My Life* (1928), p. 133.
4 *Poplar Union*. Report by J. S. Davy; 1906, Cd 3240, civ. Transcript of shorthand notes; 1906, Cd 3274, civ.
5 C. W. Key, *Red Poplar* (1925), p. 30.
6 Poplar Borough Council Minutes, 22 March 1921.
7 *The Times*, 30 July 1921.
8 *R. v. Poplar Borough Council* [1922], 1 KB 72.
9 *R. v. Poplar Borough Council, ex p. London County Council* [1922], 1 KB 95.
10 C. W. Key, op. cit., p. 19.
11 *The Times*, 3 September 1921.
12 John Scurr, *The Rate Protest of Poplar* (1922), p. 14.
13 See G. W. Jones, 'Herbert Morrison and Poplarism', *Public Law*, Spring [1973], pp. 11–13.
14 C. W. Key, op. cit., p. 21; John Scurr, op. cit., pp. 13–15.
15 John Scurr, op. cit., p. 14.
16 *Parish of Poplar Borough*, Report of Special Inquiry into the Expenditure of the Guardians (HMSO, 1922).
17 *Guilty and Proud of It* (1922), p. 3.
18 Sec. 52.
19 C. W. Key, op. cit., p. 34. Memorandum on the Rescission of the Poplar Order (1924), Cmd 2052, xix.
20 Memorandum on the Rescission of the Poplar Order (1924), Cmd 2052, xix.

21 *R.* v. *Roberts ex p. Scurr* [1924], 1 KB 514.
22 ibid., [1924], 2 KB 695.
23 *Roberts* v. *Hopwood* [1925], AC 578.
24 See, e.g., W. A. Robson, *The Development of Local Government*, 1st edn (1931), p. 349.
25 [1901], 1 KB 322.
26 *Bethnal Green News*, October 1923.
27 MS. Minutes of Consultative Committee of Poplar Municipal Alliance, 2 June 1927.
28 MS. Minutes of Consultative Committee of Poplar Municipal Alliance, 16 July 1927.
29 *R.* v. *Minister of Health, ex p. Dore* [1927], 1 KB 765.
30 MS. Minutes of Poplar Municipal Alliance, 2 June 1927.
31 Quoted in Keith Feiling, *Life of Neville Chamberlain*, p. 142.
32 211 HC Deb., col. 2121.
33 *Lansbury's Labour Weekly*, 20 June 1925.
34 Keith Feiling, op. cit., p. 142.
35 MS. letters in Birmingham University Library, NC 18/1/512–34.
36 Keith Feiling, op. cit., p. 142.
37 MS Minutes of Poplar Municipal Alliance, Consultative Committee, 17 May 1927.

Chapter V

PEOPLE IN LOCAL GOVERNMENT

The Councillors

In 1835 the Royal Commission on Municipal Corporations complained that 'those who by character, residence and property are best qualified to direct and control municipal affairs are excluded from any share in the elections or management'.[1] And in 1861 John Stuart Mill complained that 'the greatest imperfection of popular local institutions, and the chief cause of the failure which so often attends them, is the low calibre of the men by whom they are almost always carried on'.[2]

On the other hand, in 1893, an American observer, accustomed to the rather unsatisfactory standard of local administration in that country, was much impressed by the calibre of English councillors. He wrote that:

'the councillors, as a rule, are representatives of the best elements of business life. They are men of intelligence and character, and of practical conversance with affairs . . . No salaries attach to these offices, and by common consent of the community none but men of worth, who have made their way to a good standing among their neighbors, are regarded as eligible for the council. This is of course an attractive view, against which numerous individual facts might be arrayed. But it seems to me a just view.'[3]

In 1962 Dame Evelyn Sharp, Permanent Secretary to the Ministry of Housing and Local Government, said:

'I do not think that enough really able people are interested today in taking part in local government. I do not think that enough people from business, from industry, from agriculture, from the professions, are going into it. I think that the average age of councillors is a great deal too high . . . And in consequence of all these things I think that the work of authorities is often not good enough'.[4]

As there are no standards by which human worth can be accurately assessed, it is impossible to say whether the standard of councillors generally has risen or fallen over the years, but these quotations suggest that the complaint that they are not as good as they might be is fairly constant. There are, however, changes in the social background and status of councillors about which more definite evidence is available.

Some statutory changes during the twentieth century have had a clear effect on the personnel of local councils. Step by step women gained the right to become elected representatives[5] but the eligibility of married women to become members of borough and county councils outside London remained in doubt until the Sex Disqualification Removal Act of 1919 put the matter beyond any legal doubt. From that time, the number of women on the councils increased slowly, but more so in some parts of the country than in others. Welsh counties, for example, had a considerably smaller proportion of women than the counties of Southern England.

The Maud Committee on Management disclosed the figures of 1964: at that time 12 per cent of the councillors were women, although women are more than half the total population. Furthermore, 61 per cent of these women councillors were over the age of 55.[6] Even the reorganisation of 1974 made but little difference. In the county councils the proportion of women members rose from 16·4 per cent to 16·6 per cent.[7]

The need for a candidate to be qualified by the ownership of property had been abrogated before the century began. Until 1948 there was a general prohibition against paupers taking part in local elections, either as voters or candidates.[8] The right to make local decisions was restricted to those who helped to meet the burden of local expenditure. In addition, anyone in receipt of poor relief serving on a body responsible for its distribution would inevitably be faced with a conflict of interest. The disqualification was raised temporarily from 1918 to 1929 in relation to county and borough councils and this change helped Labour to win substantial victories at local elections, particularly in the East End of London and in South Wales. The end of pauperism undoubtedly made it easier for working-class candidates to become members of local authorities.

Other factors were working in the same direction. The general political and social scene in England was changing, and the Labour Party was growing in influence and power in central as in local government. But there were forces peculiar to local government which accentuated this tendency. The depression of the 1920s made the role of the guardians particularly relevant to the Labour Party, as, through the guardians, they could control the scale and forms of relief. When the responsibility for the Poor Law was passed to the county councils and county boroughs under the Act of 1929, this interest was naturally transferred to those authorities. Later, even though the Poor Law ceased to exist, and much of its work had already passed into the hands of central government, the interest did not wane. In the years after 1835, the borough councils had been concerned primarily with the administration of their corporate estates. Bit by bit they came to be more involved with sanitary services, and then with the provision of trading services – gas, water and trams. But as the twentieth century advanced, boroughs and counties were increasingly concerned with a range of personal services. Thus the work done by local authorities was coming to have a wider appeal to those with an interest in the social problems of the time.

The abolition of pauper disqualification had, in theory, opened the doors of local government to everyone, rich and poor alike. But to some it seemed that this was theory rather than practice – that access to the councils, like access to the Ritz, was open to everyone, irrespective of their wealth. For membership of a local authority could impose a heavy financial burden on a man or woman. County councils could pay their members travelling expenses, but not subsistence allowances, for attendance at council and committee meetings, and all councils could pay the cost of their members' attendance at conferences and meetings outside the area of the authority. But these powers did not touch the main cause of financial hardship: the loss of earnings due to the time spent at the town hall or council house. In 1946 the Minister of Health, Aneurin Bevan, appointed a committee, under the chairmanship of Lord Lindsay of Birker, Master of Balliol, to advise on the problem of travelling expenses and allowances for loss of remunerative time. The committee found general agreement among local authorities and their associations that the existing system was in fact excluding from the councils many people who would be valuable members. The general opinion was that some sort of reimbursement for lost wages as well as for travelling and subsistence expenses was needed.[9]

As a result, provision was made in the Local Government Act 1948[10] for the payment by local authorities to their councillors for loss of earnings 'necessarily suffered or incurred for the purposes of enabling him to perform any approved duty as a member of that body' and also for 'any additional expense to which he would not otherwise have been subject'. Maximum rates of allowance were prescribed by the minister by statutory instruments.

The effect of this change in the law was to make it possible for many people to take part in local government who could not otherwise have afforded to do so. But its impact was limited in practice to the lower paid workers who could show that they had lost wages by attendance at council and committee meetings; it did little to help the business or professional man whose earnings were reduced by his inability to give all his time to office work – though there was limited provision for payment when additional staff had to be employed.[11]

The Maud Committee on Management found that about 87 per cent of councillors did not claim, for one reason or another. Furthermore, they found that nearly all were out of pocket, and that the best remedy was to introduce an annual flat expenses allowance, payment to all elected members alike. In addition, they proposed that the members of the 'management boards' should receive substantial salaries as part-time managers.[12] These proposals for paying councillors were accepted in principle by the Labour Government, and later incorporated by the Conservative Government into the Local Government Bill; but with the difference that all councillors were to be paid, on a scale based on the number and length of meetings attended,[13] in addition to travelling and subsistence allowance.

This marked a very real change in the position of local councillors. When the Act came into force, some who sat on both county and district councils were able to draw substantial sums in the course of a year. Far from being a financial burden, service on the local council could now be a paying proposition.

Honesty and Dishonesty

Some professional and businessmen were deterred also by another disability – the rule that a councillor who is interested, directly or indirectly, in any matter under discussion must declare his interest and refrain from both speaking and voting. The law on this matter at the beginning of the century was complicated and obscure, but the general principle was that a person was disqualified from membership of a local authority if he was directly or indirectly interested by way of contract or employment in the affairs of the council.[14] To this rule there were many exceptions, and it had been the subject of a number of judicial decisions. The inadequacy of the provisions was demonstrated by a case in 1926[15] in which it was held that an alderman who was a shareholder and managing director of a company holding contracts with the corporation was not disqualified. The decision was upheld by the House of Lords, but the Lord Chancellor pointed out the dangers involved in the growth of small companies which were in practice, but not in law, owned and managed by a single man. The Onslow Commission on Local Government heard evidence from the local authorities on this matter, and came to the conclusion that the prohibition should be extended to cover all shareholders, directors and employees of companies, but that it should be a prohibition against voting rather than a disqualification from membership.[16] The Chelmsford Committee adopted this proposal,[17] and included a clause in their draft Consolidation Bill, which became the Local Government Act 1933.[18]

This legislation required any member of a local authority with a pecuniary interest in a matter under discussion to disclose immediately his interest and refrain from taking part in the discussion and from voting. It was so drafted as to include the interest of a company in which the member is a shareholder, or a partner, or of a husband or wife. The effect of these provisions was wider than was at first apparent. Shares in a company, however few, might make a member liable to prosecution if he omitted to declare his interest; membership of a co-operative society might disqualify a large proportion of councillors, particularly in a Labour area, though in such a case the Minister had powers to waive the disqualification if this would be in the public interest. Surveyors and solicitors found themselves embarrassed by the number of cases in which they were indirectly involved through the interest of a client.

The rule was slightly relaxed in 1948 by excluding the owners of small numbers of shares,[19] and again in 1953,[20] but still the main difficulties continued. Two High Court cases underlined the dangers, and increased the apprehension of candidates and councillors. In one case six councillors of Northampton Borough voted in a debate on a charge levied on council tenants who took lodgers. The six councillors were themselves tenants of council houses, but they all voted against their own interest; none the less they were all convicted, and the Lord Chief Justice, Lord Goddard, said that 'Parliament has not said that they may vote against their interest and not for their interest: it has said that they must not vote on any matter in which they have a pecuniary interest.'[21] In the second case, a Wisbech councillor was involved, who was also managing director of a building firm. Because of his position on the council, his firm did not tender for council contracts, but he voted in a debate on the employment of a direct labour force under the borough engineer, which would compete

with outside tenders from builders. It was held that in the circumstances he was guilty of an offence, as he could have changed his
mind and put in tenders for council contracts.[22]

These two cases caused considerable concern, particularly in
the Conservative Party, whose members were more commonly
affected,[23] and discussions were opened between the Ministry
of Housing and Local Government and the Local Authority
Associations. Ultimately, in 1964 a private member, Sir Hubert
Ashton, brought forward a Bill to clarify, but not essentially to
alter the existing law.[24] The basic problem remained unsolved:
how to exclude those with a conflict between public duty and
private interest, without unduly narrowing the range of people
available for service in local government.

One aspect of this problem which led to particular concern
arose out of the rising price of land. Under the Town and
Country Planning Act 1932, compensation had been paid to
landowners whose land lost in value on account of planning
restrictions. Thus the owner was in approximately the same
position whether his land was subjected to restrictions or not.
Under the Act of 1947 the position was reversed; he had to pay
a development charge if he was allowed to develop his land, but
got no compensation on account of being refused permission.
Thus still, in another way, his financial position was approximately the same, whether or not he got permission to develop.
But in 1953 the development charges were abolished, with certain
minor exceptions. The effect was that from that time the decision
of a planning committee could make a vital difference to the
value of land. Thus a favourable decision might be worth
thousands, or tens of thousands of pounds to the owner of the
land.

This change in the law came at a time of great activity in
redevelopment in the towns; there was a very heavy demand for
land for housing and offices, and town centres were being re-
planned and rebuilt. Inevitably it put a great temptation in the
way of landowners and developers, particularly in the urban
areas. Without infringing the rules about declaring interest, it
was possible for councillors to influence decisions or to profit from
advance information of planning policy. A number of cases were
reported, and prosecution ensued, in which councillors were
alleged to be guilty of offences arising out of this situation;[25]
the chairman of one county planning committee was convicted
and sentenced to twenty-one months' imprisonment. Though
such cases were not widespread, they raised the question whether
any man should be put in a position of such conflict between his

private interest and his public duty, and whether people directly concerned in real estate should be eligible to sit on local planning committees.[26]

For some time there had been rumours of corruption on a larger scale in the north-east of England, where one architect, John Poulson, had built up a very large organisation, while in Newcastle-upon-Tyne the council leader, T. Dan Smith, was presiding over massive central area redevelopment. In July 1972 John Poulson was examined in bankruptcy, and startling facts came to light. He had presided over a great empire of contacts and corruption. Between 1962 and 1970 he had made payments to various people totalling more than £334,000. Over half the money had gone to T. Dan Smith, formerly leader of the council at Newcastle, chairman of the Northern Economic Planning Council, and a member of the Royal Commission on Local Government. Other payments had been made to Mr John Cordle, Conservative MP for Bournemouth East and Christchurch; Mr Albert Roberts, Labour MP for Normanton; and W. G. Pottinger, Secretary of the Department of Agriculture and Fisheries for Scotland. The Home Secretary, Reginald Maudling, had had business relations with Mr Poulson. As the minister responsible for the police who were investigating the affair, there was a conflict of interest which led to his resignation. Others were prosecuted and imprisoned; Poulson and Pottinger for five years, Smith for six.

The repercussions of these events were many: for many years afterwards lesser actors in the drama were charged and tried; and the public confidence in the honesty of public life was severely shaken.

Social and Political Change

It was not only changes in the law that affected the composition of local authorities during this period. There were fundamental social and political changes in progress which, almost imperceptibly, influenced the membership of councils. The general change in English society affected the composition of local councils as much as it did that of Parliament itself. Most noticeably, the old respect for the aristocracy and the gentry was dying. When, in 1889, the first county councils were elected, they were composed predominantly of members of the upper class; about half the county councillors were magistrates, and many peers were elected. Moreover, in the choice of aldermen it became the practice in many counties to invite the principal landowners and the county members to serve.[27] Since then the number of such people serving on the county councils has steadily declined:[28]

Date	Members of House of Lords	Members of House of Commons
1889	131	87
1920	93	55
1930	71	43
1940	70	35
1950	54	20
1960	45	24
1975	10	6

But the change has been much more marked in some counties than in others, and the number of 'gentry' on the county councils has changed very little. In the rural counties at least, it is apparent that the change is very slow. In Hampshire, for example, in 1964, the council included three lords, four baronets, three knights, two MPs and sixteen men with military or naval ranks, but in 1975 there was only one lord, one baronet, no knights or MPs, and eleven naval or military officers. In 1964, Gloucestershire had a duke, three lords, a baronet, and twelve retired officers, but by 1975 it had no lords, no baronets, and four retired officers. This aristocratic tradition, carried over from the days of government by Quarter Sessions, showed also in the choice of chairmen of the county councils; in 1934, eleven counties had peers as chairman of the council, though by 1964 the number had fallen to two. Moreover, in many counties the tradition continued of keeping a chairman in office for many years; the Marquis of Bath was forty years chairman of Wilt-shire County Council, and Sir Godfrey Baring occupied the chair in the Isle of Wight for fifty-nine years. Perhaps the last of these long-term chairmen was the Earl of Macclesfield, who was in office in Oxfordshire from 1937 until 1967.

Not all the counties, however, have retained these traditions. Dr Lee has shown how, in Cheshire, the old land-owning families have given way to a new type of councillor who owes his status to his position on the council rather than his position on the council to his social status.[29] So, too, in Wales the land-owning class have never dominated the county councils, and such in-fluence as they had was much reduced in the struggles over denominational schools.

In the towns the story has, inevitably, been different. Two main changes can be seen. The rise of the Labour Party, the abolition of pauper disqualification and the introduction of pay-ment for lost wages have all served to bring in more people from among the poorer workers.[30] Figures for the earlier years of the century are not available, but it is clear that there has been some substantial change in this way. The other noticeable change is a reduction in the number of business and professional men on the town councils. This is due probably to several causes: there are fewer large businesses which are privately owned, and the salaried managers of public companies do not feel as free to give their time to local politics as did their predecessors, such as the Chamberlains in Birmingham, Lord Simon of Wythenshawe in Manchester, and the Mander family in Wolverhampton. In addition, the use of cars has meant that fewer of these people now live in the towns where they work – they live out in the country, or perhaps in London.[31]

The decline in the number of businessmen on the grand scale who play a leading part in municipal affairs in the provincial cities has not, however, meant a decline in the proportion of businessmen, great or small, who play a part in local government. They are, in fact, still the largest single group in the membership of local authorities. Thus the Government Social Survey has shown that, in 1964, the county councils included 45 per cent employers and managers (including farmers) and practically no unskilled labourers or agricultural workers,[32] while all types of local authorities had employers and managers far in excess of their proportion in the general population.[33]

Clearly, one of the most potent causes of change in the personnel of local authorities has been the changing political scene. It is not possible to give a statistically accurate table of the number of Conservative, Liberal and Labour members of local authorities for a number of reasons; many Conservatives, and some Labour and Liberal candidates, have stood as Independents; in the early part of the century, many Labour men were elected with a Liberal ticket, and a number of different titles have been used with varying meanings – Municipal Reform, Ratepayers, Progressive, Municipal Alliance, and others.

None the less, certain clear patterns do emerge. In 1900 the Independent Labour Party was the only organised Labour group putting up candidates in local elections. In that year it claimed sixty-three town councillors, four county councillors, thirty-six urban district councillors and three rural district councillors.[34] This contrasts with a figure in 1973 (after reduction in the number of authorities under the Local Government Act of 1972) of 1,803 county councillors and 28,183 district councillors. Inevitably, this has drastically affected the type of person elected to the councils. But perhaps the most remarkable fact in this content is not the change, but the extent to which, particularly in the more rural counties and districts, the pattern has survived of government by the professional classes, and particularly the retired and elderly. The Maud Committee found in 1964 that in the county councils 70 per cent of the councillors were over 55 years of age; 35 per cent belonged to socio-economic groups 1, 2 or 3, as against 12 per cent in the population at large.[35] Even in the county boroughs, manual labourers (groups 9, 10 and 11) were only 24 per cent of the total, as against 51 per cent in the population at large.

It is also relevant to notice how many local councillors have progressed from local government to Parliament. Colin Mellors has shown[36] how, particularly in the Labour Party, local government has become a principal ladder leading to Parliament. Of the 1,592 MPs elected at the eight general elections from 1945 to 1970, 554 – slightly over one third of the total – had been members of local authorities.

The effect of this on the personnel of local government is, however, much reduced by the fact that, unlike the pattern in France, nearly all councillors resigned from their local councils on being elected to Parliament. It is unusual to find a man serving both on his local council and in Parliament. In and around London this has been possible, but it is much more difficult in more distant areas. In Liverpool, however, there has been a long tradition of local Members of Parliament being also city councillors.

The type of person serving on local authorities has also probably been affected by the increased burden of work involved. The extent of this, however, can easily be over-estimated. While the range of functions of local councils has increased substantially, and their total expenditure has risen many fold, the amount of time involved in committee work has not apparently increased in proportion. For example, the total expenditure of Oxford County Council rose between 1900 and 1974 from £74,433 to £70,309,340.[37]

It appears, however, that the actual burden of committee work falling on an average councillor in a county borough has increased very little during the period. In Sheffield, for example, the number of committee meetings in the year rose between 1900 and 1964 from 319 to 341.[38] In Manchester, the number of committee meetings in the year fell from 372 in 1894 to 338 in 1964.[39] In Portsmouth, there were fifteen full committees in 1900, and fourteen in 1964; the number of subcommittees had risen slightly, from fifty to fifty-three, but the average size of these subcommittees fell from ten to seven. The committees met less frequently in 1964 – the average number of meetings a month declined from twenty-three to seventeen and a half and the average size of the committees declined from seventeen to twelve. At the same time the number of councillors among whom this reduced number of meetings was distributed increased from fifty-six to sixty-four.[40]

The Government Social Survey has shown[41] that in 1963-4 county councillors would spend an average of 67·9 hours a month on their council work; county borough councillors, 76·6 hours, and rural district councillors, 34·4 hours. This adds up, in the counties and county boroughs, to nearly half the normal working month, and thus to a very serious inroad into one's earning capacity. It is as yet too early to assess the effect of the reforms of 1974, but it is doubtful whether they have done much, if anything, to reduce the number of hours involved.

These figures are statistically inexact, and they do not take into account the duties that fall on a councillor outside the regular committee meetings. These include not only informal discussions and political meetings, but also membership of other official bodies which follows as a consequence of being a borough councillor. Thus the University of London Centre for Urban Studies has shown[42] that in 1959 'on the average, almost six public posts (excluding those inside the Council) are held by each member of the LCC, and almost seven by each county councillor in Middlesex and Surrey'. The extent of this has probably increased since the beginning of the century.

Thus, in the first three quarters of the twentieth century, there were real changes in the composition of the local councils of England. In the counties, the noblemen and squires had slowly – very slowly – been elbowed out by the new businessmen. In the provincial cities, the large-scale businessmen, at the head of their great family undertakings, had moved away, and given way to businessmen on a smaller scale. The social and legal changes of the period had led to a great increase in the number of manual workers on the councils – but still far below their proportion in the community at large. Women had at last been admitted to the councils, but had not occupied the proportion of places that their numbers might have justified.

Staff

Meanwhile the pattern of the councils' staff was changing, but slowly and reluctantly. The major authorities had inherited from the nineteenth century a system which had its roots even further back. At the head of the staff was the town clerk, or county clerk, usually a solicitor, who had served his articles in local government, moved once or twice from authority to authority, and then settled down. Some of these were men of great authority and ability – such as Sir Samuel Johnson of Nottingham (town clerk, 1870–1908), C. W. Potts of Cheshire (clerk, 1890–1931) and Sir Horatio Brevitt of Wolverhampton (town clerk, 1882–1919).[43] In the previous century, many of these solicitor-clerks were also in private practice, and employed their own staff to help them. Many held a wide range of other offices, such as coroner, clerk of the drainage board, registration officer, steward of the manor, and so on. But as the new century advanced they became, more and more, full-time professional officers. However, in some of the smaller district councils and boroughs the part-time clerk continued; the numbers were dwindling, but in 1962 there were still 110 such, mostly in the very small urban districts and boroughs![44] In a few cases, one chief officer served as such for two authorities, as, for example, the small borough of Montgomery and the surrounding rural district of Forden.

The town clerk or clerk of the county council was, since the early nineteenth century, a great man, drawing a handsome salary; in 1906 the town clerk of Liverpool was paid £3,000 a year, but his clerks only received £40 to £175 a year.[45] The clerk of the county council was similarly placed, and usually served also as clerk of the peace, clerk of the lieutenancy, and in several other offices.[46]

But there was a great gulf between these professional men and the ordinary clerks, who were commonly recruited as office boys on leaving school at 14, and served in the town hall until they retired half a century later. They were untrained, except by years of experience, and unorganised. There had, however, emerged over the years new technical bodies for treasurers and engineers,[47] which gave a professional status to these officers. Medical officers were qualified doctors, often in private practice at the same time; chief constables in the towns were usually promoted police constables, but in the counties were nearly always ex-army officers of high social standing but not necessarily much knowledge of police matters.

The system as a whole had grown in a haphazard way. The recruiting was a matter of patronage and chance; admission to the privileged ranks of the town clerks and clerks of county councils depended on being able to buy one's articles, and so qualification as a solicitor. There was little prospect, if any, of the ordinary clerks making their way into these circles. It was like the officers and the NCOs of the regular army.

But change was at last beginning; in 1905 there was founded the National Association of Local Government Officers. It aimed at winning for local government officers the right to pensions, appointment by open examination, regular salary scales, and promotion by merit. It was essentially an organisation of the clerical staffs, rather than of the chief officers, and it looked with some resentment at privileged groups such as solicitors and university graduates.

There had, meanwhile, been a growing volume of criticism of the pattern as a whole. In particular, Ernest Simon[48] was challenging the assumption that town clerks needed to be qualified in law rather than in administration, and was criticising the haphazard way in which the staff was recruited. He also urged the recruiting of more university graduates, despite the opposition of NALGO and the existing staff.

The Royal Commission on Local Government heard evidence on these matters from Graham Wallas, Ernest Simon and others. They came to no clear conclusion, but fell back on the customary policy of recommending the appointment of another committee of investigation.[49]

So, in September 1930, the minister appointed a departmental committee, under Sir Henry Hadow, a former Vice-Chancellor of Leeds University, with Evelyn Sharp, a young civil servant, as secretary. The committee accepted the main arguments put forward by NALGO for post-entry training, for a regular system of examinations, for a national system of Whitley councils, and for the abolition of premiums for articles. It also urged the need for town clerks to be trained as administrators rather than lawyers.[50]

The status and prospects of the general administrative staff had not, in the past, been high, though their organisation, NALGO, was doing much to raise them. Their pay was low, and their conditions of service depended very much on the goodwill of each individual employing council. The Hadow Committee had pointed the way towards a better system: established grades and scales of pay; defined conditions of service; a proper system of training; and prospects of promotion.

For some years before the Hadow Committee was appointed, NALGO had been active in developing the idea of 'Whitleyism' – the settlement of questions of wages and conditions of work through permanent joint industrial councils of employers and employees. Progress, however, had been slow, and the first attempt had failed. But the Hadow Report gave a new impetus to this movement, aiming at a structure of provincial councils negotiating such matters over the whole country. Ultimately, in 1946, there emerged, after much delay and conflict with the employers, the National Scheme of Conditions of Service, commonly known as 'The Charter', which laid down a general pattern, applicable to all staff, except those who were in the professional categories. The Charter covered recruitment, training, examinations, conditions of service and scales of pay, promotion, and codes of conduct.

There was immediately set up a Local Government Examinations Board and, six years later, the Diploma in Municipal Administration was established, in the hope that it would prove to be a qualification regarded as equal to a university degree, or a professional qualification, and thus serve as a passport to the senior appointments.

The Charter has done much to improve the conditions and pay of the general administrative staffs of local authorities; whether it has done much to improve the intellectual and academic standards is less easy to assess. The Diploma in Municipal Administration proved to be something of a disappointment. It did not open the doors to the most senior posts. The local authorities still demanded the accepted professional qualifications. The future chief officers still climbed up the separate professional ladder, and the committee clerk did not find himself in the running for promotion to the town clerk's chair.

So the harshness of the old pattern was softened; premiums for articles were abolished; new opportunities were opened up; none the less, the basic shape of the service was the same. Solicitors held a practical monopoly of the town clerkships; other departments were headed by professional men – architects, accountants, doctors, etc. There was really no place for the general administrator, nor ladder of promotion for the university graduate unless he had also a professional qualification. It was a strange contrast with the Civil Service, based on the predominance of the general administrator, usually with an Oxford or Cambridge degree.

The Maud and Mallaby Committees
The critics of local government had, for a long time, attacked the boundaries, the structure and the finance. Only a few, such as John Stuart Mill,[51] and Lord Simon of Wythenshawe,[52] had criticised the people in local government. Now, a hundred years after Mill had written on the subject, more was being heard of this form of criticism. Dame Evelyn Sharp, who had been secretary of the Hadow Committee, and was now Permanent Secretary of the Ministry of Housing and Local Government, began to question the calibre of local councillors.[53] The Conservative Party in its annual conference in 1961 was highly critical of the system

of aldermen,[54] and a number of writers were attacking both the aldermen and the mayor.[55]

Dame Evelyn Sharp invited the chairmen of the principal local authority associations to meet her, and put to them a proposal for a departmental committee on the question of the people in local government. Out of this evolved a decision to appoint two committees, one to inquire into how local government could best attract and retain people of the necessary calibre, and the other into the recruiting and training of local government officers. In due course these committees were appointed under the chairmanship respectively of Sir John Maud[56] and Sir George Mallaby.

Both committees found themselves working in circumstances of change. There was already a growing interest in modern management techniques, and a tendency to move away from the traditional conception of the lawyer town clerk; Newcastle upon Tyne had just appointed an executive from the Ford Motor Company as town clerk and principal city officer, to work under the council leader, T. Dan Smith;[57] computers were being introduced into local administration, and the principal emphasis in the services provided by local government was shifting more and more towards education, social services and planning. Proposals for radical reform of the structure were in the air, and the traditional pattern of recruitment of officers had failed to keep pace with the changing education service.

The Mallaby Committee, which was heavily weighted with local authority members and officers, reaffirmed the principle that the town clerk should be a manager rather than a lawyer, and that he should be head of the council's paid service, with a general authority over the other chief officers. They did however get into some confusion about the 'lay administrative officer'. The chairman, who had been Deputy Secretary to the Cabinet, tended to equate him with the administrative grade civil servant; some members saw him rather as the unqualified local government clerk.

They agreed however on recommending a move away from reliance on the strictly professional officer towards the general administrator, at much the same time as the Fulton Committee was recommending just the opposite movement in the Civil Service.[58]

The total result of this report was probably little more than to accelerate a tendency which was already visible, to break the monopoly of the lawyers, and open the way for a few accountants to become town clerks. There was certainly no dramatic change. It did, however, make it more difficult for a young graduate entering local government to discover how best to get onto the first rungs of the ladder that might lead him in due course to the office of town clerk – or, as it came to be called, chief executive.

The Maud Committee supported the view that the clerk should be trained as an administrator rather than as a lawyer, and should have authority over the other chief officers. It also proposed that aldermen should be abolished, and that each authority should appoint a 'management board'. This would be in effect a cabinet but including members of the Opposition party. Thus the councillors would be divided into those on the board, who would play a major part in the administrative work, and be paid, and the other 'back benchers'.

One member of the committee, Sir Andrew Wheatley,[59] wrote a Note of Dissent, arguing that, by stripping the committees of executive power, one would no longer give to the majority of the elected councillors a worthwhile role to play. Thus local government would cease to attract members of the quality needed. He proposed instead a pattern of management in which the committees would still exercise executive powers, reporting direct to the councils, except on matters of major policy, on which they would report to the management board.

The committee's proposals were received by local authorities with interest rather than enthusiasm. Those councils that made any change in their organisation tended to prefer Sir Andrew Wheatley's scheme, which involved less alteration to existing patterns. But there was unmistakably a current running in favour of new administrative methods. The Institute of Local Government Studies at Birmingham University was preaching the doctrine of 'corporate management', and others were advocating a bewildering collection of administrative nostrums. In May 1971, before the Local Government Bill was introduced, the minister, Peter Walker, appointed a committee to advise the new local authorities on management structures.

This committee, under the chairmanship of Malcolm Bains, Clerk of the Kent County Council, produced a report which was widely accepted as a pattern for the new authorities. It did not follow Maud in centralising power in a 'management board', but it did accept the conception of 'corporate management', and recommended that local authorities should appoint a chief executive with no departmental duties, working with a 'management team' of chief officers, concentrating on plans and programmes for the long-term objectives of the council.

The concept of 'corporate planning' was avidly accepted by most local authorities, though, a year or two later the pendulum of opinion began to swing the other way, and critics questioned whether it left sufficient scope for the elected councillors, and whether it did not unduly blur the responsibility of expert professional officers.

One side-effect of the report was a move away from the traditional titles of town clerk, treasurer, public health inspector (formerly sanitary inspector) and borough engineer, in favour of more impressive designations like chief executive, director of environmental health services, and director of technical services.

NOTES

1 Report of the Royal Commission on *Municipal Corporations* (1835), vol. 1, p. 35.
2 *Representative Government* (1861), p. 351. See also D. Read, *The English Provinces* (1946), pp. 237–43, and S. D. Simon, *A Century of City Government* (1938), pp. 395–405.
3 Albert Shaw, *Municipal Government in Great Britain* (1895), pp. 53, 54.
4 *Public Administration*, Winter 1962, vol. 40, p. 383.
5 See pp. 18, 19.
6 Report, vol. 2 (HMSO, 1967), p. 16.
7 S. L. Bristow, 'Women in county government', *County Councils Gazette*, April 1975.
8 See pp. 19, 20 for fuller discussion.
9 Report of the Inter-Departmental Committee on *Expenses of Members of Local Authorities*, 1946–7, Cmd 7126, xiii.
10 Secs. 111–19, amended by Public Authorities (Allowances) Act 1961.
11 See Mary Stewart, *Unpaid Public Service* (1964); some councillors claimed to be £500 to £1,000 out of pocket through serving on the council. See also Maud Committee on *Management of Local Government*, vol. 1, Appendix D.
12 Report of the Committee on *Management of Local Government* (HMSO, 1967), para. 217.
13 Local Government Act 1972, sec. 173.
14 Municipal Corporations Act 1882, sec. 12; Local Government Act 1888, sec. 75; Local Government Act 1894, sec. 46.
15 *Lapish* v. *Braithwaite* [1926], AC 275.
16 Final Report of the Royal Commission on *Local Government*, paras. 327–42; 1929–30, Cmd 3436, xv.
17 *Local Government and Public Health Consolidation Committee*, paras. 44–57; 1932–3, Cmd 4272, xiii.
18 Sec. 76.
19 Local Government Act 1948, sec. 131.
20 Local Government (Miscellaneous Provisions) Act 1953, sec. 15.
21 *Brown* v. *Director of Public Prosecutions* [1956], 2 QB 369.
22 *Rands* v. *Oldroyd* [1959], 1 QB 204.
23 *The Times*, 16 April 1959; 14 February 1964.

24 Local Government (Pecuniary Interests) Bill 1964.
25 *The Times*, 31 October 1962, 12 December 1962, 16 May 1963, 3 June 1964; *Guardian*, 9 December 1964; *The Times*, 29 December 1964 (Frimley and Camberley Councillor acquitted); *Daily Telegraph*, 13 January 1965 (Salford).
26 See, e.g., F. V. Corfield, MP, speech to the Rating and Valuation Association, *The Times*, 28 October 1961; *New Society*, 18 April 1963.
27 See J. M. Lee, *Social Leaders and Public Persons* (1963), p. 227.
28 Sources: Year Books of the County Councils Association and *County Councils Directory*, 1889; information from Association of County Councils.
29 J. M. Lee, op. cit. See also G. W. Jones, *Borough Politics* ([Wolverhampton], 1969).
30 See A. M. Rees and Trevor Smith, *Town Councillors*, a study of Barking, 1964; *Current Topics*, March 1963, vol. 2, no. 8; and E. P. Hennock, *Fit and Proper Persons* ([Birmingham and Leeds], 1973).
31 J. M. Lee, op. cit., p. 93; G. W. Jones, op. cit., pp. 116–19; Brian D. White, *A History of the Corporation of Liverpool* (1951), pp. 188–9; A. H. Birch, *Small Town Politics* (a study of politics in Glossop), (1959), p. 115; D. Read, *The English Provinces* (1964), pp. 232–8.
32 Report of the Committee on *Management of Local Government* (HMSO, 1967), vol. 2, p. 23.
33 ibid., p. 21. In the general population, employers and managers were 11 per cent of the whole; among councillors, 31 per cent.
34 H. Tracey (ed.), *The British Labour Party* (1948), vol. II, p. 177.
35 Report of the Committee on *Management of Local Government* (HMSO, 1967), vol. 2, pp. 21, 23.
36 'Local government in Parliament – 20 years later', in *Public Administration*, Summer 1974, pp. 223–9.
37 Including all expenditure (capital and revenue) net from specific grants, general grants and rates and other income, but not including expenditure from special funds such as Superannuation Fund, Motor Licensing etc.
38 These figures (which do not include sub-committees) are based on Redlich and Hirst, p. 313n., and information from town clerk. The number of sub-committees in 1900 was fifty-three; in 1964, sixty-four. These figures do not allow for changes in the length of meetings, nor for the number attending.
39 A. Shaw, *Municipal Government in Great Britain* (1895), p. 148, and information from Town Clerk. The number of sub-committees has fallen from 'nearly a hundred' in 1894 to seventy-four in 1964.
40 Information from town clerk. In Oxford the numbers of meetings appear to have been approximately; 1900, 230; 1930, 611; 1964, 430 (information from town clerk). Plymouth shows a moderate increase in the number of meetings, but the picture there is confused by the merger of the two county boroughs of Plymouth and Devonport.
41 Report of the Committee on *Management of Local Government* (HMSO, 1967), vol. 2, p. 93.
42 Statement of Evidence to the Royal Commission on *Local Government in Greater London* (written evidence), (HMSO, 1962), vol. V, p. 9.
43 See J. M. Lee, op. cit., pp. 67, 68; and G. W. Jones, op. cit., pp. 269–72.
44 Information from Urban District Councils Association.

45　Alec Spoor, *White Collar Union* (1967), p. 5. Redlich and Hirst, vol. I, p. 337, refers to the salary of a town clerk in 1900 'rising in large towns to upwards of £2,000'.

46　See Report of the Select Committee of the House of Lords on *Charges of the County Rates* (1835) (206), xiv. Even then, some clerks of the peace received very large remuneration: Lancashire, £4,329 p.a.; Sussex, £1,985 p.a.; etc. In 1899, the Clerk of the West Riding County Council had a salary of £1,500 plus £264 as Clerk of the Peace (Redlich and Hirst, vol. II, p. 38).

47　The Institution of Municipal Engineers, founded 1873; the Institute of Municipal Treasurers and Accountants, founded 1885.

48　Later Lord Simon of Wythenshawe; see Ernest Simon, *A City Council from Within* (1926), p. 136.

49　Final Report, paras. 408–13; 1929–30, Cmd 3436, xv.

50　Report of the Committee on the *Qualifications, Recruitment, Training and Promotion of Local Government Officers* (HMSO, 1934).

51　*Considerations on Representative Government* (1861), p. 351.

52　Ernest Simon, op. cit., p. 136.

53　Address to the Association of Municipal Corporations, the *Municipal Review*, November 1960; a lecture at Bristol, published in *Public Administration,* Winter 1962; address to Ham and Petersham Ratepayers' and Residents' Association, referred to in 669 HC Deb., 13 December 1962, cols. 557–8.

54　*Guardian* and *Daily Mail*, 11 October 1968.

55　e.g. B. Keith-Lucas, *The Mayor, Aldermen and Councillors* (1961).

56　Created Lord Redcliffe-Maud in 1967. This committee came to be known as the Committee on the Management of Local Government, although management was not mentioned in its terms of reference.

57　The Newcastle experiment began to crumble when Mr Smith resigned to become Chairman of the Northern Economic Planning Council in 1965; the Principal City Officer, Frank Harris, resigned in 1969. In 1972 Mr Smith was convicted of fraud. See also J. Elliott, 'The Harris experiment in Newcastle upon Tyne', *Public Administration*, 1971, vol. 49, pp. 149–62.

58　Report of the Committee on the *Civil Service*, 1967–8, Cmnd 3638, xviii.

59　Formerly Clerk of Hampshire County Council.

Chapter VI

PARTY POLITICS

The Situation pre-1914

'The English nation is still led by Society, and if religious qualifications have been almost swept away and the advantages of birth
reduced, the superiority conferred by wealth and education has
rather increased than diminished.'

Dr Redlich's concluding comment in his chapter on 'Municipal
Electioneering'[1] illustrates the limited extent to which a wider
franchise had affected local elections by the turn of the century.
Political parties were most highly organised in the towns. Here
the rival Conservative and Liberal parties would vie for control
of the borough council. West Ham was the sole authority to have
experienced a Labour majority by 1900. In rural areas the party
element in local elections were normally unknown; leading
citizens offered themselves to serve on local authorities and
unopposed returns were frequent. Many boroughs had seen some
party competition at elections since 1835. Yet not all wards were
contested each year. Sitting councillors were often allowed an
unopposed return. When a seat was fought it was common for
the challengers to adopt a Conservative or Liberal label. Once
elected, councillors were little restrained by party allegiance and
tended to act as individuals, speaking and voting as they thought
fit. An example of this atmosphere is to be found in *The Times*
report of the election in the Borough of Appleby in 1900. 'No
Contest. A Conservative has retired and the vacancy has been
filled by a Liberal. The two political parties are about equally
represented on the new council.' In a situation of this type, local
government becomes virtually non-political.

Of course, in the large industrial cities the parties were more
vigorous than in Appleby. The greatest contrast would be found
in the London County Council. Even in 1900 it was rare for any
seat to be uncontested. Two teams of rival candidates were
assembled. The team that won most seats took control of the
council. It appointed one of its number to be chairman. The

election of aldermen was conducted on party lines. The winners chose all the chairmen of committees. Party groups of councillors and aldermen met separately to decide policy and tactics. Voting at council and committee meeting was predetermined on the basis of party allegiance. The chairmen of committees developed considerable personal authority in relation to their sphere of responsibility and devoted a substantial amount of time to council business.

The Appleby model was, however, more common than the London one. In 1900 there was no contest at all at the elections in about 350 boroughs. Some seats, but not usually all seats, were fought in 140 boroughs. Again, some of these contests were not party political. At county council elections the parties were even less involved. The 1901 county council elections were not reported at all in *The Times* as they were of such little importance. This inertia was due partly to a feeling that local administration was not a political matter. Even in the larger towns there was often little to divide Conservative and Liberal councillors. Where party groups were formed, the minority would accuse the majority of extravagance and emphasise the need for economy. Then if the balance of power changed the new minority would start to make the same sort of speeches as had previously been made by its opponents. In urban areas a major issue was often a tussle over areas – should Council A take over the whole or a part of the territory of Council B? An argument of this kind stimulated geographical loyalties rather than political loyalties.

However, during the first decade of the twentieth century, party ardour was aroused by two controversies, denominational education and municipal trading, which achieved wide importance.[2] But there were occasions when local issues aroused remarkable passion. In Bradford, the Independent Labour Party campaigned successfully for the development of school welfare services, first on the Bradford School Board and after 1902 on the borough council. At Wolverhampton in 1902 and 1903 the borough was occupied with bitter exchanges about the best method of tram propulsion.[3] In 1904, the administration of the new Licensing Act led to a clash in Liverpool between the Liberal supporters of temperance and Conservatives associated with the drink trade.[4] Also at this time Alderman Salvidge[5] began to build a working-class Conservative organisation linked to Protestantism as the tempers aroused by the clash in Ulster between Catholics and Orangemen began to spread across the sea. This religious issue greatly hindered the growth of the Labour Party in Liverpool:

Labour did not win control of Liverpool until 1955, long after it had conquered other major cities.

The argument over education concerned support for denominational schools out of the local rate funds. School boards were abolished by the Education Act 1902 and their duties passed on to the county authorities with the medium-sized boroughs and urban districts receiving responsibility for elementary education only.[6] In addition, the 1902 Act made the county education authorities responsible for the running costs of schools provided by the churches. Without such assistance many church schools would have had to close. So the rates paid for teachers' salaries and the maintenance of buildings; in return the county nominated one third of the managers of the church schools assisted in this way. This legislation caused a storm of protest from Nonconformists since the schools concerned had almost all been established either by the Anglican Church or by the Roman Catholics. As the majority of the church schools were in the countryside and the smaller towns, rather than in the great industrial centres of population, the issue concerned the county councils rather than the county boroughs.

English counties were predominantly Conservative in sympathy and could be expected to support the policy of giving financial assistance to church schools. Welsh counties were essentially Liberal and Nonconformist. Here the policy of the 1902 Act was anathema. In 1903 the Carmarthen County Council refused to provide financial aid for any school that was not under the full control of the council. Merioneth adopted a similar policy. The issue dominated the county council elections in Wales in 1904 and the Liberals were triumphant throughout the principality. The response of the Conservative Government was to secure the passage of a further measure, the Education (Local Authority Default) Act 1904, which authorised the Board of Education to act where a local authority refused to carry out its duties and to impose a charge on the local rate fund. The Liberal Opposition strenuously resisted the Bill in Parliament. However, once the Bill was passed it effectively killed the revolt among the Welsh counties. In England the controversy was less acute. The West Riding County Council refused to pay for that proportion of teachers' salaries which it calculated was used to give denominational instruction, but this action was held to be illegal by the courts.[7] Elsewhere many nonconformists refused to pay the whole or part of their rates and were served with warrants to appear before the magistrates. The great Liberal victory at the 1906 general election led, in the same year, to the introduction of an

Education Bill which sought to remove public aid from denominational schools. This measure passed through the Commons but was rejected by the Lords where Anglican interests were deeply entrenched. At this time the Lords still had an absolute veto over legislation and so the church schools remained.

Parliamentary politics had a steadily increasing influence over local elections, especially in the boroughs. As early as the 1870s the Chamberlain Liberal organisation in Birmingham had realised that annual elections provided an ideal stimulus for keeping party sympathisers alert and active. If local contests were fought each year the local party machine was in much better condition to fight a perhaps unexpected parliamentary election. George Jones in his study of Wolverhampton quotes a letter from Alfred Bird MP, dated October 1912 to the president of his local Conservative association in which the MP argued: 'The policy of contesting seats has to be considered with relation to the effect that may be produced upon our Parliamentary prospects and *nothing else.*'[8]

The Labour-Conservative Conflict

The Labour Party did not gain significant strength on local authorities until after the First World War. At the 1919 elections the Labour representation on London borough councils was increased from 46 to 572. In the same year Labour won control of Durham County and Monmouthshire; the full tally of its victories amounted to 236 county councillors, 1,776 borough councillors, 1,828 urban district councillors and 1,245 Poor Law guardians. Throughout the inter-war period this advance was continued and Labour replaced the Liberals as a major political force. Merthyr Tydfil was captured in 1920, Walthamstow in 1921, Sheffield in 1926. Labour did exceptionally well in 1927, taking control of Barnsley, Barrow, Nelson and Mansfield. Notable victories in 1933 were those at Leeds and Norwich. By 1939 Labour majorities existed on 4 county councils, 18 county boroughs, 24 non-county boroughs, 17 London boroughs and 100 district councils. Its position was especially strong in the county boroughs where the party held one third of the council seats.

The rise of the Labour Party greatly strengthened the element of party conflict. Labour candidates made more specific proposals in their election addresses and, if successful, tried to get their policies accepted by the local authority. Labour councillors met together to decide what they should do and then acted and voted in concert to a degree which, outside London, had been unknown. There is a common belief that Labour first brought party politics into local government. Stated in a simple form this proposition is untrue since there had been a party element in borough elections since 1835 and a fully developed system of voting on party lines with party control of policy and appointments had operated in the London County Council since it was established in 1889. The protagonists then were the Moderate and Progressive groups. It was not until 1934 that Labour obtained a majority on the LCC. But outside London the emergence of highly disciplined Labour groups of councillors stimulated their opponents to organise themselves more effectively both at local elections and then in terms of deciding policy on the local council.

In many of the larger boroughs the first substantial challenge from Labour came after the First World War. Often the Conservatives and Liberals coalesced to try to repel the new invader. They developed a theory that party politics should be kept out of local government because local issues were different from national political issues. The councillors from the traditional parties also resented the high level of co-ordination amongst Labour councillors which was inimical to independent individual action. No doubt, it was also felt that 'No party politics in the council chamber' would be a good election cry. In 1920 all the members of the Southampton Council, apart from the Labour members, signed the following declaration:

'We, the undersigned members of the Southampton County Borough Council, have honourably and unanimously agreed that, as far as we are concerned, party politics shall no longer be a factor in local municipal life. We believe that the great majority of Ratepayers will welcome this change and at the approaching municipal elections they will support the no-party candidates.'

Thus the Southampton Independent Party was born. Four years later similar events in Bristol led to the formation of the Citizen Party. The titles adopted by the anti-Labour organisations varied; the most common names were Independents, Ratepayers and Moderates. Sometimes the names were changed for reasons of local tactics. In 1934, the Southampton Independents became the Ratepayers Party.

Conservative organisation in London was in the hands of the London Municipal Society which always supported faithfully the Conservative Party, yet stood apart from it. In essence, the society was a Conservative 'front' designed to conciliate the substantial body of opinion that felt party politics should be kept out of local government affairs. The society began to achieve a wider significance in 1921 when ratepayers associations in the provinces started to be accepted as institutional members. Its name was changed to the London Municipal Society and the National Union of Ratepayers' Associations. Between 1921 and 1935 eighty-eight provincial bodies joined. They were of widely differing size and importance, varying from the Birmingham Ratepayers' Association to the Headley Parish Ratepayers' Association. Hove was represented by a Ratepayers' Association and a separate Private Residents' Association. Most of these local groups were situated in the Home Counties and southern England.[9]

Relationships within this 'front' were uneasy. The steadily rising tide of Labour success in the boroughs during the 1920s strengthened the desire of some Conservative enthusiasts to fight local elections on a straightforward party basis. The basic purpose of the society, to defeat Labour, had little practical appeal for many ratepayer groups for they flourished in areas where few Labour candidates had a serious chance of winning. The concern of the ratepayers to curb expenditure could lead them into conflict with Conservative national policy. Occasionally Conservative and Ratepayer candidates opposed each other in local contests. By 1936 the internal strains were sufficient for the National Union of Ratepayers' Associations to emerge as a separate body.[10] It prospered until 1939. Then the cessation of local elections in war-time sent NURA into a decline from which it could not recover.

The Conservatives were shattered by their defeats at parliamentary and local elections after 1945. However, they soon started to rebuild their organisation under the leadership of Lord Woolton and continued to debate whether to nominate party candidates at local elections or whether to assist sympathetic non-party candidates and associations. By now the pressures in favour of direct party involvement were much stronger; it was claimed that to build an efficient organisation to fight local contests would greatly strengthen the party in crucial marginal constituencies at parliamentary elections. Some ratepayers' associations were formally merged into the Conservative machine: this happened at Southampton in 1954. At Wolverhampton the Penn Ratepayers' Association fought a number of electoral battles with the Conservatives before it succumbed.[11] The London Municipal Society, although increasingly dominated by Conservative Central Office, managed to maintain itself until 1963 when it was submerged in the reform of London government. Yet where Labour could not provide a strong challenge, many Conservative-minded councillors were most reluctant to adopt party labels.

The old ways lingered especially in rural areas where the system of triennial elections for county councils did not offer such a valuable spur to political activity.[12] The same was true for rural district councils and many urban districts. So the annual elections in provincial boroughs for one seat in each three-member ward affected but a minority of the population.[13] These elections were expensive. Where a party system was clearly established they could be frustrating in that a party group with a large majority was certain to remain in command whatever the verdict of the electors might be. It is arguable that the regularity of elections produced boredom and apathy among the public. In spite of these drawbacks there was never any serious move to change the pattern of annual elections. The party organisations found it convenient. Apart from the desirability of an annual challenge, there could be serious difficulty in finding sufficient suitable candidates to contest all the seats for councillors instead of one third. Triennial general elections could also have led to single-member wards: smaller electorates would make it easier for local personalities to be elected as non-party or minor-party candidates. There can be no justification whatever for the system used in London boroughs of multi-member wards combined with triennial general elections, for they both deny an annual opportunity to test opinion and help to obliterate minority views. The result has been, on occasion, that some London councils have consisted entirely, or almost entirely, of supporters of one political party.

It has been often argued that party politics are good for local government as they stimulate wider public interest in local elections and so make them more democratic. In fact, this claim is a half truth. A comparison of the post-1945 period between the most political group of local authorities, the county boroughs, and the least political, the rural districts, shows that the turnout at elections for both types of council was virtually the same, averaging around 40 per cent. The great contrast was in the proportion of seats contested; for rural districts the figure was below 30 per cent; in county boroughs nearly 90 per cent of vacancies produced a contest. So the party dog-fight leads to a challenge for council seats but is less successful at getting voters to come to the polling booths. Possibly the boredom induced by annual elections in the boroughs was a major factor in reducing turnout.

Meanwhile the party fight has spread slowly from the towns and the industrial areas to the countryside. In 1951, J. H. Warren[14] estimated that the party system existed in about 90 per cent of the counties and the large towns, in about one half of the urban districts and one quarter of the rural districts. He also recorded that the party element was stronger in the north of England than the south. Party activity extended further in the 1960s and received a fillip from the 1972 reorganisation. The number of Independent or non-party councillors has dwindled. In rural areas, councillors known to be sympathetic to the Conservative Party have been told to stand for election under the party banner or face the prospect of being opposed by an official candidate. Some resisted the threat; some submitted; some dropped out of local government. Yet the move towards two-party councils has been slowed down because, particularly since 1963, the electors have shown some lack of enthusiasm for the major parties. There has been some resurgence of support for the Liberals; opposition to higher rates has stimulated the nomination of candidates by ratepayers' associations. In some areas a particular local controversy, e.g. a development scheme or adding fluoride to the water supply, has secured the election of a few candidates who concentrated on a particular issue. At Andover in 1957 the success at the polls of a few anti-fluoride candidates succeeded in forcing the borough council to change its policy. But in councils where the two-party system was well established it was rare for the minor groups to be able to influence the balance of power.

Before the 1972 reorganisation the general pattern was for councils in rural areas to remain largely non-political. Now party influence has spread to all large authorities. The *Municipal Year Book* shows how far political organisations had come to dominate local councils after the 1973 elections. Party activity had full sway in all metropolitan authorities, including London. Five counties still retained a majority of councillors styled as Independent – Cornwall, Dyfed, Gwynedd, the Isle of Wight and Shropshire. At district level, nineteen authorities reported no party organisation while another seventy-three had Independents as the largest group on the council. So the parties are still not in command of a significant proportion of the 333 non-metropolitan districts in England and Wales.

Local elections become more and more an aspect of the national political struggle. The national parties arrange the timing of part of their ration of television and radio broadcasts in an attempt to influence local election results. The electorate have reacted by voting in accordance with their views on national issues. Local issues, even local personalities, tend to be ignored. The government tends to become unpopular during its term of office, so its supporters at local elections do badly. As a general rule, the longer a Cabinet remains in office the less political support it will have from local authorities and, therefore, from the local authority associations.

Parties and Local Administration

Political parties are unknown to the law. In theory everyone elected to a local council has the right to express his individual opinions on the issues that come before the authority. The appearance of party candidates at elections pledged to follow particular lines of policy could be inimical to fully independent action by councillors. In general, Conservative and Liberal organisations accepted that, once elected, every councillor should act as he saw fit. The Labour Party saw things differently: Labour councillors should not only be loyal to election pledges, they should also represent the views of party supporters. Clearly, they would have the biggest impact on local policy if they acted in unison so, normally, they were expected to speak and vote together. Since the local Labour Party paid the expenses of its candidates, this gave the party a further claim to loyalty: Conservative and Liberal candidates had more often paid their own expenses.

As party activity has become more firmly established at elections so, after lapse of time, has party group discipline become accepted by councillors. Of course, there have been variations and a range of local conventions. It has been easier to establish discipline in urban areas than in rural areas because, in the latter, differences may arise out of geographical loyalty rather than political philosophy. It has been easier to establish discipline once a party has gained a majority of seats for then it can clearly control a council and its opponents are encouraged to organise themselves more forcibly to gain power for themselves. Even these generalities conceal exceptions. The extent of party penetration has been much greater in London than Manchester. From 1889 onwards, the London County Council has been dominated by party allegiance. E. D. Simon's description of Manchester in 1926 recorded that party issues hardly ever arose in committee business and that, while committee chairmen were initially chosen by the majority party, they were not replaced if the political balance of the council changed.[15] Bulpitt's study of Manchester thirty-five years later found that the liberal-style tradition had been maintained. Except in relation to secondary school selection and the over-all level of local expenditure, a genuine attempt was made to run municipal affairs on bi-partisan lines.[16]

Throughout this period one quarter of county and borough

councils were aldermen elected by the councillors and, before 1910, non retiring aldermen. (In London, the proportion of aldermen was one seventh.) Aldermen had normally been chosen from among the councillors with the longest periods of service. When Labour first gained a footing on local councils they, quite naturally, had no aldermen. But as years passed, Labour councillors, entitled on grounds of seniority to elevation to the aldermanic bench, were often passed over for political reasons. Then as a party system became firmly established the opposing groups tended to reach a concordat that the aldermanic seats should be shared out *pro rata* to the number of councillors supporting each party. Occasionally these agreements broke down where the filling of aldermanic vacancies could affect the control of the council. Such disputes caused great bitterness. The 1972 Act abolished the office of alderman, and so eliminated the problem.

As the number of Labour councillors increased efforts were made to improve liaison between them and the party's national headquarters. An advisory committee on local government matters was created after the end of the First World War. It discussed issues of contemporary importance, e.g. rating, municipal banking and housing finance. In 1932 it was replaced by a Local Government Sub-Committee of the Policy Committee of the Party's National Executive. The role of these national bodies has been limited. Their task has been to ventilate issues and to advise rather than to control or instruct. Transport House has been forced from time to time to take some action on the pattern of organisation in local Labour Parties, but it has lacked both the resources and the inclination to become involved in local disputes on policy.[17]

In 1927, a special conference was held to discuss problems of local government and it was agreed that each group of Labour councillors should appoint a corresponding member who would report monthly to Head Office on local activities, problems and policy. At this period, Labour councillors were often subjected to strong pressure from party supporters in relation to decisions on council business. It was felt that Labour councillors should act as delegates from the party rather than as representatives; they should, therefore, accept instructions from local party organisations on how they should vote at council and committee meetings. Obviously this could lead to a situation in which effective decisions were being made by people uninformed about the details of the business, and who were not answerable to the electorate. The Labour Party ultimately felt compelled to take action at national level to avoid these difficulties. In 1930, Model Standing

Orders were issued to local Labour groups.[18] They authorised
three representatives of the local Labour Party to attend, but not
to vote, at the group meetings of Labour councillors which were
to decide policy. The Labour group should meet privately before
each meeting. 'Members of the Group are expected to abide by
Group decisions and not to vote or speak in opposition in the
Council unless the Group has decided to leave the matter to a
free vote.' It was made clear that free votes should be exceptional except on 'issues of conscience', e.g. religious matters and
temperance.

However, the relationship between Labour councillors and
their party supporters continued to cause trouble. The local
party was responsible for the local election manifesto. How far
should the manifesto control the actions of Labour councillors?
A Transport House document issued in 1938, *Labour Groups on
Local Authorities*, laid down clear guide-lines:

'While it is the function of the appropriate section of the Party
to determine election policy, it is the definite responsibility of the
Labour Group to decide Group policy and action on the Council.
Although Group policy is determined within the general framework of election policy, questions of practical application con-
tinuously arise and not infrequently decisions have to be taken
on matters not specifically covered by election policy. On all such
matters it is the definite responsibility of the Labour Group to
take decisions.'

Motions at the 1939 Party Conference unsuccessfully attempted
to increase local party influence over council groups. The debate
gave evidence of more dissension, particularly at West Ham and
also at Nottingham over the municipal gas supply.

Labour councillors did not always impose strict discipline on
themselves, especially where their strength was weak. Glossop
Labour Party in the 1950s was still ignoring the Standing
Orders.[19] Bulpitt's studies a few years later found divergences of
practice. At Middleton and Macclesfield the Standing Orders were
strictly applied. At Manchester, Rochdale, Salford and Sale there
was greater flexibility in that an item of council business only
became a 'whip issue' if the caucus specifically decided it should
be so.[20] Another feature of tight party organisation is that a
majority party takes all committee chairmanships and vice-
chairmanships; when not in a majority it refuses these offices in
order to disassociate itself from the policies being pursued. Again,
where the Labour Party was weak, these ideas have been accepted

slowly if at all. Even in Leeds, with a long tradition of politics on the city council, the controlling Labour groups did not take over committee vice-chairmanships until 1953.

Strict discipline invited the possibility of rebellion. A Labour councillor who opposed his colleagues in public could have the whip withdrawn and thereby suffer expulsion from the Labour group. Such action could be the subject of an appeal to the party's National Executive Committee. In the most highly regimented Labour groups party discipline was even stronger than in the House of Commons. By the end of the 1960s there was a growing feeling that discipline had become too severe and that the greater laxity allowed in Parliament might be extended to local government. A harsh régime could disincline able people from standing for election. It magnified some petty squabbles so that they were widely reported and became an embarrassment. It could enhance the power of local leaders to an undesirable extent by discouraging backbench councillors from challenging the leadership even in the privacy of party meetings. So there has been a mild reaction in recent years. The emphasis has been placed on rather more flexible discipline combined with encouragement for councillors to exercise personal initiative on matters that do not involve party policy.

Opponents of the Labour Party felt forced to organise themselves on similar lines in self-defence. Often they did so with reluctance. Partly this was due to distaste for party-style organisation in local affairs. Perhaps Conservative businessmen found it more difficult to find time for private pre-council meetings. Perhaps also the individualist capitalist ethic made its adherents less willing to accept the restraints of party discipline. Thus the groups formed by Conservatives and their allies were less rigorous. It was less unusual for Conservatives to vote on opposite sides at council and committee meetings. Dissident councillors did not lose the whip; they were not invited to stand again at the next election.

Conservative Central Office has played a much less active role in local government affairs than has Transport House. The inhibition was caused by the widespread feeling in the party that politics should be kept apart from local council business. However, a Local Government Advisory Committee was established in 1944. The following year saw the resumption of local elections after the war and the executive committee of the Conservatives' national organisation adopted the following resolution:

'As the Socialist Party have now made it impossible to exclude party politics from local government elections, the Conservative

Party organisation should take a full and effective part in all contested local government elections; and while the Conservative Party does not seek to control the independent judgement of candidates when elected to local authorities, it is as a general rule desirable that candidates receiving the support of the party should stand as Conservatives.'[21]

To strengthen links between Conservative headquarters and their local councillors a local government officer was appointed in 1947 when the first Conservative Local Government Conference was held. Lord Woolton, as Chairman of the Party, encouraged these developments. Yet many influential Conservatives, particularly from rural areas, viewed the invasion of party activity into local affairs with distaste. The local Government officer was allowed but modest status in the hierarchy of Tory headquarters.

In places where local elections were fought on party lines, the Conservative associations made no attempt to influence the decisions of Conservative councillors. Conservatives have never issued model standing orders to tell their councillors how to organise themselves. There are no appeals to national level against local sanctions for indiscipline because local discipline is informal. Central Office policy has been to avoid entanglement in disputes among Conservative councillors. In recent years the work of the local government officer has developed, but it is still essentially concerned with the organisation of consultation on policy matters between the parliamentary party and councillors. Tactical questions as to whether council elections should be contested on a party basis or whether a sitting Independent should be supported are left to local associations; any advice from the party organisation comes from regional offices and not headquarters.

At local level the activities of groups of every party have become steadily more complex. Pre-council party meetings were not always sufficient to co-ordinate policy. If an important issue comes before a council committee which had not been considered by the party group, the councillors belonging to the majority party might come to a decision of which their party group as a whole disapproved. Alternatively, they might disagree among themselves and allow other committee members to have a crucial voice in the decision made. Such incidents were embarrassing if a majority party assumed that it should have monolithic control of all council decisions. To ensure party domination worked smoothly, various measures were adopted. Sometimes the members of a party group on a committee would meet together before the formal committee meeting to concert their views on items on the agenda. Or committee chairmen would try to ensure that the whole party group got a chance to discuss a major question of policy before it cropped up on a committee agenda. These party meetings held in private raised a further difficulty – that vital decisions might be taken in the absence of officers who could give professional advice. A way out of this dilemma, which has been adopted by a few authorities, is to form a central policy committee on which only the majority group is represented: if this committee is an official council committee, it is then quite in order for council officials to attend and advise.

The growth of party loyalty transformed the nature of council meetings. In the early years of the century it was assumed, apart from the London County Council, that a council meeting was a forum of debate that would determine the decisions reached. A powerful speech might sway opinion and alter policy. There was some element of unpredictability. What was done, or not done, could depend on the presence or absence of members. It could even be said that decisions were a matter of chance. The Local Government and Public Health Consolidation Committee commented in 1936, 'If a council wish to take advantage of the enabling provisions of the Local Government and Other Officers Superannuation Act 1922 . . . it is clearly right that a decision of such importance should not be taken by a chance majority of members attending an ordinary meeting of the council.'[22] The committee ignored the possibility that such an issue would have been considered beforehand by a majority group and that the decision of the council meeting would merely record what had been agreed elsewhere. By 1936, this possibility was the reality in many urban authorities in industrial areas. By 1974, most county and district council meetings were summoned to register formal approval of the decisions of the political majority: in the remainder which had no majority group or which still avoided party discipline, all important questions were carefully reviewed by the central policy committee whose advice was rarely rejected at a full council meeting.[23]

What effect did the development of party organisation have on the influence of permanent officials? Any answer must be in general terms which conceal important local exceptions. Yet there can be little doubt that the growth of disciplined party groups inhibited clerks and treasurers. No longer was it adequate to win the confidence of the chairmen of major committees. Important policy discussions were held at meetings which officials could not attend and which might take place before advice could be fed into sympathetic ears. Yet the restraints on officials imposed by party activity have been masked and sometimes overtaken by a countervailing pressure – the growing volume of local authority business and the decisions that have to be taken. Inevitably this has forced councils and committees to delegate wider discretion to their officials. Even in relation to major policy issues, the growing complexity of data which provides the essential background for decisions means that the advice of professional staff becomes more influential. The general picture to emerge is that in the early years of the century the senior officials in the largest boroughs had more opportunity to exercise initiative than their colleagues in the county councils which were responsible for a narrower range of functions. Then in later years, especially after 1945, the position was reversed. Borough officials became more constrained by party groups which were not so active in most counties. In addition, the powers of the counties increased while those of non-county boroughs declined.

NOTES

1 *Local Government in England*, vol. I, p. 277. The same theme is followed in J. M. Lee's study of Cheshire, *Social Leaders and Public Persons* (1963).
2 On municipal trading, see pp. 38–41 *supra*.
3 G. W. Jones, *Borough Politics* (1969), pp. 40–1.
4 B. D. White, *A History of the Corporation of Liverpool* (1951), pp. 190–1.
5 His biography, S. Salvidge, *Salvidge of Liverpool* (1934), is largely concerned with national politics.
6 For fuller discussion, see E. Eaglesham, *From School Board to Local Authority* (1956), chs. VI and VII.
7 *Att. Gen. and the Board of Education* v. *the County Council of the West Riding* [1906], 2 KB 676; [1907], AC 29.
8 G. W. Jones, op. cit., p. 47.
9 A complete list is given by Ken Young, *Local Politics and the Rise of Party*, (1975), app. 2.
10 For full description, see Ken Young, op. cit., ch. 5.
11 G. W. Jones, op. cit., pp. 211–19.
12 See p. 22 *supra*.
13 A few very small boroughs were not divided into wards but still had annual elections for one third of the councillor seats.
14 *Parliamentary Affairs*, Winter 1951, p. 180.
15 Ernest Simon, *A City Council from Within* (1926), ch. XIII.
16 *Party Politics in English Local Government* (1967), pp. 59, 76.
17 For fuller detail, see J. Gyford, *Local Politics in Britain* (1976), pp. 16, 18.
18 They were drafted by Herbert Morrison and based on the practice of the London Labour Party. B. Donoughue and G. W. Jones, *Herbert Morrison* (1973), pp. 135–6.

19   A. H. Birch, *Small Town Politics* (1959), p. 64.
20   *Party Politics in English Local Government* (1967), p. 100.
21   Quoted in J. D. Hoffman, *The Conservative Party in Opposition, 1945–51*, (1964), p. 68.
22   Second Interim Report, 1935–6, Cmd 5059, xi, p. 17.
23   The Maud Committee on Management, which reported in 1967, urged that a local authority should have a central policy committee or management board, but it also urged that minority political groups be represented on the board.

Chapter VII

FINANCE

The Pattern of Rising Expenditure

The growth of local authority expenditure provides quite dramatic evidence of the growth of local authority services in the twentieth century. There are, however, a number of difficulties in presenting the figures. It is necessary to distinguish between revenue and capital expenditure. It is not possible in the general area of poor law, hospitals and welfare services to provide an unbroken series of figures owing to the changes in the extent of local responsibilities. Above all, the unvarnished statement of amounts of money spent tends to lose meaning in recent years because of the decline in the purchasing power of sterling. So the expenditure figures have been supplemented by index numbers which take account of changes in the value of money and so demonstrate, in real terms, the pace of development of local services.

Table 7.1 shows the total revenue expenditure of local authorities in England and Wales at the start of each decade. It also gives the corresponding figures for the major local services. Table 7.2 provides parallel information in relation to capital expenditure.

These tables require further explanation and qualification. In the first place, one must remember that the period 1900–70 saw a 50 per cent increase in the population of England and Wales from 32 million to 48 million. Thus the growth of expenditure, *per capita*, either in financial terms or in real terms is substantially less than the figures might indicate. Over the same period, measured in current prices, the national income rose from £1,750 million in 1900 to £39,375 million in 1970. This huge rise is far less than it seems for, when allowance is made for the change in the value of money, it emerges that national income multiplied by a factor of three. *Per capita* it only doubled. But Table 7.3 shows that over the same time-span local government expenditure in real terms became eleven times as great as it was at the start of the century. Local councils have claimed a vastly increased share of total national resources.

The figures for Poor Law expenditure are potentially misleading. Their relatively slow rise is due to the development of alter-

Table 7.1   Revenue Expenditure of Local Authorities
England and Wales (£m).

	Total Expenditure	Education	Libraries and museums	Poor relief	Housing	Highways and lighting	Fire service	Sewerage and refuse	Police
1900	76·0	8·8	0·40	8·4	0·05	10·6	0·4	3·5	5·1
1910	125·8	27·5	0·71	12·4	0·58	16·3	0·6	6·9	6·7
1920	265·5	56·4	1·0	19·2	1·4	28·8	1·4	13·8	17·4
1930	423·7	83·7	2·0	33·9	35·1	55·2	2·3	17·2	21·7
1940	578·8	98·6	3·2	35·3	47·5	47·8	3·4	21·5	31·0
1950	849·1	257·1	8·3	—	80·8	71·3	13·8	38·3	48·6
1960	1,865·7	696·8	19·6	—	279·1	130·4	27·1	78·1	108·2
1970	5,405·2	1,894·6	58·2	—	797·1	305·1	66·9	227·6	303·1

Source: *Annual Abstract of Statistics.*

Table 7.2 Capital Expenditure of Local Authorities
England and Wales (£m).

	Total expenditure	Education	Workhouses, etc	Housing etc.	Highways and bridges	Sewerage and water services	Welfare services
1900	24·9	2·1	1·2	0·8	3·2	6·2	—
1910	40·6	2·9	0·4	0·4	1·9	4·7	—
1920	23·9	0·7	0·1	4·8	1·2	2·6	—
1930	108·9	6·0	0·9	42·8	16·2	9·6	—
1940	117·0	14·4	1·0	29·3	9·8	12·0	—
1950	331·1	28·0	—	233·8	5·1	24·8	2·9
1960	571·5	89·2	—	321·2	26·5	63·3	4·9
1970	1,707·9	222·1	—	831·2	181·9	178·5	16·7

Source: *Annual Abstract of Statistics.*

Table 7.3   Index Numbers of Real Growth: Revenue Expenditure

	Total Expenditure	Education	Libraries and museums	Housing	Highways and lighting	Fire service	Sewerage and refuse	Poor relief	Police
1900	100	100	100	100	100	100	100	100	100
1910	173·5	284	177	1,758	140	136	178	134	119
1920	145	231	90	1,684	98	126	141	83	123
1930	364	541	284	6,660	296	327	279	330	242
1940	381	561	400	4,750	225	425	307	210	304
1950	362	821	604	7,570	200	970	307	—	267
1960	496	1,593	989	18,810	248	1,365	450	—	428
1970	1,121	2,942	1,990	36,340	394	2,294	890	—	812

Table 7.4   Index Numbers of Real Growth: Capital Expenditure

	Total Expenditure	Education	Housing etc.	Highways and bridges	Sewerage and water services	Workhouses, etc.
1900	100	100	100	100	100	100
1910	148	125	45	54	62	33
1920	35	117	208	135	15	3
1930	248	162	304	288	88	43
1940	235	343	183	153	97	33
1950	374	375	820	45	112	—
1960	462	857	810	167	206	—
1970	938	1,445	1,422	778	394	—

native provisions by the national government which eased the strain on local revenues. Old age pensions were introduced in 1908; compulsory health insurance followed in 1911; unemployment relief became the responsibility of the Unemployment Assistance Board after 1934. It should also be noted that the housing figures include advances made under the Small Dwellings Acquisition Act 1899 and later housing legislation to assist house purchase by individuals.

Index numbers do exaggerate the importance of the base date. Thus, in table 7.3, the astronomical figures for housing are the result of very low expenditure in 1900. Yet, irrespective of the base date chosen, the figures demonstrate revenue expenditure on housing has grown at a remarkable pace. The major features to emerge from the statistical analysis are the check on local government expansion caused by two world wars and the burst forward in the period after 1950. Naturally services have advanced with unequal speed and at different periods. In terms of revenue expenditure, highway maintenance has tended to lag behind other services. So also, to a lesser extent, have the police, sewerage and refuse services. The fire service developed greatly in the period of its nationalisation during and after the Second World War. The expansion of education after the local authorities replaced the school boards in 1902 is also notable. Table 7.4 illustrates the decline in workhouse construction after 1940 and the boom in highway construction in the 1960s.

Statistics based on decennial intervals are open to the objection that they may not reveal short-term changes. However, in relation to figures of local expenditure this criticism has little validity. The detailed year by year accounts show, with few exceptions, a steadily rising level of expenditure on all services. There are few dramatic ups and downs. In 1926, the cost of Poor Law relief rose by a third, but in the following year the expenditure fell to the 1925 level; this peak was a result of the general strike. The biggest proportionate jump in activity came in 1953 when the sum spent on land drainage and coast protection was nearly double that of the previous year, a result of the east coast floods in January 1953. Housing is the area where the pace of activity does fluctuate but these changes are concealed in the figures of revenue expenditure which are dominated by the cost of debt maintenance and repayment for houses built in the past. The major gap in the figures presented here relates to the social services. The reason is that the complex evolution of the functions carried out by the social services departments makes it difficult to produce a long run of truly comparable figures.

The rising tide of local expenditure has placed increasing burdens on the taxpayer. The following sections of this chapter review the changes in policy over the distribution of liability between local rates and the national Exchequer as well as the administrative problems of local rating. Capital expenditure raises rather different issues concerned with the nature and purpose of central control and how local councils borrow money to meet capital outgoings.

Capital Expenditure
At the start of the twentieth century, government concern over local debt was concentrated on the financial stability of local councils. Now the government is determined to ensure that local capital expenditure reflects its own priorities and does not conflict with national economic policy.

With minor exceptions local authorities finance their capital expenditure by borrowing. In the nineteenth century, borrowing powers were commonly obtained through private Bills. However, since 1875 there has been less use of private Bills for this purpose except for the special case of the London County Council and now the Greater London Council. The Public Health Act of 1875 gave a general power to borrow subject to a maximum of twice the annual rateable value of the local authority. Many later items of legislation allowed borrowing for a particular purpose which was exempted from 1876 limits – examples are the Electric Lighting Act 1882, the Allotments Act 1887 and the Education Act 1902. The Municipal Corporations Act of 1882 placed no limit on the sum corporations could borrow in terms of rateable value. The Local Government Act of 1888 stipulated that when a county council proposed to raise a loan that exceeded a tenth of its rateable value then permission would have to be obtained direct from Parliament through a provisional order. Controls were imposed not simply on the amounts borrowed, but also on the period of loans. Parliament was anxious to ensure that debts were repaid within the useful life of the assets financed by each debt. Accordingly, government departments were authorised to fix a maximum duration for each loan depending upon its purpose. An overall limit of sixty years was placed on borrowing by boroughs and district, but county councils were restricted to thirty years. This differentiation could cause difficulty if a county combined with other authorities in a joint enterprise. A parliamentary inquiry in 1902 decided that the Local Government Board was not unduly restrictive when imposing limits on loan periods.[1]

With the continued growth of local capital expenditure and wider confidence in the ability of local councils to meet their financial obligations, the controls over borrowing were slowly eased. In 1921, borrowing by bank overdrafts was permitted; in earlier years the legality of this practice had been challenged with confusing results.[2] The derating of industry and agricultural land in 1928 ended the limit on total borrowing by reference to rateable value, a restriction already undermined by various exemptions. Finally, the Local Government Act 1933 gave local authorities a comprehensive power to borrow subject to a general sixty-year maximum for each project, but eighty years was permitted on land for allotments, smallholdings and housing. But in spite of these relaxations the need for ministerial loan sanctions remained and Whitehall could hold an inquiry into any loan application that was unusual or controversial.

The immediate effect of the Second World War was to strengthen greatly government control not only over the amount of local borrowing but also over the methods used to raise money. Local authorities had developed a variety of means of raising capital, through mortgages, debentures, internal borrowing, bank overdrafts and stock floatations on the money market. Smaller authorities commonly used the services of a government agency, the Public Works Loan Board. At the outbreak of war it was decreed that, with minor exceptions, local borrowing must be through the PWLB. The policy was continued by the Labour Government in the post-war period. It believed that firm control was necessary in order to secure optimum use of scarce resources required by the building industry. It also believed that the coordination of borrowing through the PWLB would reduce competition for capital and help to keep down interest rates.

The succeding Conservative Government favoured a greater degree of financial freedom. In 1952, local authorities were again allowed to use initiative in methods of raising capital. This immediately created twin problems – how to borrow and for how long a period. The initial period of a loan need not, of course, coincide with the maximum duration of the debt permitted by the government. Thus the capital debt involved in building a new school must be repaid over sixty years, but the capital can be borrowed initially for a much shorter period, say two years, and then be reborrowed. Whether it is wise to borrow for long or short periods depends on a forecast of the future pattern of interest rates. In the 1950s, local authorities tended to hope that interest rates would fall so there was a large demand for short-term capital. The Radcliffe Report on the working of the monetary system was published in 1959 and criticised the amount of short-term local authority debt which it felt tended to push up interest rates.[3]

In 1955, the Government had restricted the use made by local authorities of the Public Works Loan Board. The policy was that a local council should make application to the PWLB only if it had tried and failed to find other means of raising capital. So the PWLB became a lender of last resort and was used almost entirely by the smaller authorities. Quite clearly the withdrawal of PWLB facilities had encouraged the spate of short-term borrowing. It was some time before the Government took firm action on the Radcliffe Report, but as from July 1964 restrictions were placed on the amount of short-term debt a local authority could incur but as a compensating factor all authorities were allowed to obtain at least part of their capital requirements through the PWLB.

Firm ministerial control was retained over total amounts of local government capital expenditure. Thus each year education authorities, highway authorities and housing authorities would have to negotiate with the appropriate central department over the size of their capital programme. In the 1950s, the purpose of the control slowly changed. During the post-war years, the aim was to secure the optimum distribution of real resources; subsequently the aim was to impose a ceiling on public expenditure. At this stage the controls became more flexible and reflected the contemporary economic policy of the government. Whenever ministers were alarmed about the balance of payments or inflation, capital expenditure was discouraged; if ministers were worried about unemployment, then there was no discouragement. The loan sanction system remained the mainstay of ministerial influence over local spending. It is much easier for central departments to control new construction projects than items of current expenditure because the latter can be financed by an increase in the local rate. Loan sanction is not an essential prerequisite of capital expenditure because capital works may be financed by means other than external borrowing, e.g. by the use of internal superannuation funds or by raising the rate, but these alternatives offer limited scope. So the ability to control local borrowing remains a powerful weapon.

More recently, moves were made to streamline the procedure for loan sanction. During the 1960s, instead of giving sanction to individual schemes, block approvals began to be given which covered a whole programme of capital works. As from 1969, small sums could be borrowed without the need for a ministerial approval. From 1971, local capital expenditure has been divided between key sector schemes and other schemes. The key sector covers services for which ministers feel a direct responsibility for maintaining standards and co-ordinating development, e.g. education, housing, principal roads, police, social services; for these functions specific loan sanctions are still required. For non-key sector schemes local authorities are permitted to borrow to finance capital expenditure as they wish within a total sum approved annually, the amount of which can be adjusted to suit the government view of the national economic situation.

The Rating System

Local authorities have traditionally obtained the revenue they need to carry out their duties by the imposition of a rate on occupiers of property. To an increasing extent, monetary grants have been received from the national Exchequer but even at the end of the nineteenth century these central grants covered but a small proportion of local expenditure. So the methods of collection and assessment and the size of the rate poundage were matters of major importance to local communities.

Until the Rating and Valuation Act 1925 rationalised the situation, there were two distinct local rates. The explanation is historical. The major local function had been the relief of the poor; the major financial burden had been the poor rate. Each parish had its overseer who was responsible for the collection of the poor rate. As other local functions developed, they were paid for by making additions to the poor rate. Technically this was known as precepting. The counties precepted on the guardians, so did the boroughs in relation to functions shared with counties, e.g. education and police. The second rate, known as the general district rate, was limited to urban areas. It originated from the activities of Improvement Commissioners and the sanitary legislation of the 1840s. In amount, the district rate was significantly less than the multi-purpose poor rate.

This dual system was obviously unnecessary and wasteful. In urban areas there could be two sets of officials collecting rates. Indeed, between 1896 and 1923 the liability to pay the two rates was not equal in that agricultural land was taxed on the basis of half its rateable value in relation to the poor rate, but only on one quarter for the purpose of the general district rate. In London and many towns, a single collection system for the two rates had been established, but in the provinces this reform required authorisation by a private Bill.

In the towns the rates were usually gathered by officials

appointed by the local council; in rural areas the task was undertaken by assistant overseers paid by the guardians. But in small parishes it was still possible to find remnants of the eighteenth-century system of unpaid public service with the poor rate being collected by the parish overseer. The overseers were personally liable for the rates they were empowered to collect, so the office was not only unpaid, but it could result in personal loss. An overseer was in the same position as a juror in that, if nominated, he had a statutory obligation to serve. Inevitably, this duty had become highly unpopular and, to avoid the necessity for nominating overseers, paid assistants were appointed, except in small rural communities.

The task of rate collection had also been eased by the device known as compounding. In the case of rented property, the owner could accept liability for obtaining the money from the occupiers, i.e. his tenants, in return for a commission. The liability extended to property whether occupied or not, so the owner stood to lose if the property was empty. However, the commission terms were generous – 15 per cent to 30 per cent in the case of the poor rate and 50 per cent for the district rate. So although the system was convenient for local authorities, it was also extremely expensive in that it reduced the rate yield substantially and ensured that owners made a good profit from rate collection so long as their properties were not empty.

Levels of property assessment had for long been a source of controversy. Originally each parish, through its overseer, was responsible for its own valuations. But as soon as the area of assessment became smaller than the area of charge, there was a strong inducement to undervalue. Thus where a group of parishes contributed towards the cost of a union workhouse, a parish which imposed low valuations could escape its fair share of the burden. To avoid abuses, the parish valuation lists had been since 1862 subject to the approval of the guardians. Similarly, the counties had been empowered to make their own block assessment of a parish which had to be applied to the rate levied for county purposes. This separate county valuation could impose a harsh penalty on a small parish because the liability was collective and not related to individual properties. It followed that the ratepayers had to make good any deficiencies arising from empty property. If the manor house was unused or the factory was deserted, the extra burden could be severe.

Neville Chamberlain, Minister of Health between 1924 and 1929, was determined to rationalise the legislation which controlled the work of his department. The reform of local rates was but one item in a comprehensive programme of twenty-five measures, covering local government finance, Poor Law, public health, housing and health insurance, which he prepared immediately upon taking office in 1924.[4] The Rating and Valuation Act 1925, based on the London model of the Valuation (Metropolis) Act 1869, secured a great simplification in local administration. 12,000 overseers lost their valuation duties to some 1,700 rating authorities. The task of scrutiny of valuation lists was transferred from 600 Poor Law Unions to 343 area assessment committees. Clearly, this was to be a preliminary to the abolition of separate Poor Law authorities. Not surprisingly the guardians resisted; so did MPs who felt that change would be to the detriment of the poor; so also did some Conservative MPs who disliked the idea that Labour-controlled boroughs would have responsibility for valuation.[5]

After a parliamentary struggle the legislation was passed. Separate poor rates and district rates were abolished. Boroughs and districts were made responsible for collecting a single all-purpose rate. Other local authorities, the counties, the Poor Law guardians and the parishes were to issue precepts to the rating authorities. The commission paid to landlords for compounding was cut to 15 per cent. Alternatively, landlords could collect rates without accepting liability for empty property; in such cases the commission was to be 5 per cent. Provision was made for the quinquennial revaluation of properties by the rating authorities so that valuation lists should be kept up to date. In fact, due to the outbreak of war in 1939, the changes of valuation policy and administrative difficulties, this regular review has never been achieved. Perhaps the weakest feature of the Act was the attempt made to equalise standards of valuation. Decentralised assessments continued in order to mollify the guardians and other potential critics of national bureaucracy. County boroughs were to be wholly independent when making their assessments, but the other rating authorities had to submit their lists for the approval of area assessment committees covering two or more rating authorities. These committees consisted of representatives of the county council, the guardians and the rating authorities. This clumsy device to try and promote uniformity was also supported by a county valuation committee with merely advisory powers. At national level, a further advisory committee was nominated, but the ideal of achieving uniform standards of valuation throughout the country was not realised.[6]

The extent and consequences of uneven valuation were reviewed in two reports which appeared in 1944. One contained the results of the labours of an official committee;[7] the other was a research study commissioned by the National Institute of Economic and Social Research.[8] Both showed the valuers, who in theory exercised judgement in an independent judicial manner, had been affected by local pressures. Where property values and therefore rents were low, rateable value was low and rate pound-ages tended to be high. In such areas, the rating assessments were close to the market view of the annual value of property. The intention of the rating law was honoured because under-assessment would have led to even higher rate percentages. Prosperous areas with lower rates could afford the luxury of under-assessment as its effect on the local poundage was less serious. These variations had a number of unfair effects. During the twentieth century the Inland Revenue had come to use local valuations for the purpose of Schedule A income tax: so under-assessment benefited the ratepayer as taxpayer. If districts within a county had unequal standards of assessment, then this influenced their share of the cost of county services, a matter of increasing import-ance due to the growth of county services. Thirdly, the payment of national grants on the basis of deficiency in local rateable value per head gave a further powerful incentive to under-value. The third factor ultimately proved crucial. The distribution of the block grant introduced in 1929 had reflected to a limited extent local rateable values. In the post-war period the revised general grant adopted deficiency in local rateable value as the basic criterion for the receipt of central aid. Thus the nationalisation of assessment, strongly urged as early as 1914 by an official report,[9] became essential and was secured by the Local Government Act 1948.

The 1948 Act also proposed to change the principles of property valuation. The traditional method had been to base valuation on the rent a property could command. A deduction was made for maintenance and insurance, and the 'pure' rent then became the figure on which the rate poundage was charged. The operation of the Rent Restriction Acts and the distortions in the property market caused by the destruction of homes, particularly in London during the 1939–45 war, meant that the rental basis was felt to be increasingly arbitrary and unrealistic. The scheme in the 1948 Act was to retain the rental basis for dwellings con-structed before 1918 and to use a cost of construction figure for post-1918 properties. Aneurin Bevan, Labour Minister of Health, also proposed to introduce an element of discrimination to favour council house tenants: rate poundage would be charged on 5 per cent of the cost of construction of council houses and 5½ per cent of the cost of construction of other residential properties. However, this scheme was never put into practice because of the massive administrative difficulties of producing valuation lists based on building costs. The law was amended in 1953 to retain the theory of the rental basis for assessments, but to soften the shock for ratepayers, assessments were related to 1939 values. On this basis the first post-war valuation list became effective in 1956. In the next list, produced in 1963, current values were used.

The distribution of the rate burden between different categories of ratepayer has been a long-standing source of controversy. Farmers have claimed special treatment on the grounds that to rate agricultural land increases the cost of food and that the land is, in essence, the farmer's raw material. Factory owners were not required to pay rates on the raw material that passed through their premises. So in 1896 the Conservative Government gave farmers some more relief: agricultural land was rated at half its value for the poor rate and a quarter value for the general district rate. In 1923 the figure was unified at a quarter for both rating systems – a move which slightly simplified the task of collection. Finally, in 1928, agricultural land was derated completely. It is notable that each of these favours came from Conservative Governments. In addition, assessments in rural areas were low compared with those in the towns. At the beginning of the century this could be justified in terms of property values and the lack of some public services, notably sanitation: in later years the disparity of services has been greatly reduced. Rural property values increased rapidly, but this change has been only slowly reflected in local rating assessments.

Derating in 1928 extended beyond agriculture to industry and the railways, both of which were relieved of three quarters of their liability for rates. Railways received this bounty in return for an undertaking to lower charges for carrying coal and steel. The aim of this policy was to strengthen the competitive position of British industry in international trade by cutting costs and thereby reduce unemployment. Local government was partially compensated for the loss of rate revenue by additional financial aid from the Exchequer. The overall effect of the scheme was to provide an indirect subsidy to industry and to use the mechanism of local authority finances to conceal what was done. Churchill, the Chancellor of the Exchequer, strongly supported the scheme. Chamberlain opposed the plan but failed to convince his Cabinet colleagues. A letter to his sister Hilda confided,

'The permanent plan under which we pay the subsidy to the local authorities . . . [is] . . . so complicated and so completely contradictory of the opinions universally expressed a little while ago that State subsidies were economically unsound, that I could not imagine that it would not be torn to pieces at once. S.B. on the other hand was always attracted by the scheme, and thought the camouflage was sufficient to enable us to get away with it.'[10]

In essence, the derating technique was being used to circumvent the principles of Free Trade. For local authorities the incident is an example of how their finances can be manipulated by the central government to buttress its basic economic policies.

Since 1945, the rise in rate poundages has caused increasing concern. The failure to revise assessments every five years ensured that they had fallen far behind current property values, and they had failed to reflect the fall in the value of money. Inevitably, rate poundages had increased substantially. If dwellings were to be revalued at current prices, then the assessments would shoot up dramatically. In pure theory this need not matter. If valuations are quadrupled and the rate poundage is cut to a quarter of the previous figure, the local authority receives the same amount and each ratepayer contributes the same amount. In reality, the effects of such a change are more complex. A massive increase in rateable value could encourage more local spending so that rate poundages would not fall *pro rata* with the rise in assessments. Then not all properties would be affected equally. The revaluation would be certain to decide that some properties had been either over- or under-assessed in the past so there would be some transfer of burden between individual ratepayers. Finally, it was feared that a massive increase in assessments would be a severe shock that would arouse public resentment. Accordingly, to minimise the effect on residential ratepayers, the 1956 valuation list was made on the basis of hypothetical rental levels in 1939. Other properties were assessed at current values, but since factories paid rates on one quarter of their assessed values it followed that the only properties paying rates on full contemporary values were shops and offices.

The next few years saw various shuffles which slightly altered the balance of incidence between different classes of ratepayer. Occupiers of shops and offices complained that theirs was the only category of property paying rates on current values. To appease them, in 1957 shops and offices were derated to the extent of one fifth of their new assessments. The Local Government Act 1958 reduced the derating of industry from 75 per cent to 50 per cent. Arguments used thirty years before about the need to reduce the rating burden on industry to reduce unemployment no longer had any force. But as far as local authorities were concerned, the effective rateable values still failed to reflect current price levels and the base of their sole source of independent revenue was being eroded. In 1961, the government grasped the nettle: the Rating and Valuation Act of that year required future rate liability to be on the basis of assessment at current values for all classes of property. The next valuation list appeared in 1963. It caused much discontent, especially in south coast areas, to which a lot of people retire who are forced to live on relatively fixed incomes. The 1961 Act had empowered the Minister of Housing and Local Government to issue orders, subject to parliamentary approval, which would have authorised reductions in dwelling house assessments in areas where householders had been affected very adversely by the new valuations because the share contributed by residential property to local rateable value had been significantly increased. Any such orders would have created local anomalies, and in the event, none were made. The protest caused by the 1963 revaluation caused the government to nominate a committee headed by Professor Allen to investigate the rating system. This report and its consequences are considered at the end of the following sections. Meanwhile the political unpopularity of reassessment ensured that the principle of quinquennial reviews is never honoured. The list due in 1961 was postponed until 1963; the list due in 1968 became effective in 1973.

Central Grants
At the start of the twentieth century the financial relationship between central and local government was based on the 'assigned revenues'. This concept had been part of the major reform contained in the Local Government Act 1888. Goschen, then Chancellor of the Exchequer, wished to create a clear separation between national revenue used for national purposes and national revenue used to assist local services. Such a distinction, it was hoped, would deflect ever increasing local requests for greater financial aid. Accordingly, the 1888 Act terminated a large number of grants which had been devoted to particular local purposes and replaced them by a system which gave local authorities the benefit of certain national taxes – the assigned revenues. Not all the specific grants disappeared, for the separate education grant remained. But most of the principal grants were ended, including those related to highways, police and the Poor Law. In

return, the local authorities received the revenue from a wide variety of licences, notably those relating to the sale of intoxicating liquor and game licences and taxation of beer, spirits, wine, tobacco and carriages. Local authorities also received a 40 per cent share of the probate duty. When the scheme was introduced the sum total of these revenues was estimated to amount to about £5·6 million. This money was to be paid not to the consolidated fund but into a new local taxation account; it would then be distributed to local authorities, partly in proportion to the amount collected in each area and partly in proportion to the share that each authority had enjoyed of the discontinued grants.

The assigned revenues rapidly became a potent source of controversy. The initial theory was that natural growth in the sums realised should provide adequate expansion of local services. But as new financial burdens were placed on local authorities, e.g. to provide police pensions and some rudimentary technical education, the level of some of the duties had to be raised. The 50 per cent derating of agricultural land in 1896 would have caused serious financial loss to rural authorities, so the government paid full compensation for this loss by a fresh grant derived from national taxation. The method of distribution of the assigned revenues according to the formula of the 1887 fraction caused discontent especially to needy areas and those with a growing population. There was also some dispute about how far the central government should finance local services. Agricultural interests were broadly more in favour of national financial aid than business interests in urban areas; the pressure of the local rate was more strongly felt in the countryside.

A Royal Commission on Local Taxation was appointed in 1895. Its final report appeared in 1901.[11] The commission was split in its opinions and produced majority and minority reports. But all members agreed that local services were capable of division into two categories – national and onerous, local and beneficial. The onerous services were those which had to be provided as a matter of national policy including the Poor Law, police, highways and education. Local services were either optional or of direct benefit to the properties that were taxed to finance them. This curious distinction implied that only people who lived in houses connected to sewers obtained benefit from modern sanitation, as if germs could distinguish between different categories of ratepayers. However, the theory of national and onerous services led the commission to support Exchequer aid for these functions at the level of broadly half their cost. The majority report advocated the retention of the assigned revenue system with some modifications; the minority wished to end it, with grants for the national services being a charge upon the consolidated fund and being paid from that fund into the local taxation account. The minority also wished the money to be distributed locally on the basis of a needs formula related to rateable values which tended to equalise the financial situation of councils in poorer and well-to-do areas. This minority view gained the support of the Departmental Committee on Local Taxation,[12] which urged that national grants should seek to reduce inequalities in local taxation.

No direct action was taken as a result of these reports. Meanwhile the assigned revenues formed a steadily decreasing fraction of the total of Exchequer aid. The theory on which they were based was effectively abandoned before 1914. The separate education grant was increased in 1902 and again in 1906. The Finance Act 1907 provided that the assigned revenues should again be paid into the consolidated fund and that equivalent sums be then transferred to the local taxation account. The Finance Act 1910 imposed a fixed limit on the yield of the more important assigned revenues that were to be passed on to local government. A part of the proceeds of the car and carriage licences was allocated to local authorities, not through the LTA, but through the road fund established in 1909 to promote major highway improvements. At the same period the Liberal Government were introducing new discretionary grants for smallholdings and drainage and capital grants for the construction of sanatoria to combat tuberculosis. In addition, the introduction of old age pensions together with health and unemployment insurance made a contribution towards easing the local burden of the poor law.

So the assigned revenues faded. It became impossible to isolate central financial aid for local authorities in a separate box due to the pressure for improved local services and the desire of the national government to influence the use of resources at the local level. The assigned revenues almost entirely disappeared in 1929; by then they amounted to only £4·5 million out of the total of £90 million of Exchequer aid for local government. Trivial examples, like licences for dogs and dealers in game, still remained after 1929.

The outbreak of the First World War stimulated concern over the physical strength of the nation. This paved the way in 1915 for new grants for maternity and child welfare; in the following year new grants were made for the care of mental defectives and the treatment of venereal disease. In the immediate post-war period there was strong political pressure to improve many local services. 'Homes for heroes' was a popular cry. The most generous of all grant regulations was that under the Housing Act 1919 where the financial contribution expected of a local council was the product of a penny rate (or 0·4 of a new penny). Education and police grants were also increased. The level of assistance varied considerably as between different classes of local authorities. In the financial year 1919–20, grants, when expressed as a percentage of local rates plus grants (i.e. excluding fees, rents and other charges), amounted to 48 per cent in the case of county councils, 33 per cent in county boroughs, 26 per cent in non-county boroughs, 18 per cent in urban districts and only 10 per cent in rural districts.[13] These figures reflect the fact that the most highly subsidised services were the main county functions, education, police and roads. In 1923, another grant was made to compensate local authorities for the further derating of agricultural land.

This array of separate subventions focused attention on the question whether central financial aid should be itemised or paid in lump sums. The Geddes Committee proposed a fresh review of central-local financial relationships as part of their attempt to curb public expenditure.[14] Accordingly, in 1922 a departmental committee was appointed under the chairmanship of Lord Meston to review the problem. The curious feature of this committee is that it failed to produce a report. It was widely believed that the Treasury had managed to avoid publication because the recommendations were contrary to Treasury policy which favoured block grants.[15]

Ultimately, the Treasury was victorious. The partial derating of industry and the total derating of agriculture in 1928 inevitably required fresh Exchequer assistance for local government. It provided a natural claim for more government money not specifically related to a particular service. So the Local Government Act 1929 introduced a new block grant to compensate for loss of rate revenue, the loss of assigned revenues still paid under the 1888 Act and the termination of specific grants for various health services and some, but not all, highway grants. The block grant was to be distributed on the basis of a formula which took into account the characteristics of a local authority area rather than the expenditure of the local council.[16] By this means most help could be given to areas of greatest financial need. The factors which were recognised as giving a claim for greater assistance were the number of children, the rateable value per head of population, the level of unemployment and sparsity of population. However, to smooth the transition to the new system, the new system of distribution was to have effect by stages. It was to come into full operation by three five-year periods during which the formula would control the distribution of 25 per cent, 50 per cent and 75 per cent of the money available. In these quinquennia 75 per cent, 50 per cent and ultimately 25 per cent of the money would be allocated in terms of the loss of existing grants.

So the growth of specific grants was checked and some were withdrawn. But the separate grants for education, police, housing and the main county roads remained. Indeed, there were strong pressures which favoured the allocation of central aid to a particular purpose. Only in this way, it was argued, could central government influence how local authorities used their resources. By attaching conditions to the grants, it was possible to insist on the maintenance of standards of service. The Treasury view was that percentage grants for a particular local activity could encourage extravagance. A 50 per cent grant meant that local councils had to find but half the cost of any marginal extras on a scheme covered by the grant. To monitor effectively grant claims by local councils caused more administrative costs. The alternative, a lump-sum grant fixed in advance, meant that councillors had full responsibility for raising any additional amounts they chose to spend.

After a moderate interval, fresh specific grants were introduced. The failure to reduce maternal mortality, and the varying experience of different parts of the country, produced a demand to strengthen maternity services. The Midwives Act 1936 gave a fresh percentage grant to local authorities. Other grants were given in 1937 under the Physical Recreation and Training Act and the Air Raid Precautions Act. During the war the range of grants extended further to cover civil defence and all aspects of local wartime emergency services including British restaurants and the supply of milk and meals in schools. The Rural Water Supplies and Sewerage Act 1944 opened the possibility that the countryside could obtain grants to meet part of the capital cost of installing these basic amenities.

At this period the specific grant was again in favour. It was widely agreed that Exchequer aid should be used to stimulate local provision thought to be desirable or necessary. The distinction made in 1901 between national and onerous, local and beneficial services had faded: an increased range of functions was provided at the behest of the government and it was accepted that few services produced benefits that were purely localised. The policy of the post-war Labour Government was to give selective encouragement to local activities. It had no inhibitions about extending central intervention. The National Health Service Act 1946 contained a 50 per cent grant for local authority health services. Other grants were made available for the redevelopment of bomb-damaged areas. The post-war housing drive was stimulated by central financial aid. The fire service was returned to counties and county boroughs after the period of wartime nationalisation with a 25 per cent grant. By now the general grant was out of fashion. The Local Government Act 1948 ended the 1929 block grant and replaced it with the Exchequer Equalisation Grant. This change was quite fundamental. Whereas all authorities had obtained some benefit from the block grant only selected councils gained revenue from the EEG. Councils with a rateable value per head lower than a notional national average were credited with sufficient additional rateable value to bring them up to national average and the Exchequer paid the local rate on this credited rateable value. Thus the councils with the lowest rateable value per head obtained large sums; those just below the national average gained little; those above the average got nothing. The effect was sometimes dramatic. Cardigan – now Ceredigion – was the extreme case where the rate demand was cut by £1 3s or £1·15p. Clearly, this was a measure designed to promote social equality. It could be justified only if rateable value per head was accepted as a fair test of prosperity. To ensure that local valuation authorities did not artificially depress assessments to attract more central aid, the 1948 Act also had to nationalise valuation for local rating.

The decade 1948–58 was the high-water mark for specific grants. But they were subject to increasing criticism. Certainly they did not discourage extravagance. The grant for education was based on a formula, but the general effect was that local education authorities received a national grant of 60 per cent of approved expenditure. But where an authority had low rateable values, further help was received under the Exchequer equalisation grant. To take a fairly extreme case: if local rateable value per head was half that of the notional national average, then the credited rateable value would equal actual rateable so that half the rate-borne expenditure would be met by the Exchequer. In such circumstances some 80 per cent of approved educational expenditure would be a national charge and councillors had a strong inducement to make generous provision for local needs.

Grant regulations provided detailed rules about standards of permissible expenditure, but these were difficult and expensive to monitor. They could also involve more central interference in local decisions, a trend always resented by local government. In 1957, the Conservative Government announced its intention of ending the grants for education, the fire service and certain domiciliary health and welfare services,[17] which would be replaced by a new general grant. A major part of the case presented in favour of this change was the need to set local authorities free from so much detailed central control. The general grant would be fixed in advance. Local councils would know how much central aid was coming to them, and then would be free – within the rules of *ultra vires* and the restraints on capital expenditure imposed by loan sanctions – to spend as they wished. Under this plan, additional marginal expenditure was wholly borne by the local rates. The government intended to force local authorities to take a more responsible attitude to their expenditure which was increasing far more rapidly than the national income.

This proposal brought a storm of protests, especially from local education committees.[18] It was claimed that the standard of educational provision would suffer. Education was, and still is, by far the most expensive local service. It was feared that without the support of the 60 per cent grant education estimates would be severely pruned by local finance committees. The Conservatives persisted with their plan. The Local Government Act 1958 replaced the specific grants for education, fire, health and welfare by a new general grant. The Exchequer equalisation grant was continued in an adjusted form as the rate deficiency grant. The formula which controlled the disbursement of the general grant was on similar lines to that used in 1929, except that no allowance was made in relation to local employment because Poor Relief had ceased to be a local responsibility. The size of the fresh grant was unexpectedly generous and allowed a modest increase in the resources made available to local authorities. So fears expressed about cuts in expenditure were not realised. However, the Labour Opposition promised to restore the separate education grant when it had the opportunity.

Everything pointed to a straight party conflict over the issue with Conservatives favouring general grants and Labour wedded to specific grants. But the dispute faded away. When Labour regained office in 1964, Richard Crossman, Minister of Housing and Local Government, consulted local authorities over a projected reorganisation of the grant system. He found broad support for existing methods. The general grant was far easier to administer. It also provided greater promise of flexibility. So the Labour Government came to accept the concept of a general grant. Subsequently Crossman suggested two criteria which justified

separate aid for particular functions: the need for central supervision of a service and an uneven distribution of burden between
authorities. The police are an example of the first category, and
coast protection of the second.

In the 1960s the central issue about grants was their amounts.
Growing public opposition to increases in rates imposed strong
political pressure on the national government to reduce the rate
burden by making bigger grants to local authorities. Public irritation was stimulated by the reassessment of properties in 1963,
when some occupiers suffered dramatic increases from the revaluation of their property. It was argued that elderly people and
those on fixed incomes were hardest hit. The approach of a
general election made the question highly sensitive politically.
Accordingly, the Conservatives produced the Rating (Interim
Relief) Act 1964 which provided for an additional grant to be
made to local authorities at the rate of £5 per head for people
over 65 where this age group comprised more than 10 per cent
of the population. This Act was a curiously ill-conceived piece
of legislation in that it did nothing to ensure that this extra
financial assistance went where it was most needed. A grant paid
to a local authority benefits all its inhabitants, not just those
above retirement age. And there is no evidence that the greatest
concentration of poverty is to be found in places with the higher
percentages of older citizens. The 1964 legislation was a minor
Act of limited duration, but it showed how sensitive politicians
had become to discontent over the rates. Similarly, the Crossman
Diaries demonstrate the extent to which electoral considerations
influenced the 1966 reform of the rating system.[19]

The Labour Government met the problem of the burden of
the local rate in two ways. A system of rebates gave special
relief to the lower income groups. A new element in the general
grant allowed residential ratepayers some relief as compared with
other ratepayers. So in 1966 the general grant was renamed the
Rate Support Grant. The RSG had three parts: the needs element
based on a formula mainly related to population gave assistance
to all authorities; the resources element based on rateable values
replaced the rate deficiency grant and gave extra help to the
poorer areas; the domestic element compensated local authorities
for reducing the rate poundage demanded of residential occupiers. In subsequent years the latter form of relief grew rapidly.
When it started in 1967–8 the domestic element cost £30 million
and allowed a domestic rate reduction of 5d – a little more than
2p. By 1974 the cost was £446 million and permitted rate reductions of 13p in England and 33·5p in Wales.

Recent years have thus seen a dramatic increase in the size of national grants. To a degree the figures became meaningless and misleading because they reflect not so much real changes in distribution as the loss of value in the currency due to inflation. But the general grant concept is now dominant. The rate support grant supplies over 90 per cent of the money that local authorities receive from the Exchequer. On average, local authorities receive nearly twice as much revenue from the Exchequer as they do from the local rates.

The Weakness of Local Taxation

An outstanding feature of local rates has been their unpopularity. Both the Royal Commission on Local Taxation, which was appointed in 1895, and the departmental committee appointed in 1912 were established primarily to see if superior alternatives to the local property rate could be discovered. All taxes must be resented, but local rates have stimulated far more irritation than national taxes. Why should this be? Perhaps the central government, supported by its association with the Crown, is felt to have superior moral authority to demand contributions. Perhaps the services it provides are felt to be of greater importance. For the first half of the century it was assumed that the Exchequer could and would provide the finance necessary to provide national security. It may also be felt that local taxation should be under effective local control, whereas the level of council spending is increasingly a response, not to local opinion, but to policy directives from Whitehall. Rates are also a disincentive to property development; they may deflect expenditure to other and less desirable alternatives.

Since the end of the last war fresh causes for complaint have emerged. The extension of universal franchise to local government in 1945 gave votes to people who are not ratepayers. These new voters could support candidates who favoured expensive policies without themselves having to pay, at least directly, the higher rates. In equity, this made a strong case for extending the ambit of local taxation so that it affected all voters. The introduction of Pay As You Earn for national income tax meant that the local rate was the main form of direct taxation not collected at source. In the case of indirect taxation the tax element tends to be subsumed in the price of the commodity purchased. So the rate became a uniquely visible tax. Money had to be saved up to meet what was normally a twice-yearly demand. Further as noted above, there has been a steady rise in rate levels caused partly by improvements in local services and partly by the infrequency of reassessments which therefore failed to keep pace with changes in the value of money. When reassessments did take place, as in 1956 and 1963, they created a fresh impetus for protest. Above all, there has been a growing realisation in the post-war period that rates are unfair in the sense that there is little correlation between liability to pay and ability to pay. Income tax is progressive in the sense that the higher the level of income the greater proportion of income will be claimed by the Inland Revenue. With local rates the proportion has worked the other way; the lower the level of income the higher the proportion to be claimed by the local authority. This was demonstrated very clearly in 1965 by the report of the Allen Committee. Households with a disposable income of £6 a week were shown to pay 8·2 per cent of it in rates; with disposable income between £6 and £10 a week the proportion fell to 6·2 per cent; at £30 a week the figure was down to 2·2 per cent.[20] So the burden fell most heavily on the poor. Since the introduction of rate rebates in 1966 this is no longer true, assuming that those entitled to rebates claim them. Now the rates bear most heavily on the section of population whose income is just above the level at which rebates are available. And it is also the case that some of those entitled to this relief may not claim, either through ignorance or through pride.

The political pressure against the rates was strengthened by the feeling inherited from the nineteenth century that a local impost should be under local control. It was accepted that the level of national taxation, partly determined by the necessities of defence, must be beyond the influence of the individual. But ratepayers should not be powerless in relation to local levies upon them: their elected representatives were expected to curb expenditure. Any ambitious schemes, especially in relation to public buildings or cultural or sporting activities, were certain to meet criticisms of extravagance. Some forceful municipal leaders with far-sighted schemes for development tended to lose popularity, as in the case of Sir Sidney Kimber in Southampton.[21] The concept that the council was the trustee of the rate fund was readily linked with the view that councillors should carry out their duties with Gladstonian prudence. Naturally it has been Conservative opinion rather that left-wing opinion that has shown greatest concern with the agonies of ratepayers. The National Union of Ratepayers Associations, formed in 1921, was certainly Conservative in sympathy: very largely its inauguration was a reaction against Labour victories at local elections. The Labour Party has been less worried about the amount of council expenditure which it saw as a minor but useful means of obtaining a more equal distribution of wealth.

Sensitivity about the rates has weakened the independence of local authorities as it made them more willing to accept increasing financial aid from the Exchequer. When central government wished local authorities to take on some fresh responsibility, an expectation developed that national funds would meet part of the cost. Central grants became stimulators. Councils that might have been reluctant to use new powers agreed to do so, for otherwise they would lose the proffered grant and their services would fall behind those of their neighbours. After 1945 there was a change of attitude towards public expenditure. The philosophy of the Welfare State required local authorities to provide for steady improvements in education, health and social services. Fewer advocates of retrenchment were to be heard, but the rise in expenditure increased keenness for more government aid.

Meanwhile there was no serious attempt to replace the rating system or submit it to drastic reform. It was patched and propped. Neville Chamberlain made rating more efficient by a great simplification in the methods of collection, but his Rating and Valuation Act 1925 left the essentials of the system unaltered. The derating measures already described were designed to meet the plaints of various interest groups at the cost of weakening further the local tax base. After the Allen Committee had demonstrated how people with the lowest incomes suffered most from the rate demands, the rate rebate machinery was developed to alleviate this cause of distress. The monetary inflation of recent years, not fully reflected in levels of assessment, has sent rate poundages soaring and produced still stronger claims for even more Exchequer assistance.

In view of the widespread hostility to the local rate it is a little surprising that the system has remained unaltered. Indeed, throughout the period 1900–74 there has been no serious challenge to it. On this subject the Labour Party has kept quiet. The obstacle to change has been the lack of agreement on an alternative form of local taxation. Both the Royal Commission report in 1901 and the departmental committee report in 1914 concluded that the administrative objections to a local income tax were insuperable. The Royal Commission and a majority of the Departmental Committee opposed the rating of site values. The broad conclusion of these enquiries was that the rate must remain as the foundation of local taxation. Certainly the rates have important advantages. Since they are levied on immovable property it is difficult to evade payment. The cost of collection is

relatively low. They have a flexible yield in that it is easy to alter
the rate poundage. The yield is also stable in that increases in
the rate poundage have a negligible effect on the amount of
empty, and therefore untaxable, property.

For forty years following the departmental committee report
of 1914 there was little serious discussion about alternatives to the
rating system. Interest in the subject was revived in 1956 when
the Royal Institute of Public Administration published a research
study, *New Sources of Local Revenue*, which advocated that
local authorities be empowered to impose an entertainments tax,
a restricted income tax and that vehicle licences and driving
licences be transferred to them.

A rather different issue was raised by the Royal Commission
on the Constitution when it argued that a high level of central
grants does not affect the sense of financial responsibility among
local councils. Indeed, the commission asserted that high levels
of grant actually increase local financial sensitivity because where
a low percentage of the cost of local services is raised locally then
any additional expenditure has a bigger proportional effect on the
rate poundage.[22] This, of course, is a logical extension of the
case for the block grant which claims that local authorities will
take greater care over marginal expenditure if the whole of it
falls on the rate fund. The whole conception depends on the
assumption that extra local expenditure has no effect on the
amount of the general grant. But the annual haggles over the size
of the general grant that developed in the 1960s tend to undermine this assumption. A tendency has emerged for local authorities to agree to spend in the hope and expectation that central
government will give them more money to minimise the political
storm caused by yet more severe increases in rate poundages.

Whitehall has steadily resisted the claim that the financial
weakness of local authorities undermines their independence. The
rating system, although widely assailed, has remained. On each
occasion of national economic difficulty ministerial policy has
been that the pace of local activity should be adjusted to fit the
needs of the situation. So councils are expected to amend their
ways in response to inflation, the balance of payments, or unemployment. Government exerts influence by exhortation and
through the grant system. A stronger form of local taxation
might make local authorities less responsive to national guidance.
So if rating has been a weak vessel, it has become increasingly
convenient in the context of promoting a Cabinet's economic or
social programme. From the 1901 Report of the Royal Commission on Local Taxation to the 1971 Green Paper, *The Future*

Shape of Local Government Finance, the official documents on this subject have evaded the issue by escaping into technicalities. The crux is not technical feasibility but political will.

Audit

Expenditure of public money inevitably raises questions about scrutiny of payments. Should there be an audit? Who should appoint the auditor? What power should the auditor have? During the nineteenth century local government developed two distinct traditions regarding the checking of accounts. The Municipal Corporations Act of 1835 had provided that boroughs were to have three auditors: one was to be a member of the council nominated by the mayor while the remaining two were to be elected by those entitled to vote at local elections subject to the stipulation that the elected auditors were not to be members or officers of the council. The alternative consisted of district auditors appointed by the government, a system evolved from the need to check Poor Law accounts and which was applied thereafter to each new type of authority as it was established, including the London boroughs.

These separate arrangements differed in style, in authority and in philosophy. Borough audit was amateur: district audit was professional. It was assumed that borough audit was only a matter of concern to local ratepayers. They were entitled to a guarantee that borough accounts were properly kept and that there had been no peculation of the funds. District audit assumed that the government had a legitimate interest in local accounts, not merely in the context of probity but also to ensure that money had been spent in a reasonable manner. The district auditor had powers to surcharge council members who had authorised illegal *ultra vires* expenditure; he could surcharge council officials who made improper payments; he could also impose surcharges for unreasonable expenditure. It was possible to obtain ministerial sanction for an item of expenditure which excluded it from the power of surcharge. It was also possible to appeal to the minister or to a court of law against the district auditor's decisions. An appeal to a court was restricted to legal grounds. An appeal to the minister was not restricted; the minister could decide the appeal on the merits of the case. Nevertheless, the system of district audit enabled an official appointed by the central government to ride roughshod over the views of locally elected representatives. It was arguable that the auditor was both unaccountable to the ratepayers and less well informed than council members of the need for expenditure in dispute.

No clear pattern can be found in the legal decisions on audit cases.[23] Some appeals were successful while others failed. In 1908 an important case, *R.* v. *Roberts*, went in favour of the Westminster City Council which had accepted a tender other than the lowest submitted for a particular contract. In the course of his judgement Lord Justice Fletcher Moulton commented that the task of local councillors was unpaid and thankless and that no self-respecting man would take part in municipal affairs if his conduct could be 'pronounced upon and their character and property injured by decisions, not of any Court of Law . . . but of a special tribunal consisting of an official chosen by a government department without any powers or qualifications for holding a judicial enquiry and discharging those functions without any of the securities which protect an individual before our Courts.'[24] This judgement was a powerful encouragement to councillors and a warning to the auditor.

Controversy about district audit revived sharply in the 1920s as a result of the activities of the Poplar Borough Council described in Chapter IV. Herbert Morrison, who was entirely opposed to the lawbreaking activities of Lansbury and his associates in Poplar, was united with Lansbury in condemning the powers of the auditor. Morrison felt that Whitehall bureaucracy was using audit as a means of restricting the discretion of elected councillors.[25] There is no doubt that the Minister of Health, Neville Chamberlain, and his advisers felt that audit was a valuable weapon to use against the spendthrift guardians. Meanwhile, the fact that the auditor was said to be independent of the minister and exercised his powers in a quasi-judicial role merely enabled the minister to evade parliamentary questions on this topic. But the ultimate effect of the Poplar struggle was to increase the power of the auditor. The Audit (Local Authorities) Act 1927 decreed that anyone surcharged for more than £500 should also be disqualified from membership of a local authority for five years. This extra sanction was essential since councillors too poor to pay a surcharge otherwise suffered no penalty and could continue to act as councillors and agree to expenditure in defiance of the law. The disqualification could be remitted, on appeal, either by the minister or by a court. But the 1927 Act also restricted the power of the minister in that appeals against a surcharge above £500 had to go to a court.

Provincial boroughs were not entirely spared the attentions of the district auditor since he was entitled to inspect accounts for certain services which attracted a central government grant. For the rest the system of elected auditors was of dubious efficacy and impossible to defend. A few towns voluntarily submitted to district audit either by including an appropriate clause in a local Bill or through a Provisional Order under Section 303 of the Public Health Act 1875. The Municipal Corporations (Audit) Act 1933 at last provided an alternative to elected audit; boroughs could choose to use district audit or employ professional auditors instead of retaining the elective system. Professional auditors, of course, had no power to surcharge. Accordingly, many boroughs opted for this arrangement in the knowledge that it could not disturb local traditions of municipal hospitality or, in the case of resorts, of expenditure on advertisements to attract holiday-makers.

The extent of the penal sanctions imposed by district audit declined steadily throughout the century. Figures for the number of items disallowed and surcharged in selected years, and of the number of appeals to the minister, are given in Table 7.5. Also included are the number of applications made to the minister for a certificate which would exempt a particular item from the auditors' purview.

Table 7.5   *District Audit Surcharges and Ministerial Exemptions*

Year	Number of surcharges and disallowances	Number of appeals to ministry	Exemption applications	
			Granted	Refused
1902–3	3,372	1,228	2,836	456
1912–3	2,554	571	1,916	428
1922–3	958	135	3,381	487
1932–3	185	21	2,439	180
1938–9	111	16	1,406	297

Source: *Annual Reports of the Local Government Board and the Ministry of Health.*

The result of appeals to the minister was that decisions of the auditor were usually upheld. Thus in 1912–13 there were 120 appeals by Poor Law authorities, but only in a single case did the president of the local government board quash the decision of the auditor. However, appeals were not fruitless. Indeed, the normal practice was for a surcharge to be remitted because this course was held to be fair and equitable. Of the 120 Poor Law appeals in 1912–13, in only three instances was the surcharge not remitted. In sum, the authority of the auditor was upheld and those surcharged were let off with a caution.

After 1939 similar details are not available as the reports of the Ministry of Health were issued in a truncated form. By 1958

the number of surcharges had fallen to fifteen.[26] The contrast
between this total and the corresponding figures for the earlier
years of the century is dramatic. A major reason for the change
must be a great improvement in the quality of local administration. Sophisticated methods of internal audit were developed.
Some of the smaller and weaker authorities disappeared. The
elimination of separate authorities was also a major contributory
factor. Over 40 per cent of the surcharges in 1922–3 concerned
Poor Law accounts. The auditors also began to go about their
duties in a more discreet way. When they found a dubious item
the tendency was to initiate discussions which could either lead
to a repayment of money or prevent a similar charge arising in
subsequent years.

Against this background the Labour attitude to the district
auditor underwent a complete reversal. The idea faded away that
he was an irresponsible bureaucrat who, at least potentially,
could interfere with the rights of democratically elected representatives. Largely this was because district auditors avoided surcharging expenditure they felt to be unreasonable. Perhaps controversy was diminished because local authorities, including those
controlled by Labour, avoided illegal or adventurous policies.
After the abolition of the guardians the 1930s were relatively
peaceful and the district audit became essentially a check against
corruption and malpractice. Professional audit seemed something
of a privilege and an unnecessary departure from the normal
rule that accounts should be submitted to government auditors
experienced in local authority finance. A combination, arguably
a worthy combination, of egalitarianism and puritanism made
district audit acceptable to Labour opinion.

The case of the Mid-Northamptonshire Water Board
symbolised this change of view. The parliamentary committee
appointed in 1949 to consider details of the order establishing
the board passed a number of amendments that were not acceptable to the Labour Government. One such amendment was that
the board's accounts should be sent to professional auditors
rather than district audit. Under the special parliamentary procedure that applied to orders of this type, the government used
its right to transform the order into a public Bill: the Labour
majority in the Commons was then able to reimpose district audit
on the board in face of Conservative comments about 'jobs for
the boys'.[27]

Meanwhile district auditors developed a useful role as management consultants. They observed different methods of carrying
out the same tasks and so could advise authorities with less

efficient routines how to effect improvements. The legislation of 1963 which allowed a local authority to incur expenditure up to the amount of a penny rate for any purpose which it felt would be beneficial to the area (provided the activity was not contrary to other statutory limitations) introduced an element of flexibility into the *ultra vires* rule. Thereafter the cases of surcharge fell to about three a year; most of these related to trivial items relating to the claims for expenses. So the issue of unreasonable expenditure faded away. No doubt central influences helped to condition local councils towards orthodox spending policies. But the standard doctrine that local authorities are subject to an ever-increasing degree of central control is certainly not supported by the history of district audit.

The Local Government Act 1972 gave local authorities outside London the right to choose between district audit and approved professional auditors. Labour MPs objected. They argued that approved auditors would be less expert in local government matters; that they would be employed by a local authority and would report back to their employers; that they could not provide ratepayers with the same guarantee of impartial scrutiny as district audit. Conservatives supported alternative audit systems as giving a new measure of freedom to local councils. The outcome was that few authorities chose approved auditors. Perhaps this was because the 1972 Act restricted the powers of district audit so that the objections of the past can no longer apply. District audit is not now concerned with the reasonableness of expenditure. Any surcharge for illegal payments is imposed by a court after an application by the auditor. Only in the case of alleged misappropriation of funds does district audit now impose a charge, and such action may be the subject of an appeal to a court.

NOTES

1 Report of the Select Committee on the *Repayment of Loans by Local Authorities*, 1902 (239), viii.
2 C. H. Wilson, *Essays in Local Government* (1948), p. 195.
3 Paras. 596–600, 1958–9, Cmnd 827, xvii.
4 K. Feiling, *Life of Neville Chamberlain* (1946), pp. 129 and 459–62.
5 ibid. pp. 132–3.
6 For full discussion, see IMTA, *The Rating of Dwellings: History and General Survey* (1958), ch. II.
7 The Report of the Fitzgerald Committee on *Valuation for Rates* is dated 2 August 1939, but it was not published until 1944 (HMSO).

8 J. R. and U. K. Hicks and C. E. V. Lever, *The Problem of Valuation for Rating* (1944).
9 Final Report of the Departmental Committee on Local Taxation, p. 89, 1914, Cd 7315, xi.
10 Letter dated 29 April 1928 in the collection of Chamberlain Papers at the University of Birmingham.
11 1901, Cd 638, xxiv.
12 1914, Cd 7315, xl.
13 Royal Commission on *Local Government*, Minutes of Evidence, Part I, p. 40 (HMSO, 1923).
14 1st Interim Report, p. 133, 1922, Cmd 1581, ix.
15 For fuller discussion, see C. H. Wilson (ed.), *Essays on Local Government* (1948), pp. 128–31.
16 Full details will be found in D. N. Chester, *Central and Local Government* (1951), Appendix B.
17 The Policy was announced in a White Paper, *Local Government Finance*, 1956–7, Cmnd 209, xxvi.
18 The Association of Education Committees issued a vigorous challenge to the ministerial policy in a pamphlet, *The Threat to Education* (1957).
19 R. H. S. Crossman, *The Diaries of a Cabinet Minister*, vol. I (1975), esp. p. 349.
20 1964–5, Cmnd 2582, xxii.
21 Sir S. Kimber, *Thirty-eight Years of Public Life in Southampton* (1949).
22 Para. 661, 1973–4, Cmnd 5460, xi.
23 A full statement of the law will be found in W. A. Robson, *The Law Relating to Local Government Audit* (1930). See also C. R. H. Hurle-Hobbs, *The Law Relating to District Audit* (1955).
24 1 KB 419. Quoted by W. A. Robson in his critique of the powers of district audit in *The Development of Local Government* (1931).
25 G. W. Jones, 'Herbert Morrison and Poplarism', *Public Law*, 1973, p. 26.
26 The annual report of the Ministry of Housing and Local Government for 1958 had a special section on district audit, 1958–9, Cmnd 737, xv.
27 464 HC Deb., 4 May 1949, cols. 1152–72. This case is of particular constitutional interest since it was the first occasion on which this procedure had been used.

Chapter VIII

CENTRAL CONTROL

The Years of Hesitant Intervention

The nature of any local government system is profoundly influenced by the relationship between local authorities and the central government. If secondary authorities are left with full freedom of action within defined spheres, then something akin to a federal style of government will develop. If local councils are subject to a battery of legal and financial restraints and are left with little opportunity to use discretion or exercise initiative, then local government tends to become local administration of national services. British local government stands at neither of these extremes although the pressures from Whitehall and Westminster push it ever nearer the latter alternative.

The Victorian tradition had been that local government was a necessary evil. The poor are always with us; so they must be relieved. Roads fall into decay; so they must be repaired. Insanitary conditions are unpleasant and spread disease; so there must be drains. Children must become useful and responsible members of society; so they must be taught. These services were essential, but the local bodies that provided them needed to be kept in check. They should not be allowed to undertake functions other than those approved by Parliament. There should be some element of central scrutiny to see that money was not wasted and, in some services, to ensure that minimum standards of provision were maintained. Paupers were entitled to basic necessities of life. Children were entitled to competent instruction. The payment of a central grant in aid of a particular service reinforced the concern with local efficiency. The payment of the police grant was conditional on a certificate of efficiency in respect of each local force from the national police inspectors. There was also concern that public bodies should be honest, so safeguards were taken to check raids on the public till. The total picture is one of restraint from the centre but of restraint imposed in an economical manner. The basic limitation was that local bodies, apart from municipal corporations,[1] were subject to the *ultra vires* rule and needed parliamentary sanction for fresh endeavours. The legal barrier to unorthodoxy was reinforced by a limited amount of inspection of local activities including the audit of local accounts.[2]

The nineteenth century had produced four categories of local inspection: the Poor Law, public health, education and police. The Poor Law inspectors perhaps attracted the most attention. They were entitled to attend meetings of the boards of guardians where they could speak but not vote. They gave advice but could not insist that the advice be accepted. They could pass on experience of how neighbouring authorities had dealt with similar problems and would no doubt reinforce any suggestions made in circulars issued from the Local Government Board in London. Each inspector was responsible for visiting the guardians in two or more adjacent counties. They made regular reports to headquarters which were published in the annual reports of the Local Government Board, which provide a full picture of the problems of Poor Law policy and administration in the early years of the century. Initially the task of inspectors had been relatively simple – to try to develop a technique for the relief of destitution which would satisfy modest standards of humanity but which would also act as a deterrent to those seeking public relief. By the year 1900 Poor Law administration had become far more complex. Separate institutions had been established in many areas for the aged, the sick, the mentally handicapped and children and the able-bodied unemployed. The inspectors thus had to face a much wider range of problems. The Minority Report of the Poor Law Commission was very critical of the work of the inspectorate.

'Regarded as an instrument of central control, it has, in fact, of late years been wholly unsuccessful . . . It has failed to get adopted, with any thoroughness or uniformity, the authoritative views on the treatment of the sick, the children and the deserving aged to which the LGB has, since 1895, given repeated utterance. It has failed even to prevent the persistent defiance of the instructions of the Central Authority; a defiance resulting, on the one hand in continued refusals to provide new buildings deemed to be requisite, and, on the other, with a few Urban Unions, in a rising tide of extravagance and corruption'.[3]

This comment was unfair in that it overlooked the limited powers of the inspectors. Nor should their influence be under-estimated because without them the standard of Poor Law administration would certainly have been worse. In the 1920s the inspectors had increasing difficulty with boards of guardians with left-wing political opinions who were faced with the distress caused by rising unemployment. After 1930, when Poor Law responsibilities passed to county councils and county boroughs, the inspectorate declined as the new and larger authorities were felt to need less supervision.

In the area of public health the Local Government Board provided advice for local authorities on both medical and engineering matters. The medical inspectors were concerned both with Poor Law institutions and the supervision of vaccination.[4] One of the inspectors, Dr Buchanan, was given fresh duties in 1905 – to advise on the technical and administrative problems of the wholesomeness of food, especially in the context of matters referred to the Board by local public analysts.[5] The engineering inspectors were originally appointed to hold local inquiries related to the development of local sewerage systems. Their duties widened steadily to include inquiries into the reorganisation of local district boundaries, loan sanctions needed to finance sanitary improvements and housing improvement schemes in areas deemed unfit for human habitation. The Housing and Town Planning Act 1909 led to some inspection by the board of the limited amount of town planning subsequently undertaken by local authorities.

The activities of its Poor Law inspectors apart, the Local Government Board tended to stand aloof from local authorities. Communication was by correspondence rather than personal contact. The Board was concerned about the soundness of local finances and scrutinised all attempts to extend the powers of local councils. The policy of the board was to restrain rather than encourage. Its relationship to local authorities was formal and consisted largely of response to local initiatives.

The limits imposed by Parliament on local borrowing in the nineteenth century were noted above.[6] There was a real fear that local councils would borrow and spend recklessly and incur financial obligations that they would find difficult to meet. To the financial puritan, public debt had to be controlled with care. Any suggestion that a local authority might possibly default on its debts was viewed with horror since this would undermine confidence in public authorities and make it more difficult and expensive for them to raise funds. Gradually the statutory limits imposed by Parliament were eroded, but for many purposes additional local borrowing needed approval of the Local Government Board under the provisional order procedure. The Board also kept a watchful eye on any borrowing clauses in local legislation.

A wider financial scrutiny over local expenditure was maintained by the district audit.[7] The Local Government Board played an important role as arbiter between the auditor and local councils and could also issue certificates to ensure that a council would not suffer an auditor's surcharge on a particular item. This involved detailed surveillance of local policy, but this surveillance always resulted from a local request. The board also heard appeals from frontagers arising from charges for private street works. Other forms of control arose from a determination to ensure that public property was used for the public good. Some of the older corporations had accumulated substantial property over the centuries, so the Municipal Corporation Acts 1835 and 1882 required central approval for the sale and lease of corporate property, the use of money obtained from the sale of such property, and over the exchange and purchase of land.

The Board had extensive powers over the acquisition of additional powers by local councils. Under the Public Health Acts of 1875 and 1890 it could grant certain powers of urban authorities to rural districts. Similarly under the Local Government Act 1894 it could allocate parish powers – mainly the appointment of assistant overseers – to boroughs and urban districts. It gave permission to local authorities to promote and oppose local legislation. Local by-laws and allotments regulations framed by parish councils were subject to the approval of the Board. Under the Housing and Town Planning Act 1909 the consent of the Board was needed before a local authority could prepare a town planning scheme. The assent of the Board was also needed for the compulsory purchase of land for housing projects and the development of gas and water undertakings as such acquisition required parliamentary consent under provisional order procedure. All these controls were potentially negative and restraining. However, if public health was at risk the Board could require local authorities to take action. Under the Public Health Act 1875 the Board received complaints from the public that the responsible local authorities were failing to provide adequate water supplies or sewerage; the Board might then issue orders to require the necessary work to be done. The Harpenden Urban District received one such order relating to local sewerage in 1912.

Thus in the years before the First World War the role of the Local Government Board was negative and regulatory. The vigour and excitement of the Liberal Government seemed to pass it by. No action was taken on the 1909 Report of the Poor Law Commission. The establishment of national health insurance was entrusted to a new insurance commission in the more dynamic care of Sir Robert Morant. A large part of the inertia was due to the personality of the President of the Board, John Burns, who held office from 1905 until the outbreak of war in 1914. The first Cabinet minister to come from a poor working-class background and with a long record of trade union and socialist agitation behind him, Burns, on attaining high office, seemed content to administer the existing system. Thus the Local Government Board had a tradition and resources inadequate to launch the housing drive which Lloyd George had promised in the 1918 General Election. Christopher Addison, the President of the Board in the post-war period sought new men and new measures.[8] Sir Robert Morant became Permanent Secretary and the Local Government Board was merged into a new Ministry of Health. Both Morant and Addison, a former professor of surgery, had visions of a new comprehensive health service to be administered by local authorities.[9] However, this did not materialise until 1948, and, when it did, the hospital service was removed from local government to newly created regional hospital boards.

The new Ministry of Health had an unhappy start. The task of building 'homes for heroes' in a hurry was difficult because of the shortage of building resources. Local authorities were encouraged to build by a generous system of central grants. Under the Housing Act 1919 the contribution of housing authorities, the borough and district councils, was limited to the product of a penny rate; any excess cost would be met by the Exchequer. This arrangement offered no inducement to economy. Once local liability had passed the penny rate threshold the local council was spending other people's money. Local authorities pressed forward with housing programmes which were too ambitious for the resources immediately available. Competition between local councils helped to force up construction costs and the nature of the grant system did nothing to restrain this competition. The Housing Act 1919 was an example of central stimulation rather than central control, but it was an experiment that was never repeated. With the pruning back of public expenditure in 1921 under the encouragement of the Geddes Committee, Addison was moved away from the Ministry of Health. Later grants for specific services returned to a percentage basis and were subject to stricter central supervision of estimates and grant-aided expenditure.

The award of grants for particular services greatly strengthened the impetus to greater supervision of local council business. If central government provides funds it naturally wishes them to be spent in ways it approves. It also wishes to control the amount of expenditure, which may imply a determination to resist or perhaps increase the sums involved. Supervision was exercised by requiring local authorities to submit estimates of expenditure on grant-earning services for approval by central departments; such approval was necessary for the grant to be 'earned'. This mechanism could be used to stimulate or discourage local spending. When a new duty was imposed on local authorities, as opposed to an optional power, a more generous rate of grant was offered to ease any resentment caused by the new obligation. Examples of this kind are the treatment of venereal disease during the First World War and the requirement to organise a midwifery service imposed in 1936. In 1908 a 50 per cent grant had encouraged local authorities to provide land for small-holdings. When a new service was proposed the associations of local authorities pressed for a grant to minimise the added burden on local rates. The more urgently a government wanted the new service the higher the rate of grant that would be forthcoming. Between 1935 and 1937 the associations engaged in protracted bargaining with the government over the grant for air raid pre-cautions; ultimately the Exchequer met 90 per cent of the cost.[10]

When ministers wished to curb public expenditure the grant mechanism provided a relatively painless means of achieving their aim. In 1922 the Economy (Miscellaneous Provisions) Bill authorised the limitation of grants to local education authorities. This part of the Bill was dropped but rationing of local expenditure was achieved through the grant system without legislative sanction.[11] It is, of course, even easier to use the grant system as a regulator to support national economic policy if separate grants for individual services are replaced by a unified general grant. In 1958 when various grants, including that for education, were replaced by a new general grant, the rubric governing the amount of money to be made available made explicit reference to what could be afforded in the current economic situation of the country.

Sometimes central departments want to restrain local activity; sometimes they want to insist on it. A financial reward may not be sufficient inducement to local action. In any case, to give a grant for the particular service may not be current government policy. A public body may be forced to carry out its duties by an order of mandamus. But the process of law is slow and ministers have felt that they needed more immediate and direct powers to ensure that local government services are provided adequately. Default powers allow ministers to take over themselves, or pass on to another body, duties which a local authority refuses to undertake. The first example of a default power is to be found in the Sewerage Act 1866. Other examples come soon after in the Education Act 1870, the Public Health Act 1875, and the Elementary Education Act 1876, in respect of compulsory school attendance. These powers were rarely used but in 1899 three Lincolnshire school boards were declared to be in default for failing to insist on attendance at school.[12] A difficulty for central departments was that they did not have the resources simply to take over scattered parcels of local administration. A convenient alternative, therefore, was to require one local authority to take over those duties which another local authority refused to carry out. The obvious move was to pass on the obligations to a larger authority. The Local Government Act 1929 provided that when a county district failed to carry out certain public health duties, these should be transferred to the county council. However, these powers have never been used. Of course, the technique of passing responsibilities upwards to a bigger local authority could not be applied to counties or county boroughs. The Education (Local Authority Default) Act 1904 authorised the Board of Education to recognise the managers of any elementary school as the local education authority for that school. In this case the potential transfer was to a smaller unit but, again, these powers remained unused. The default clause weapon is only wielded in extreme circumstances. The Boards of Guardians (Default) Act 1926 authorised the Minister of Health to replace local guardians with his nominees.[13] Three orders were issued under this Act and represented the climax of the struggle between the Conservative Government and Labour-controlled boards of guardians over the administration of the Poor Law.

The guardians disappeared in 1930 and the following decade was a relatively peaceful period for central-local relationships. The Local Government Act 1933 restated the basic law relating to local authorities but, as it was a consolidation measure, their position *vis-à-vis* the central government was unchanged. However, this decade saw one major struggle between a local authority and the central authorities which ended in a complete local victory. The victor was the London County Council and the issue Waterloo Bridge. The need to replace the old bridge became evident in 1923 when emergency repairs were required. The arguments over its replacement dragged on for over a decade. Conservationists urged that the old structure was a masterpiece and should be preserved. There was dispute about the width and design of a new bridge. The government intervened in 1926 by appointing a Royal Commission to review alternatives; its report proposed a double-decker road and rail bridge to Charing Cross.[14] Further delay was caused by the Southern Railway which agreed to move its terminus to the south bank of the Thames. In 1931 the Labour Cabinet refused to make a grant towards the building of Charing Cross Bridge because of the serious financial position. The following year the National Government offered a 60 per cent grant for a new bridge, but the Commons struck out the clause in the Bill sponsored by the LCC which authorised borrowing to finance the scheme. The LCC was in a unique position in that it required to obtain borrowing power annually from Parliament by means of a private Bill: other authorities obtained loan sanctions simply by application to a government department. So any other major highway authority wishing to build a bridge could expect to obtain permission to borrow capital with little trouble. Meanwhile the government felt it must support the view of Parliament, so the offer of a grant towards the cost of a new bridge was withdrawn; a grant would only be made for widening the existing structure.

The LCC accepted the widening plan but its policy changed when Labour won a majority at the 1934 election. Labour were determined to go ahead with a new bridge even if it had to be paid for out of rate revenue. The scene was set for a confrontation between the LCC and the central government. Herbert Morrison, the Labour leader of the LCC, dramatised the situation by personally starting the demolition of the old bridge. There followed a campaign led by Herbert Morrison to get borrowing powers from Parliament and a grant from the government to finance a new Waterloo Bridge. In 1936 borrowing powers were obtained and in 1937, when at last work was ready to start, the government agreed to make a grant of £400,000.[15] This incident is an outstanding example of the frustration and delay that can be caused when powerful organisations are at cross-purposes; it also illustrates how effective a powerful local authority can be when it is led with imagination and determination.

The Development of National Policies for Local Services

Since 1945 there has been a marked increase in central supervision over the activities of local councils. The trend has not been continuous. During the 1950s there were positive efforts to remove petty controls and encourage local responsibility. But the growing political tensions and economic difficulties since 1964 have inevitably increased central pressures on local administration.

The sharing of the hazards of war, particularly on the home

front, gave great impetus to the idea of equality. The inevitable shortages of the reconstruction period led to demands that resources be shared out fairly. So the concept of the need for minimum standards in local services was replaced with stronger concern to achieve equal standards. Housing was the key example. More houses were an urgent necessity. To ensure that the resources of the building industry were properly distributed between competing claims and to avoid the chaos of 1920, a system of building licences was instituted in addition to a rigid system of sanctions for local borrowing. To ensure that a local authority built as many houses as possible from its ration of loan capital and building resources, a maximum was fixed for the size of new council houses and a maximum-cost yardstick was imposed which affected the quality of construction.

The Labour Government was faced with an insuperable dilemma. Its instinct, its philosophy and its programme all demanded that local authorities be encouraged to proceed with a wide range of social provision. The harsh reality was that the lack of means available to implement these ideals required a regime of delay, restraint and rationing. So a gap developed between the intentions of legislation passed through Parliament and what, in practice, Whitehall was able to permit local authorities to do. Successive statutes required local authorities to think ahead in relation to particular responsibilities and to set out a formal programme of how they proposed to develop a service over a long period, often fifteen years. These programmes were then submitted to central departments for approval. There was some utopian stimulus to this activity, a belief in the need to plan a better Britain for the post-war world. No doubt also Labour ministers feared that a Conservative backlash might develop, aimed at restricting public spending. If local authorities were firmly committed in advance to long-term development programmes it might be more difficult for the advocates of retrenchment to halt the pace of progress. But while local councils were encouraged to think expansively about the future, their immediate activities were constrained by edicts from Whitehall permitting only the construction of so many houses, schools, etc. Some element of unreality was evident in the longer-range planning. To ask a local authority how it proposed to develop its health services or how many primary schools it proposed to build over the next fifteen years was to require a forecast about the birth rate that could be no more than a guess.

Labour Ministers when drafting legislation designed to give local government a positive sense of direction had a useful precedent in the 1944 Education Act passed by the war-time coalition government. This Act appeared to give the central ministry a dominant position *vis-à-vis* the local education authorities. Section 1 decreed that it shall be the duty of the Minister of Education 'to promote the education of the people of England and Wales . . . and to secure the effective execution by local education authorities, under his control and direction, of the national policy for providing a varied and comprehensive educational service'. Section 68 empowered the minister to give directions to any local education authority if he or she felt it was acting unreasonably. The authority of the minister was further reinforced by section 99 which authorised him to make an order declaring a local education authority to be in default because of failure to carry out its duties: such an order was to be enforceable through an application to a court for an order of mandamus. These powers sound draconian but exactly what they mean was not tested in the courts during the period covered by this history. They were felt to be insufficient to enable subsequent Labour governments to insist that local authorities should abandon selection for secondary education. However, the language of the Education Act was followed elsewhere. Section 1 of the Water Act 1945 reads 'it shall be the duty of the Minister of Health . . . to secure the effective execution by water undertakers under his direction and control, of a national policy relating to water'. The Children Act 1948 provides another example: section 42 requires that 'local authorities shall exercise their functions . . . under the general guidance of the Secretary of State'.[16]

Major legislation passed by the Labour Government covered police, the fire service, the national health service, town and country planning, the children's services, national assistance and civil defence. These measures had a common style. A minister was nominated to be generally responsible. Local authorities were responsible for the application of national policy to the particular situation in their own areas. Each function was to be the concern of a separate committee of the local authority and a chief officer would be responsible to it for the local administration of the service. Statutory Instruments could be issued by ministers under the powers conferred upon them by the principal Acts to enable them to control the evolution of a service. In extreme cases of local disobedience, ministers could declare local authorities to be in default, take over their responsibilities and charge the local ratepayers with the cost. The need for central approval of loans was maintained. Local development plans were subject to ministerial consent. In the case of town and country planning any decision to refuse planning permission could be the subject of an appeal to the minister. Not every Act contained every type of control outlined above, but a common pattern of *dirigisme* was very clear.

The selection of some chief officers was felt to be so sensitive that central departments obtained a right of veto to prevent unsuitable persons from being appointed. This had long been applied to the office of chief constable. In 1944 the veto power was extended to the chief education officer, in 1947 to the chief fire officer and in 1948 to the children's officer. Little controversy was provoked by this form of supervision because it was rarely exercised yet it remained as a powerful weapon in reserve. A curious feature was that it did not extend to the clerk or the treasurer, usually thought of as the two most influential local officials. The explanation is that control of local appointments was a central departmental technique to control a specific function: the clerk and the treasurer were concerned with all facets of local authority work and were not so susceptible to the scrutiny of any one ministry.

Increasing requirements were placed on local authorities to inform ministries about their activities. A detailed report on progress in council house building had to be sent to the Ministry of Health every month. Great importance was attached to this return, not simply because it enabled civil servants to oversee the pace of local endeavour but also because it enabled the minister, Aneurin Bevan, to give full replies to parliamentary questions. The parliamentary aspect illustrates an element of inconsistency in the distribution of responsibility. Without doubt the Minister of Health was regarded as being responsible for the national house-building programme. The minister personally accepted this view. But he had no responsibility for the actions of individual local councils although the accumulated total of their efforts constituted the progress of the national programme. Meanwhile, information was collected from local authorities for parliamentary purposes in fields other than housing. A witness from the Ministry of Housing and Local Government explained to the Select Committee on Estimates that his ministry kept a central register of local loan sanctions, not with a view to restricting borrowing by a local council, but because the information was sometimes needed at question time.[17]

The end of the period covered by the Attlee government saw a general review of relations between central and local administration. To some degree, this review was accidental. In 1947 the Ministry of Health issued a circular to local authorities urging economy in administrative manpower. Local councils responded by claiming that the growth of office workers was largely caused by central supervision and requests for information. Many checks had been imposed to ensure fair rationing of scarce resources during the war and in the post-war years. The government and the local authority associations then agreed that the methods of control should be examined with a view to their relaxation wherever possible. A Local Government Manpower Committee was established and issued two reports, the first in 1950 and the second in 1951.[18] Detailed work was done by sub-committees consisting of civil servants and chief officers of local authorities. Some of these sub-committees dealt with the functions of a particular central department, e.g. the Ministry of Transport or the Ministry of Education. Other committees were concerned with a particular problem area, e.g. the control of building resources. Inevitably the committee was something of a battle-ground between central and local interests. However, the committee accepted that the basis of its approach should be

'To recognise that local authorities are responsible bodies competent to discharge their own functions and that, though they may be the statutory bodies through which Government policy is given effect and operate to a large extent with Government money, they exercise their responsibilities in their own right, not ordinarily as agents of Government Departments. It follows that the objective should be to leave as much as possible of the detailed management of a scheme or service to the local authority and to concentrate the Department's control at key points where it can most effectively discharge its responsibility for Government policy and financial administration.'

This statement has been much quoted by local authorities when attempting to repel fresh attempts at surveillance.

Thus the efforts of the Manpower Committee had nothing directly to do with manpower. The issue became central controls. As a result of its labours many controls were removed. Some were so detailed that it is surprising that they were ever imposed. Even the relaxations were often timid. A concession from the Home Office relating to the fire service was that its prior approval would not be required for the installation of hydrants 'where the capital cost does not exceed £500, provided that no departure is contemplated from prescribed standards'. The fire service was perhaps a special case. It had been nationalised during the war to secure co-ordinated action against incendiary bombs.

When it was returned to local government in 1947 all procedures and equipment had been standardised and the Home Office was keen that uniformity should be maintained. But the same defence cannot be made of the supervision of child care. To quote from the Manpower Report again: 'The Home Office will replace the existing control of expenditure on an individual child boarded out by a more general financial control related to the total number of children boarded out.' On some matters local councils suffered a double scrutiny. The representatives of government departments on the Manpower Committee made it clear that ministries were not prepared to accept a district auditor's certificate as a basis for accepting a local authority claim for grant in aid of a particular service.

The replacement of a variety of specific grants by a new general grant in 1958 led to the disappearance of a large number of central controls. Education was the major grant to disappear. The children's service provides a useful example of the type of relaxations introduced. Four important controls were terminated. Local authorities were given full freedom to decide rates of payment to foster parents; they were no longer expected to inform the Home Office if they spent above a given figure per head on people above the age of 18 who were being given assistance under the Children Act 1948; they could decide whether to remit parental contributions in aid of children in care; they could make grants to voluntary bodies without the need for the Home Secretary's consent.[19] So councils could make their decisions without reference to Whitehall. If, as a result, local expenditure increased, the result would be to increase the local rate. Since the Exchequer aid was fixed and bore no relation to the detail of local action, there was no need for civil servants to scrutinise. This followed the Manpower Committee's view that control should be concentrated at key points. The key financial control was the amount of the Exchequer grant which remained securely in the hands of the Treasury. This being so, it mattered little if some local authorities were a little more generous than others.

A similar philosophy underlay the relaxation of the *ultra vires* rule in 1963 when the Local Government (Financial Provisions) Act allowed the spending of a penny rate for any purpose 'which in their opinion is in the interests of the area or of its inhabitants'.[20] In similar vein the system of loan sanctions was made more flexible in 1972,[21] subject to strict Treasury control over the total amounts that local authorities could borrow.

While the need for administrative economies helped to ease

the amount of detailed supervision from Whitehall there were even more powerful forces tending to integrate local and national government. These pressures were political and economic. It has been shown in Chapter VI that party politics had an increasing role in local affairs. A parallel tendency was for local government matters to assume greater importance in national politics. Ministers would claim credit for building more council houses, more schools, more old people's homes. The Opposition would claim that more should be done to promote particular local government services. On some issues a clear division of opinion emerged between the major parties in the 1960s: leading examples are the sale of council houses and selection in secondary education. If a party appeals to the national electorate on the basis of a programme that includes items that involve local government, it is inevitable that the party, if successful, will take steps to see that its policy is put into effect. Such a course is wholly justified in terms of democracy. Yet where a local political majority is opposed to the national political majority, there can be a conflict. Indeed, the national policy of a party need not always coincide with the views of its local supporters. Some Conservative education authorities ended secondary school selection in rural areas many years before the idea became a *bête noire* to the party. But all the time the pressures for conformity became stronger. If party political broadcasts take a firm line on a matter that falls within the ambit of local authorities, if front bench speeches in the House of Commons follow the same pattern, then it becomes politically necessary for ministers to try to make local councils toe the line.

This led to the concept 'Government by circular'. Government departments would try to press local authorities to follow a line of policy although they had no statutory power to require them to do so. The leading example is the famous Department of Education Circular 10/65 which 'requested' local education authorities to send to the department within a year their plans for reorganising secondary education on comprehensive lines. The circular then discussed six alternative forms of comprehensive education. A handful of authorities failed to respond under this pressure, and by 1970, when the Labour Government was defeated, it was preparing legislation to compel compliance with its policy.

It is difficult to disentangle purely party political reasons for greater central control from general desires for equality and efficiency. If the national taxpayer is making a majority contribution to the cost of local services, then the central government must feel a responsibility to ensure that these services are broadly uniform in quality and extent. Otherwise a taxpayer could be giving financial assistance to facilities available in other parts of the country that are not available to him. To a degree this has been the case throughout the twentieth century. It must be so if local authorities are grant aided and still have significant discretion. Nevertheless some basic standards are uniform, e.g. the ages for compulsory education, financial assistance for higher education, quality of council house construction and levels of road maintenance. In 1948, valuation for local rating had to be removed from local authorities because the distribution of Exchequer aid to compensate for low rateable values would have given local valuers a powerful incentive to under-assess. Fairness and equality demanded unification.

Professor Griffith, writing in 1966, suggested that government departments had different traditions in dealing with local authorities and that these could be divided into three categories; *laissez-faire*, regulatory and promotional.[22] The *laissez-faire* attitude emerged most strongly in the attitude of the Ministry of Health towards local health and welfare services. These services had unequal facilities between separate local authority areas. The ministry seemed to take the view that local authorities were spending their own money and so should take their own decisions. There may also have been reluctance to interfere as this might be interpreted as a challenge to the professional judgement of local medical officers of health. The Ministry of Housing and Local Government also had something of a *laissez-faire* relationship with housing authorities. It is true that after both world wars, and also in 1951 and 1965, the ministry gave vigorous encouragement for local building programmes. But local authorities have never been required to make an assessment of the housing needs of their areas, there has been no central direction on tenant selection and no action whenever local authorities decided to stop building council houses. From a detailed study of housing administration in Lincolnshire between 1919 and 1958, Dr Owen Hartley has concluded that it was generally possible for the central department to frustrate a local authority that wished to innovate, but that it was far more difficult to force an inert council into action.[23]

The Home Office was used by Professor Griffith as the prime example of the regulatory model. It supervised the police force and the children's service largely through the use of inspectors whose task was to ensure local efficiency by making sure that regulations were obeyed. The Ministry of Transport had a similar approach but this had become more promotional in that the ministry has had to develop a more positive approach to secure the development of a network of major roads designed to meet national needs rather than the susceptibilities of local councils.

The Department of Education is treated as the example of a ministry with a promotional approach. The department has positive policies about the organisation of schools and the supply of teachers, the quality and style of school buildings, which are pressed upon local authorities. But it is notable that the promotional role has not extended to questions of syllabus nor the organisation of examinations.

These alternative models of the central-local relationship are valuable for the purposes of analysis but they need to be treated with caution. The regulatory style can involve more detailed supervision of local administration than the promotional style: there is more central control over the police force than over any other local function.[24] Attitudes do change over time. As noted above, a promotional element has sometimes interrupted the generally *laissez-faire* relationship with housing authorities. And since Griffith was writing in 1966, the *laissez-faire* element had declined substantially. At this time public opinion and politicians became increasingly sensitive to the needs of deprived children, the elderly, the sick and the disabled. Local arrangements to help these groups had grown in piecemeal fashion and were divided between separate departments of a local authority. The report of the Seebohm Committee[25] urged major changes and led to quite rapid action. The Social Services Act 1970 was an example of authoritarian local government law. It required these duties to be carried out by a separate committee, imposed restraints on the type of business coming before that committee, required local authorities to act under the general guidance of the Secretary of State and empowered him to veto the appointment of the chief official appointed by a local authority to supervise the execution of these services. The Act was passed in a hurry in order that it should reach the statute book before the General Election. But it was not contentious between the parties. As with education in 1944, the feeling was that central government must act as an overlord to promote greater equality in local provision and to insist on minimum standards of efficiency in a field in which professional expertise was felt to be variable in quality.

Opposition spokesmen on local government affairs, particularly among Conservatives, occasionally deplore the extent of central interference in local affairs. When in office the major parties are equally willing to override local opinion. After 1965 the Conservatives complained bitterly about Labour attempts to bully local education authorities into creating comprehensive schools. After 1970 Mrs Thatcher as Secretary for Education vetoed plans for school reorganisation on comprehensive principles which had the genuine support of local authorities. The Conservative dislike of direct labour organisations was evident in DoE Circular 90/72: it decreed that above a cost limit of £40,000 (excluding the cost of land) direct labour could not be used for road improvement schemes unless the work was won in competition with contractors. In this case political principle was happily married with concern for efficiency.

The need to combine economy with a broad equality of local provision has been greatly reinforced by the serious economic difficulties which the country has faced, particularly since 1961. The problems of the balance of payments, inflation and, most recently, unemployment, have made governments feel the need to exercise firm control over the economy. Keynesian theories were accepted by ministers irrespective of party. The public sector was used to set an example. The nature of the example varied with the content of the most recent economic statistics. Most often the outcome was squeeze and freeze: the traditional first step was to inform local authorities that no loan sanction could be given for less essential facilities like town halls and swimming pools. Whether these were the least necessary items was never seriously argued: they were items that never got included in ministerial speeches about the need to develop local services. Similarly, local authorities were required to conform with the requirement of contemporary wages policy. In the case of teachers' salaries the government could exert commanding influence through the Burnham Committee. On the less frequent occasions when the economic climate was brighter or government policy was dominated by fear of unemployment, then local authorities would get some encouragement to spend. The school building programme would be expanded; cost yardsticks would be raised; particularly in areas of economic depression, a start would be made on building new roads. The establishment of the general grant in 1958 gave the government a central regulator which could be adjusted much more readily than a series of specific grants each supported by separate institutional and professional pressures. The negotiations over the general grants and, after 1966, over the level of the rate support grant further increased the influence of the associations of local authorities. The individual local council could do little but sit back and await the outcome of discussions between the government and their representatives. Due to their complexity, the arguments are commonly conducted by officials. On the one side of the table are civil servants; on the other are the financial advisers of the local authority associations, usually the treasurers of some of the largest local authorities.

In spite of the centralisation it was broadly accepted that the poundage of the local rate was a matter for local decision. It might be affected by local factors. It might be affected by local wishes. Certainly ministers did not wish to accept any responsibility for rate levels. To do so would be to incur unpopularity and to suffer criticism for matters not fully under their control. So while national politicians would urge local authorities to do this or that, or claim credit for some things that local councils had done, they tended to look the other way when the rate demands were issued. Ultimately this convenient bifurcation began to break down. In the conditions of a wage and price freeze, a rise in local rates became a challenge to government policy. It became an important political factor, not in terms of votes but in terms of obtaining the necessary trade union support for continued wage restraint. In 1973 the government decided that a rise in local rates could be a serious menace to its economic strategy. Accordingly, rate levels were 'monitored'. Local authorities were instructed to inform the government of the rate they intended to impose. The idea apparently was that if the rise was felt to be too much, then a local authority would be asked to think again.[26] There was no statutory basis for such 'monitoring'. Nevertheless, it was a logical consequence of what is now a traditional policy of using the public sector of the economy as a whole to support the national economic policy.

How have the local authorities responded to the increasing pressure from central government? Countervailing forces have been set at work. The growth in the influence over local officials has helped to secure greater local acceptance of Whitehall guidance. It is not in the nature of bureaucracy to promote revolt against properly constituted authority. Wherever a local council rebelled, it was apparent that a group of politically motivated councillors were dominating local policy. As party organisation came to play an increasing role in council affairs, it was inevitable that, at any time, a large number of local authorities would be controlled by the political opponents of ministers. On issues where party policies were in conflict, local councillors could claim that they had a local mandate to oppose and obstruct government wishes.

It is important to make a distinction between cases where

local councils defied statutory authority and those cases where they simply resisted strong central persuasion. The latter category may create problems, but it is wholly respectable in terms of democratic theory; of the former category there are only three recent instances. Local authorities are law-abiding bodies. They do not engage in outright defiance of the state. However, at Coventry in 1954 and at St Pancras in 1957 the local councils refused to carry out their civil defence duties: they argued that to do so was a waste of money as effective protection against nuclear attack was impossible. The Home Secretary thereupon invoked his default powers, appointed local commissioners to organise civil defence and charged the local authorities with the cost. Not surprisingly, they repented fairly quickly. The third case arose when the Clay Cross UDC refused to operate the fair rents clauses of the Housing Finance Act 1972. Initially, a significant number of Labour-controlled councils threatened similar action. It seemed as if the Conservative Government had to face a widespread revolt. One by one the other councils changed their minds and Clay Cross was left alone and isolated. The government appointed a commissioner to administer the council houses there and the problem disintegrated when the Clay Cross authority disappeared in the reorganisation of local government in 1974.

The importance of Clay Cross is that it became the sole rebel. Why did the other protesting authorities retreat? There were serious moral doubts in the Labour Party about the wisdom of resisting lawful authority; there were doubts about the practical consequences of rebellion; there was the constant pressure of official advice urging conformity. These factors did not influence the councillors at Clay Cross because they were untypical. The community was compact but relatively isolated; the council was small; it was totally dominated by a tightly knit group of people with extreme opinions. The advice of local officials was ignored. Indeed, they were dismissed. The councillors were willing to create a degree of chaos unknown in modern English local government.

There are endless cases of local authorities which, while keeping within the law, have resisted a particular government initiative. The Conservative-controlled authorities which objected to comprehensive secondary schools failed to respond to DES Circular 10/65. A number of Labour-controlled councils objected to the Education (Milk) Act 1971, which stopped the provision of free milk to children over seven, and they sought to evade the effect of the Act by a variety of technicalities. Such activity can be very irritating to ministers. It can also be regarded as evidence of a healthy spirit of independence in local government.

NOTES

1   For discussion of how far the municipal corporations outside London
    were subject to the *ultra vires* rule, see B. Keith-Lucas, 'Municipal
    boroughs and ultra vires', *Public Administration*, 28, 1950, pp. 87–90.
    Attorney-General v. *Leicester Corporation* [1943], 1, Ch. 86, had cast
    doubt on the position. In practice, provincial boroughs acted as if
    they were subject to the *ultra vires* restriction; see pp. 28–30 *supra*.
2   Audit is discussed at pp. 153–7 *supra*.
3   Report of the Royal Commission on the *Poor Laws and Relief of
    Distress*, p. 988, 1909, Cd 4499, xxxvii.
4   Compulsory vaccination of infants caused acute controversy towards
    the end of the nineteenth century. Exemption for conscientious
    reasons was permitted in 1898, and compulsion was finally ended in
    1907. R. M. MacLeod, 'Law, medicine and public opinion: the resist-
    ance to compulsory health legislation, 1870–1907', *Public Law*, 1967,
    pp. 107 and 189.
5   John S. Harris, *British Government Inspection* (1955), p. 49.
6   p. 132 *supra*.
7   pp. 153–7 *supra*.
8   On taking office, Addison was gravely disturbed by the limitations of
    the administrative resources of the Board. R. J. Minney, *Viscount
    Addison* (1958), p. 170. Macmillan had a similar view in 1951 when
    he directed the Conservative housing drive. H. Macmillan, *Tides of
    Fortune, 1945–55* (1969), p. 375. Also Crossman, op. cit., p. 43.
9   F. M. G. Willson, *The Organisation of British Central Government,
    1914–1956* (1957), p. 151.
10 D. N. Chester, *Local and Central Government* (1951), pp. 223–7.
11 Sir Lewis A. Selby-Bigge, *The Board of Education* (1937), p. 105.
12 Report of the Committee of Council on Education 1898–9, pp. 82–45,
    1899, C9401, xx.
13 See p. 88.
14 1926, Cmd 2772, xiii.
15 Fuller accounts of the Waterloo Bridge saga can be found in Sir
    Gwilym Gibbon and R. W. Bell, *History of the London County
    Council* (1939), and B. Donoughue and G. W. Jones, *Herbert Morrison*
    (1973).
16 During the sittings of the Roberts Committee on *Public Libraries*,
    1957–9, the assessors appointed by the Minister of Education urged the
    committee to recommend the enactment of provisions similar to sec.
    68 of the Education Act in the proposed Public Libraries Bill. Mem-
    bers of the committee rejected this proposal vigorously. The Public
    Libraries and Museums Act 1964 contains less powerful provisions.
17 qq. 5, 12, and 14, 1960–1, (284), vi.
18 1950, Cmd 7870, xiii; 1951–2, Cmd 8421, xvi.
19 J. A. G. Griffith, *Central Departments and Local Authorities* (1966),
    pp. 412–4.
20 See p. 55.
21 DoE Circular, 2/71.
22 *Central Departments and Local Authorities* (1966), pp. 515–28.

23 'The relationship between central and local authorities', *Public Administration*, 49, 1971, pp. 448–50.
24 D. E. Regan, 'The police service: an extreme example of central control over local authority staff', *Public Law*, Spring 1966, pp. 13–34.
25 1967–8, Cmnd 3703, xxxii.
26 DoE Circular, 21/73.

Chapter IX

THE LOCAL AUTHORITY ASSOCIATIONS

The Convention of Royal Burghs in Scotland was established in the middle of the sixteenth century, with a general concern and responsibility for the well-being of the royal burghs; it was frequently instrumental in obtaining Acts of Parliament for the promotion of the objects in view.[1] But no such body grew up in England until the mid-Victorian period. The Association of Municipal Corporations was born on the initiative of Sir Samuel Johnson, town clerk of Nottingham, after a meeting of the representatives of the borough councils of England, called by Manchester Corporation, to protest against the restrictions which the Borough Funds Act of 1872 placed on the power of municipal corporations to promote Bills in Parliament.[2] The County Councils Association came into being immediately after the creation of the county councils in 1888, at the instigation of the Society of Clerks of the Peace of Counties, and legal doubts about the right of county councils to subscribe were removed by a special Act – the County Councils Expenses Act 1890.[3] The Local Boards Association, which had been founded in 1890, converted itself into the Urban District Councils Association in 1894, in which year the Rural District Councils Association was also established. The last of the associations – the National Association of Parish Councils – was not founded until 1947, although there had been several abortive and half-hearted attempts to start such a body earlier in the century.[4]

There was, however, a proliferation of lesser societies and associations representing local authorities, their officers and members; the *Local Government Directory* for 1906 lists 140 such, including the Institute of Municipal Treasurers and Accountants, the Local Government Information Bureau (c/o the Fabian Society), the Association of Mayors and ex-Mayors of Metropolitan Boroughs, the Municipal Officers' Association (shortly to develop into NALGO), and many professional associations of local government officers – sanitary inspectors, poor law dispensers, surveyors, public analysts and others, and pressure groups affecting local government.

At first, however, the Association of Municipal Corporations (AMC) had been the only effective association, and then, the leading one. It had been created to deal with legal problems, and it had from the start a legalistic bias. Almost from its foundation, the secretary was Goring Pritchard, a solicitor, who was also the leading parliamentary agent of his time, being involved in the promotion of a large proportion of the local Bills of the late nineteenth and early twentieth centuries. He was succeeded in 1910 by his son, Harry (later Sir Harry) Pritchard, who continued until 1944, when, at the age of 78, he was replaced by the first full-time secretary Harold (later Sir Harold) Banwell.[5] Sir Harry Pritchard was also a parliamentary agent, acting for nearly all the boroughs of England and Wales, and so involved in the great majority of local Bills; he was president of the Law Society, London agent for most of the provincial town clerks, and senior partner of Sharpe Pritchard & Co. Thus, for seventy years, the AMC was in the hands of the two Pritchards – able, learned, masters of private Bill procedure but essentially lawyers. Furthermore, in the words of Ernest Simon,[6]

'Unfortunately, this body is managed by the Law Committee, consisting exclusively of town clerks. If the individual town clerk in spite of a few brilliant exceptions, shows a lack of initiative because of his legal training, it is only to be expected that a committee consisting of thirty town clerks should not only have very little initiative, but a magnificent capacity for finding at least thirty insuperable objections to any constructive scheme that is put forward. The result is that the Association of Municipal Corporations has never been conspicuous for imagination or initiative . . . '

Ernest Simon may have been to some degree biased by his dislike of legal delays and his own forceful, somewhat impatient character. But, none the less, the criticism may be basically true of the period up to the Second World War. The association did not see itself as a policy-making body, nor as a political organisation. Furthermore, the Pritchards, both father and son, were closely involved in the tortuous process of local Bill legislation and saw the association mainly as a protective organisation, not as a powerhouse for the evolution of new imaginative and constructive schemes of social progress. They had few personal contacts with the civil servants, and rarely visited the ministries or engaged in discussion on policy and general legislation.

Another criticism which might have been made of the composition of the AMC was that it gave undue weight to the largest authorities; each of the five largest county boroughs in the country had automatic representation on the council and all the committees (except the General Purposes Committee), in addition to a number of seats reserved for other county boroughs by elections,[7] giving the county boroughs approximately half the members of all committees. This did, however, represent approximately the balance of population, rather than of the number of separate borough councils, and at meetings of the council, voting was on the basis of one town, one vote, irrespective of population.

The AMC was somewhat inhibited in its relations with the government by a tradition of the great provincial cities dealing direct with the ministries instead of through the association. The corporations of Manchester, Birmingham, Nottingham and other cities, with their close contact with their constituency members, tended to act as independent powers.

The pattern of the Urban District Councils Association followed that of the municipal corporations: from 1894 until 1950 the firm of C. E. Baker & A. J. Lees, Solicitors and Parliamentary Agents, provided the secretaries, who worked for the association part time. Power lay rather in the hands of the clerks than of the members of the district councils.

The County Councils Association followed a different pattern; from 1902 until 1918, the secretary was Montagu Harris, a barrister, employed on a part-time basis. From 1915 to 1919, he was also acting clerk of East Sussex County Council.[8] In 1918, the association appointed the first full-time secretary, Sidney (later Sir Sidney) Johnson. He was a local government lawyer, somewhat brusque and impatient, who played a major part in shaping the policy of the association until he retired, thiry-two years later.[9] The association had only sixty-two members, all of the same status, while the AMC had about 400 members, ranging from the great county boroughs of Manchester and Birmingham to small market towns of 1,000 or 2,000 inhabitants.

The Rural District Councils Association followed more or less the pattern of the municipal corporations, but with far less influence and activity in the parliamentary and civil service fields.

Thus, there existed four powerful associations, but only one of these, the AMC, was concerned with all local government matters on account of the county boroughs' comprehensive powers. In major discussion, the London County Council was often brought in as a separate force; it did not belong to the CCA, but its influence was very great.

In addition to the four principal associations, there had been founded in 1904 an Association of Education Committees. It came into being as a consequence of the passing of the Education Act of 1902, in order to play a part in the modelling of the new structure. At first, the county councils held aloof, feeling that their own association was their proper spokesman; but the boroughs and urban districts joined. It was not until 1919 that any county education committee joined. After the 1944 Education Act, the composition changed significantly, being limited to the county and county borough committees; by 1949 all of these (except the London County Council) were members.

The organisation and method of working of this association was not unlike that of the other associations. Since 1925, there have been only two secretaries, Sir Percival Sharp (1925–45) and Sir William (later Lord) Alexander (1945–   ). Both of them had previously served as Director of Education for Sheffield. They played a leading part in shaping the policies of the association, and Sir William Alexander, in particular, became known not only as a power in the ministries, but also as a trenchant exponent of his and the association's views on education.

The relations between the two principal associations were not always easy, and the period immediately after the First World War was one in which conflict was difficult to avoid. The expansion of county boroughs into the counties, and the efforts of the larger non-county boroughs to win independence from county government naturally alarmed the county councils. They saw their richest territories, the highly rated urban areas, being persistently taken over by the county boroughs. They were fighting a constant defensive action to preserve their integrity, and they were generally losing the fights; between 1889 and 1922, twenty-one new county boroughs were carved out of the counties, and 109 extensions of county borough areas resulted in a loss of another quarter of a million acres with a population of 1,700,000.[10]

Inevitably, therefore, there was some resentment between the representatives of the counties and of the major boroughs. The County Councils Association was pressing the government for action to stop this territorial erosion of its members, and, from 1921, was urging the minister, Sir Alfred Mond, to appoint a Royal Commission to investigate the matter; he tried to settle the conflict by discussions between the two associations, but made little progress.[11] So, reluctantly, he agreed to the appointment of a commission, and inevitably this became, in fact, an arbitrator between the two parties. The associations had per-

suaded the minister to take this action; the majority of the
members were chosen from the principal officials and office
holders of the associations.[12] The great bulk of the evidence submitted to the commission came from the associations. Thus, to a
great extent, the associations were sitting in judgement on themselves, in a tribunal appointed at their behest.

It is not surprising, in these circumstances, that, when the
commission reported, its proposals were rather a concordat
between the conflicting parties than a bold new solution to a
major administrative problem. The process of extension of
county boroughs and the creation of new boroughs was slowed
down and made more difficult.[13]

This was probably the largest single episode in which the
associations were concerned in the first half of the century, but
they were throughout the period involved in many other matters.
Not least among these was the problem of the organisation of
council staffs. The National Association of Local Government
Officers (NALGO) had been founded in 1905, and, after the war,
its leaders were attracted by the possibility of its playing a major
part in the system of 'Whitleyism' – the new pattern of joint
councils of employees and employers established to settle problems of wages and other matters of common interest. This
would involve not only the recognition of NALGO as a national
body authorised to speak for all local government officers, but
also a corresponding organisation on the employers' side, to be
based on the associations. Inevitably, this would imply the
development of the concept of local government officers as
members of a national service, rather than as employees of
hundreds of separate local authorities.[14] This would mean the
adoption of national rates of pay, and the surrender of individual authorities' right to fix their own salary scales.

The CCA was opposed from the start to these proposals, and
disliked the whole conception of a local government service
organised on a national basis; in 1920 it refused to recommend
its members to accept the negotiated national scales. Early in
1921, the AMC followed this lead, and the urban and rural
districts also refused to accept the scales. The whole exercise
was defeated by the opposition of the associations. Though
some limited degree of Whitleyism developed through provincial
councils, the associations maintained their general opposition
until the Second World War.

Then, under the impact of compulsory arbitration in wage
disputes, the associations realised that rates of pay might be
fixed at very different levels up and down the country. So, at

last, the associations were persuaded to accept a national system
of settling wages and salaries, but they had fought a successful
rearguard action for twenty-two years.[15] Moreover, the employees
were moving towards a demand for a closed shop. Durham
County Council, under Labour control, was only prevented in
1951 from enforcing this by the refusal of the teachers to co-
operate and the intervention of the Labour Minister of Education, George Tomlinson.

During the years up to the outbreak of the Second World War,
the associations were performing a variety of other functions,
mostly concerned with their relationship with central government;
their secretaries and chairmen were constantly in communication
with the ministries on a wide variety of matters; but they had
not yet achieved the status and degree of acceptance that they
reached after the war, when in the hands of two powerful full-
time secretaries – Sir Harold Banwell and W. L. Dacey – they
became almost part of the constitution, with an accepted right
to be consulted on both policy and detail of proposed legislation
and in almost daily contact with the senior civil servants, or with
the ministers themselves.[16] They also did much to help their
individual members, through dissemination of information, and
the giving of legal advice. But there was always a restraint in the
relationship between the two major associations – the CCA, in
which the squirearchy still had a dominant voice, and the AMC
with its roots in the great cities.

The AMC was from the start dominated by its secretary and
the Law Committee, composed exclusively of solicitor town
clerks. It was not until just before the Second World War that
the General Purposes Committee (composed primarily of elected
members) came to supersede the Law Committee as the real
centre of power, under a dominant chairman, Sir Miles Mitchell
of Manchester, who held office for twenty years,[17] and then under
Sir Francis Hill, chairman for another ten years,[18] both of whom
worked closely with the secretary, Sir Harold Banwell.

In 1964, the chairman of this committee became *ex-officio*
chairman of the association. This came, however, to be to some
extent a political office, depending upon the party complexion of
the majority of the constituent authorities; after the Conservative
gains in the municipal elections of 1967, the balance of power
in the AMC changed accordingly, and the Labour Chairman,
Sir Mark Henig, was replaced by a Conservative, Alderman
(later Sir) Frank Marshall of Leeds. This was in part a consequence of the growing influence of Cecil Dawson who had been
appointed to the Conservative Central Office to look after local

government matters. Sir Frank Marshall in turn gave way to a Labour nominee in 1973 when the control of the association passed back to the Labour Party. Thus there was developing a clear party pattern in the association with a convention similar to that of Parliament, that the leadership should go with the political majority of the members. The CCA has not been subject to such fluctuations in control, as the majority of the county councils have been consistently Conservative or Independent, though several of the counties with the largest populations, in the industrial Midlands and North, have been Labour strongholds. But the constitution of the CCA did not give them power in proportion to their populations.

Another important constitutional change within the AMC was the rise of the office of vice-president. Originally, there had been one vice-president whose function was to preside at council meetings in the absence of the president. But, from 1911 on, there developed a practice of electing a number of vice-presidents, chosen from members of both houses of Parliament.[19] These became, in fact, part of the machinery of the association in its relation with the central government. They were relied upon not only for advice but to act for the association in moving amendments to Bills, asking parliamentary questions, leading delegations to ministers, and introducing private members' Bills. The number of these vice-presidents steadily increased; in 1955, there were eight peers and eleven MPs. By 1973, the numbers had risen to eleven peers and nineteen MPs.

This pattern of appointing a platoon of vice-presidents for parliamentary duties was copied by the other associations, with the exception of the CCA, which normally has a number of peers and County Members on its executive council, and relied on their aid in parliamentary matters. As with the AMC, the members appointed as vice-presidents of the other associations tended to increase as the parliamentary business increased, and as the threat of reorganisation grew. For example, the National Association of Parish Councils had, in 1954, one peer and two MPs. By 1974, these had increased to four peers and five MPs; between 1901 and 1955 the Rural District Councils Association increased its parliamentary vice-presidents from three to twenty-five.

This representation in Parliament was of major importance to the associations. They did not pay their vice-presidents, and had no sort of hold over them. But they were chosen from among those peers and MPs who were sympathetic to the associations, and generally from among those who had served, at some time in their careers, as councillors in the relevant sort of local authority. Thus, the associations could be sure of friendly support, unless there were powerful influences the other way, such as matters of clear party policy and party loyalty. To a great extent, the contact with the parliamentary vice-presidents was in the hands of the secretaries of the associations, who helped them by drafting amendments to be moved, supplying statistics and facts to support resolutions, and keeping them fully informed on all matters relevant to the associations. Much of this work never appeared in official reports or minutes, and the vice-presidents, in speaking in the House of Commons or the Lords, rarely admitted that they were speaking to a brief from one of the associations, though there was no secret about their position, and some of them were well-known as exponents of the associations' points of view. In this parliamentary work, Sir Harold Banwell of the AMC established a personal position and influence which, though entirely informal and unofficial, gave him a unique position in the process of government at that time. Much of his influence, however, was exercised not through these parliamentary channels but through direct but informal discussion with the civil servants and ministers. Sir William Alexander of the Association of Education Committees played a similar, but perhaps more public, part in the field of educational policy.

In the years after the Second World War, the newly formed National Association of Parish Councils, under its energetic secretary, Charles Arnold-Baker, was coming to play an increasing part in parliamentary work. Whereas the major authorities promoted their own private Bills when they wanted new powers, the parish councils had neither the legal status nor the money to do this. Sometimes they would get clauses relating to their affairs included in private Bills being promoted by county councils;[20] more often the National Association, operating through its secretary, would get private members' Bills introduced. Between 1956 and 1971, the association successfully sponsored five such Bills,[21] as well as getting, like the other associations, a large number of amendments to government Bills, usually as a result of the activity of parliamentary vice-presidents.

In addition to this, the associations have had a growing influence in nominating members of other bodies. They have commonly been consulted informally about names for members of Royal Commissions and departmental committees. This again is never formally recorded. But officially they have nominated members of a great number of other bodies; in 1953, the AMC formally appointed members of 100 assorted bodies, including the River Board Areas Consultative Committee, the Welsh Tourist and Holidays Board, the Ministry of Labour Standing Committee on Staggering of Holidays and the Central Midwives Board.

In the immediate post-war period, there was a flood of social legislation which profoundly affected the working and services of local authorities. Among these statutes were the Education Act 1944,[22] the National Health Service Act 1946, the Town and Country Planning Act 1947, the National Assistance Act 1948, the Children Act 1948 and also the Acts to nationalise gas and electricity. At that time, the modern device of 'Green Papers' or consultative documents had not been developed. Instead the government held confidential discussions with the associations before the first reading of each Bill. These were conducted privately, so as not to break the rule that the contents of a Bill are secret until it is given a first reading. So small sub-committees of members and officials conducted the discussions, reporting later to the councils of their associations on what they had done, for confirmation or rejection. At a later stage, the vice-presidents would be called in to put the point of view of the associations at second reading or in committee. But many drafting proposals were passed direct to the government departments rather than the associations having to get their vice-presidents to put down formal amendments. Inevitably, this process, at that time of extreme legislative activity, led to the secretaries of the associations, and particularly Sir Harold Banwell, being drawn more closely into the internal working of central government.

Since the end of the war, the associations have been very much involved in such informal discussions with civil servants and ministers. Their work has had little publicity except when they have issued manifestos on reorganisation, but much the greater part of their time has been spent on less dramatic but important negotiations on innumerable matters of general interest. Nearly every item on the agendas of the associations referred to some matter of discussion with the central ministries, ranging from heavy lorries and footpaths to gambling, airports and social services. Among the most significant of these has been the series of discussions with successive ministers to settle the level of the rate support grant, paid by the Treasury to local authorities, and amounting in 1972–3 to over £2,000,000,000.

So, too, the associations have been involved in negotiations with the central ministries on revision of the boundaries of local authorities; the manpower question; finance of local government;

the proposed removal of a number of functions from the control of local authorities, including hospitals, gas, electricity; and valuation and the return of fire brigades to the local authorities.[23]

Probably the most important domestic problem in the post-war years was housing, with the allied questions of subsidies and slum clearance. In all the discussions the AMC played a dominant role, as it was only its members, with the districts and the LCC, that were concerned. All the subsidies that were paid by the central government in that period were negotiated by the associations, and settled before the Bills were introduced. So, too, the slum-clearance policies were negotiated, and based on the experience of the big cities. All in all, the secretaries of the associations gave more time to this than to any other subject during these years.

The Education Bill 1944 also involved the associations in protracted discussion and argument. Much of this revolved round the future of the 'Part III authorities' – non-county boroughs and urban districts. The Bill proposed to concentrate responsibility in the hands of counties and county boroughs. Inevitably, the AMC was divided on this matter; so, too, was the Association of Education Authorities, whose membership included only 28 counties, but 169 Part III authorities.

One of the first topics to be raised after the war was that of the general shortage of manpower to do the work and business of the country. It was not solely a local government problem – indeed, it was more acute in industry. In 1947, the Ministry of Health invited all local authorities to carry out a review of their organisation and staffing policies, with a view to reducing the number of people they employed.[24] The associations replied that one of the main reasons for their employing so many people was the degree to which the central ministries concerned themselves with the details of local government, including the statistical and other returns they demanded, such as a half-yearly return showing how much each authority had reduced its staff since the previous return.

A series of discussions took place between the associations and the Ministry of Health, and out of these emerged a proposal to appoint a committee composed of nine civil servants and thirteen representatives of the associations, and no outsiders. This had as its terms of reference:

'To review and co-ordinate the existing arrangements for ensuring economy in the use of manpower by local authorities and by those Government Departments which are concerned with local government matters; and to examine in particular the distribution of functions between central and local government and the possibility of relaxing departmental supervision of local authority activities and delegating more responsibility to local authorities.'

This, it will be observed, covered two quite distinct topics: manpower and central control, which the associations had contrived to get treated as if it were the principal cause of the manpower crisis.[25] Furthermore, despite a very strong Civil Service team, including Dame Evelyn Sharp and Mr W. Armstrong,[26] the two reports[27] of the committee almost completely ignored the first half of the terms of reference, and concentrated on how to reduce central control and interference. So the attack was not only warded off, but a counter-attack, on different ground, was developed.

Out of this emerged a large number of detailed proposals for reducing the degree of central control over local authorities, most of which were duly implemented.[28] But still the greatest tool of control was that of finance – loan sanctions and grants in aid.

The associations appear to have had no clear and agreed policy on local government finance. They wanted more money, but had no clear idea where it was to come from. They also wanted less ministerial control through the complicated system of percentage grants. But there were no clear-cut policies and no continuing discussions with the central Government on the long-term policy on the finances of local government. Instead, the existing system of rates, supported by grants in aid, was accepted with periodical adjustments and amendments to prevent its total collapse.

For some time, the AMC had been opposed to the system of percentage grants, which involved detailed control over local authorities' projects; instead, they wanted a general grant, not related to specific expenditure. This had been one of the main reforms urged by the associations in the Manpower Committee, and, in March 1957, the minister, Duncan Sandys, proposed informal and confidential discussion on this proposal. As with other such conversations about proposed legislation, it was understood that neither party would be committed, until the approval of Parliament and the councils of the associations had been obtained.

The essence of the proposals was to replace as many as possible of the existing specific grants (mostly on a percentage basis) by a general grant of an amount fixed in advance for several years, and based on the needs and resources of each authority.[29] Thus, local authorities would be more free in how they spent their money, relieved of the pressures that percentage grants involved.

But though the local authority associations welcomed this, with some detailed reservations, it was anathema to the Association of Education Committees, led by its powerful secretary, William Alexander.[30] That association saw it as a device by which the expenditure on education would be reduced. It was argued that, if education no longer had the advantage of a large percentage grant, local authorities would be less inclined to put money into that service rather than any other. In a polemical pamphlet,[31] they roundly condemned the proposals and everyone who supported them.

For some time, the CCA and, to a lesser degree, the AMC, had resented the fact that the Association of Education Committees purported to speak for all educational authorities, while they themselves claimed to do so, too, as the general representatives of local authorities. Moreover, it was Sir William Alexander who spoke for the employing authorities on the Burnham Committee, and not the representatives of the local authority associations. Now the two sides were openly opposed to each other, and yet both were supported by the same local authorities, who financed them both.[32]

The associations – and particularly the CCA – were determined to put an end to the anomalous situation; the CCA developed an education office of its own, directly aimed at superseding the AEC and making that body redundant. However, Sir William Alexander and the Association of Education Committees survived the attack.

But there was conflict also between the CCA and the AMC, as there had been in earlier years. Ever since the end of the war, they had been arguing about the principles to be employed in reorganising local government. After the dissolution of the Local Government Boundary Commission in 1949, they had been invited to put forward their own solutions. The Association of Municipal Corporations was in some difficulty because on the basic question of whether to support a one-tier or a two-tier system, it was divided. The county boroughs naturally backed the one, most of the non-county boroughs the other. After the end of the war, the General Purposes Committee had sought a compromise between the two points of view, but failed to find a solution acceptable both to the larger and to the smaller boroughs. The county borough group thereupon invoked the provision in the association's rules, declaring that a conflict had arisen between the two classes of borough, with the consequence that the association was thereby disabled from expressing any further views on the matter.[33]

Confidential talks now took place between representatives of the association to see whether it was possible to find a generally acceptable scheme. This did not prove possible and the AMC withdrew from the discussions.

The CCA, together with the urban district councils and rural district councils associations, was in favour of a two-tier system, but was aware of the great influence of the AMC, representing as it did the urban areas from which the Labour Party drew most of its strength. It sought the support of the newly formed National Association of Parish Councils and produced a policy statement endorsed by the four associations. Only the AMC was excluded.

The four associations adopted a scheme based on the continuation of the existing system with two main modifications; first, all the county boroughs of under 75,000 population (nineteen) and those in the conurbations (twenty-two) should cease to be county boroughs; and secondly, there should be statutory schemes of delegation to both the district councils and the parish councils, guaranteeing them substantial responsibilities.

This would have meant the immediate reduction of half the county boroughs in England to non-county status. The AMC reacted rapidly with a detailed critique of the scheme,[34] and a set of proposals of its own, in which it roundly declared the one-tier system to be 'the simplest, the most economical, the most democratic and the best', though it threw in a sop to its own second-tier members in a reluctant admission that 'upon local investigation, it will probably be found necessary, for various reasons, in some parts of the country to have a form of two-tier government'. The larger boroughs had, however, taken control, and were shaping the policy of the association.

Battle was thus joined – though, in fact, the officers of the associations remained on good terms with each other, and collaboration continued in many other fields. The associations had proved that they were unlikely ever to reach agreement on substantial reforms, and that, meanwhile, they were more inclined to devote their efforts to attacking each other, like the Kilkenny cats.[35] None the less, the government was reluctant to initiate any major changes in local government structure which did not command the general support of the associations. Their disagreements had at least the negative effect that, for several years, they prevented the government taking any action towards reform.

It was against this background of conflict that Mr Duncan Sandys, when he became Minister of Housing and Local Government in 1954, invited representatives of the five associations to meet him and try to find a basis on which even limited agreement could be reached. As in other matters, he relied on his own ability to bring conflicting points of view into concord, and to produce an agreed solution. This proved to be possible only on the simple principle that any reform should not upset the balance between counties and county boroughs. A statutory local government commission would adjust the boundaries of counties and county boroughs, but outside the conurbations, no change would be made in the general pattern.[36] These arrangements were incorporated into the Local Government Bill of 1958.

So, for a few years, there was peace between the associations; the government proposals for the reform of London government caused no conflicts between them, for only the AMC was substantially involved. It had internal conflicts, which led to Herbert Morrison's resigning the presidency in protest against the association's decision to accept the proposals of the Royal Commission as a basis of discussion.

During this period of peace, the collaboration between the associations grew closer in a number of ways. A joint Local Authorities Management Services Advisory Committee (LAMSAC) was established, and a joint publicity service was set up – the Local Government Information Office. The Local Authorities Conditions of Service Advisory Board (LACSAB) was formed to bring together into one office the administration of the employers' side of all the main negotiating councils and committees, including the police. So, too, were established the Local Government Training Board and the Joint Advisory Committee on Local Authority Purchasing (JACLAP). In all these bodies the associations were able to work together without conflict.

Meanwhile, at the ministry, Dame Evelyn Sharp had been considering the need for a closer look at the calibre and training of people in local government, and, at her suggestion, the associations had agreed to the appointment of two committees to investigate and report on such matters.[37] The statement at the beginning of the Mallaby Committee's report that the committee was appointed by the minister 'at the request of four of the local authority associations'[38] was technically correct, but disguised the fact that the impulse came not from the associations themselves, but from the permanent secretary.

On these matters the four associations were in accord, and

between them they suggested the names of most of the members of the committees. But, before these had reported, the period of comparative calm in their relations with each other came to an end. In 1965, Richard Crossman suddenly announced his intention to reform local government from top to bottom through the medium of a Royal Commission.[39] The associations had once more to look to their defences, and to consider what evidence they should give. Circumstances were, however, different from those of the 1950s. The need for drastic reorganisation was now more widely accepted, and the associations were less secure in their policy of defending their entrenched positions. Some of them feared that the new regional economic planning councils would supersede the elected local authorities, becoming the main subordinate organs of government in the country.[40] The associations each gave evidence to the Royal Commission, and, as before, the County Councils Association recommended what was basically a two-tier system, and the AMC was in favour of a one-tier pattern, under provincial authorities. In broad outline the policy of the CCA was that ultimately adopted by the Conservative Government and formed the basis of the Local Government Act 1972. (A description of the events that led to the acceptance of this form of organisation is given in the final chapter.) Thus the last conflict between the CCA and AMC resulted in a clear victory for the former. Indeed, after reorganisation the AMC ceased to exist as boroughs became indistinguishable from district councils, save in regard to formal status.

When the legislative framework for the new system was being prepared, detailed discussions took place with the associations on such matters as electoral arrangements, civic dignities, the distribution of functions, the allocation of property and the protection and appointment of staff. Naturally the associations were not wholly content with the Bill. They organised a large number of amendments as it went through Parliament; the National Association of Parish Councils alone initiated some 280 amendments affecting the future status and powers of parish and community councils, of which 170 were accepted. All the other associations were busy in the lobbies, jointly or separately, trying to get amendments written into the Bill; the AMC was somewhat embarrassed by the activities of the non-county boroughs group, led by the representatives of Kidderminster, who independently of the association, were lobbying for wider functions for the new district councils.

The constant disagreements between the associations did much to reduce their influence on government policy, as, to a great extent, they balanced each other on the major questions of structural reform. The failure of the associations to speak with a common voice had impressed itself on the Redcliffe-Maud Commission, which said in its report that:

'The associations of local authorities number five (not including the Greater London Council, which belongs to none of them, or the London Boroughs Association). The four main associations do take common action on many local government matters; but representing different types of authority and different kinds of area – counties, towns, urban or rural districts – they are seldom able to present a united front in dealing with central government or to take a collective initiative in national policies. Local authorities ought to be able, on occasion, to present a common local government view and to take the lead in discussions with central government, both nationally and in particular parts of the country affected by common problems. As independent political bodies, representing local interests, they cannot always be agreed on the policies they want. But there are many matters on which they have a common interest and should be able to present it, and to do so forcefully . . .'

'What local government needs is a single, powerful association to look after its interests and to speak for it. Reorganisation will provide the opportunity. We hope that all the new main authorities will join in one association – the metropolitan authorities, the metropolitan district councils and the unitary authorities. And we hope that the London authorities will join too. Neither the metropolitan authorities nor the metropolitan district councils will share all of each other's interests or all those of the unitary authorities. But many of their interests will be common, and they will, above all, share a common interest in the well-being of local government and in its relationship with central government. It would, we believe, be a disaster if, when the new system is established, separate associations of main local authorities were formed. We are convinced that if local government takes that road it will not achieve the right relationship with central government nor the independence and standing in the country that it ought to have.'

This exhortation was carefully considered by the five associations, and in May 1972 their secretaries met to consider whether and how such a single association could be formed, but no agreement was reached.[41] The advantages of amalgamation were obvious, but so were the disadvantages; some were afraid that their voices would be drowned by the louder voices of others; that for example the rural point of view would be overlooked in a body dominated by the more numerous townsmen. Some feared that one political party or another would dominate the new body, whereas, if there were one body for the metropolitan authorities, this would be consistently controlled by the Labour Party, while the County Councils Association, bereft of its more industrial members, would continue much as before. The Parish Councils Association feared that its voice would be but faintly heard among the bellowings of metropolitan county councils. The idea of a loose federation between the associations was considered and rejected. The outcome was that, as before, there were separate independent associations, each looking after the interests of its particular type of local authority. There is still no single authority to speak for local government as a whole. Instead, there are now four associations; the Association of County Councils, direct heir to the CCA, without the metropolitan counties, but including now those urban areas which were the county boroughs; the Association of Metropolitan Authorities, including metropolitan counties and districts and also the GLC and London boroughs – very much the spokesman for the great urban areas dominated by the Labour Party. Thus, for the first time, there is an association covering both upper and lower tiers of government within certain geographical limits. There is a District Councils Association and the National Association of Local Councils which is the National Association of Parish Councils renamed because of the change of name in Wales from parish to community.

NOTES

1   General Report of the Royal Commission on Municipal Corporations in Scotland, p. 19, 1835, [30], xxix.
2   C. A. Cross, unpublished MA thesis, Manchester University, 1954, and B. Keith-Lucas, *The English Local Government Franchise* (1952), pp. 205–8.
3   *County Councils Gazette*, October 1963, p. 276.
4   J. M. Beck, unpublished PhD thesis, University of Kent. *A History of Parish Councils and their Representative Associations, 1894–1970* (1971). The National Council of Social Service played a major part in sponsoring the association.
5   A solicitor, and previously Town Clerk of Lincoln, and Clerk of Kesteven Councy Council. He was succeeded in 1962 by Mr (later Sir) James Swaffield, also a full-time secretary, a solicitor and a former town clerk.

6 Later Lord Simon of Wythenshawe; see Ernest Simon, *A City Council from Within* (1926), pp. 143, 144.

7 See C. A. Cross, op. cit., ch. II.

8 Montagu Harris was author of *Comparative Local Government* (1948), and was President of the International Union of Local Authorities, 1936–48.

9 Succeeded by W. L. Dacey, and (1964) A. C. Hetherington.

10 V. D. Lipman, *Local Government Areas* (1949), p. 170.

11 The discussions were presided over by Lord Onslow, Parliamentary Secretary, who later presided over the Royal Commission. See Lord Onslow, *63 Years* (1944), p. 178.

12 On the AMC side, Sir Harry Pritchard (Secretary), Sir Lewis Beard (Town Clerk of Coventry), Sir William Middlebrook (ex-Lord Mayor of Leeds); on the CCA side, Sir Ryland Adams (Chairman of Executive Committee), Sir Edmund Turton (ex-Chairman of Executive Committee), Lord Strachie (Vice-President), and Mr Taylor. There were also representatives of the UDCA and the RDCA.

13 For details of the report, and the subsequent Local Government Act 1929, see p. 202.

14 See Alec Spoor, *White-Collar Union* (1967), ch. 9, and J. H. Warren, *The Local Government Service* (1952).

15 See Alec Spoor, op. cit., chs. 16 and 17. The principle of compulsory arbitration in case of a dispute between a local authority and officer was established in *NALGO* v. *Bolton Corporation* [1942], 2A11 ER, 425.

16 The best account of their work since 1948 is in ch. 1 of J. A. G. Griffith, *Central Departments and Local Authorities* (1966). See also Evelyn Sharp, *The Ministry of Housing and Local Government* (1969), pp. 27, 28. See also unpublished MA thesis, *The Impact of Local Authority Associations on Local Government Reorganisation in England, 1966–72*, by L. P. Barnhouse, University of West Virginia, 1972; and K. Isaac-Henry, 'local authority associations and local government reform', *Local Government Studies*, vol. I, no. 3, July 1975. The only account of the Association of Education Committees is in the association's own publication, *The First Fifty Years* (1953).

17 Chairman of the General Purposes Committee, 1936–55, of the Housing Committee, 1929–55. See C. A. Cross, op. cit., p. 112; *Municipal Review*, 1956, vol. 27, p. 37.

18 Alderman L. G. H. Aldridge held office for a short time between Sir Miles Mitchell and Sir Francis Hill.

19 There have been a few exceptions to this: Sir Miles Mitchell, Sir William Grimshaw and Sir Francis Hill were elected in recognition of past services to the association.

20 e.g. Somerset County Council Act 1967, secs. 15, 25, 39 and 40.

21 Local Government Elections Act 1956; Parish Councils Act 1957; Physical Training and Recreation Act 1958; Parish Councils and Burial Authorities Act 1970; Dangerous Litter Act 1971.

22 In the discussions on the proposals for the Education Bill, the Association of Education Committees was divided within itself between the representatives of the counties and those of the Part III authorities.

23 The part played by the AMC in relation to the National Fire Service, and the Fire Services Act 1947, is related in detail in C. A. Cross, op. cit., ch. V.

24 Circular No. 96/47.
25 The second half of the terms of reference was drafted by W. L. Dacey, secretary of the CCA.
26 Later Lord Armstrong of Sanderstead, and Head of the Civil Service.
27 1st and 2nd Reports of the *Local Government Manpower Committee*, 1950, Cmd 7870, xiii, and 1951-2, Cmd 8421, xvi.
28 See pp. 170-1 (Central Control).
29 *Local Government Finance*, 1956-7, Cmnd 209, xxvi.
30 Created Lord Alexander of Potterhill in 1974.
31 *The Threat to Education* (1958), with a foreword by Dr W. P. Alexander and Sir Ronald Gould.
32 See *County Councils Gazette*, March 1958, p. 180. There was a similar problem on a lesser scale with other specialised bodies, representing particular aspects of local government, which threatened to break down the power of the major associations.
33 *The Association of Municipal Corporations 1873-1973*, p. 15.
34 Association of Municipal Corporations, *Reorganisation of Local Government in England and Wales*, April 1954.
35 On the controversies of 1949-58, see W. A. Robson, *Local Government in Crisis* (1966).
36 The rules of procedure for the commission were drafted by Mr Dacey, the secretary of the CCA, and, in fact, proved to be so complicated as to spin out the process to inordinate length.
37 See pp. 105-7 *supra*.
38 Originally drafted as 'at the request of the local authority association', but altered to take account of the fact that the Association of Parish Councils had not been involved.
39 See pp. 211-14. Until the Cabinet had agreed and the Queen approved, it was not referred to as a Royal Commission, for reasons of protocol.
40 On 10 November 1964, *The Times* had published a leading article foretelling that the Regional Economic Planning Councils would replace the elected local authorities. George Brown, then Minister for Economic Affairs, had made similar forecasts.
41 See P. G. Richards, *The Local Government Act 1972: Problems of Implementation* (1975), ch. VIII.

Chapter X

REORGANISATION

Boundary Problems 1900–39

When the nineteenth century came to an end, Dr Redlich felt that there was but little remaining to be done to perfect the structure of English democratic local government. There might be a case in abstract logic for some changes, such as a merger of urban and rural government, but

'there again, abstract theory must yield to knowledge and experience. Urban and rural administration cannot be fixed. A system which is condemned by logic may be approved by experience. The reformer need not disdain a picture, so common in the constitutional history of England, of two independent organisations working smoothly side by side, and of old traditions mixing well with new ideas of organisation.'[1]

But yet it was just in this field of the relation between town and country that the major conflicts were about to arise. England was in the process of change from a mainly rural to a mainly urban people; there was a dramatic increase in the population – and this increase was centred in the towns, not in the villages. Inevitably, this led to an expansion in the geographical area of the towns, and an invasion of the rural areas.

In 1888, when Lord Salisbury reluctantly introduced the Local Government Bill, it was proposed that ten major towns should be excluded from the jurisdiction of the new county councils, as 'county boroughs'. When the Bill completed its course in Parliament, the ten had become sixty-one. What had been intended as an exception had become part of the general pattern. There was no general policy of extending the county boroughs, but yet, by 1922, the number had increased to eighty-two, and, by new creations and extensions, about 350,000 acres, with a population of 3 million people, had been lopped off the counties and incorporated into the county boroughs. Moreover, this was the richest land in the counties, being urban areas, high in rateable value.

At first, the county councils had raised little objection to this attrition, but, after the turn of the century, they became increasingly concerned. First, the total expenditure of the counties rose rapidly, particularly on account of their new responsibilities in education. Thus the loss of these highly rated areas became increasingly important. Secondly, the system under which compensation was paid by county boroughs to counties for loss of rateable value was successfully challenged in the courts,[2] and so each new county borough, and each county borough extension, became more obviously a threat to the financial standing of the county.

In 1913 two cases arose which, more than any of their predecessors, affected the well-being of individual counties. Luton and Cambridge both applied for county borough status, and the Local Government Board approved their applications. The effect of this on Cambridgeshire would be to reduce the rateable value of the county to less than half, and to leave no town in the county bigger than Soham, which had a population of only 4,622 people. Luton contained 28 per cent of the rateable value of Bedfordshire, and the county council feared that, if its application was granted, Bedford itself would follow soon after.

In April 1913 the County Councils Association sent a powerful delegation to see the Prime Minister, Mr Asquith, to urge him to institute a public inquiry into the whole matter. He refused, but the County Members managed to defeat the Cambridge and Luton proposals on the floor of the House of Commons, when the provisional order Bill came up for third reading.

A somewhat similar process of urban expansion was taking place at a lower level; new urban districts were being carved out of the rural districts (270 in the period 1889 to 1927), and some 400 urban districts and boroughs had their boundaries extended. So here, too, the urban authorities were encroaching upon the rural.[3]

But not all of these urban authorities were large and substantial towns; in 1927, there were 66 boroughs, 302 urban districts, and 126 rural districts with under 5,000 people. Such authorities were scarcely adequate for the functions of the nineteenth century, certainly not for those of the twentieth. Sixteen urban districts had less than 1,000 inhabitants to support and pay for their services and staff.

The explanation of this multiplication of small district councils was twofold; on the one hand, a number of small towns or large villages provided their own water supply and sewerage. Under the Public Health Act of 1875 and the Local Government Act of 1894, they were thus entitled to be separately rated, and to claim independent status as urban districts. Secondly, when the Unions of Parishes were established for Poor Law purposes under the 1834 Poor Law Act, little attention was paid to county boundaries. By the end of the century, there were still many of these unions (now the rural district areas) which cut across a county boundary. Over a hundred new rural districts had to be created in order to avoid these anomalies, and make the districts fit into the county pattern.[4]

It is not surprising, in the circumstances, that the county councils were alarmed at the continuing erosion of their territory. In 1921, they proposed to the Ministry of Health that a Royal Commission should be appointed to investigate the question. After some hesitation and delay on the part of the minister, Sir Alfred Mond,[5] it was decided in 1923 to appoint a commission 'to investigate the relations between the Councils of Counties, County Boroughs, Non-County Boroughs, Urban Districts, Rural Districts and Parishes, and Parish Meetings; and generally to make recommendations as to their constitution, areas and functions.'[6] The chairman was the Earl of Onslow (Lord Chairman of Committees). Most of the other members were drawn from the field of local government, carefully balanced in numbers between the contending parties. It was an expert, rather than an impartial, commission.

As was to be expected, the outcome of their lengthy deliberations was not a drastic or radical change in the pattern of local government, but rather a compromise between the parties involved. The conflict between the urban and the rural authorities was not resolved, but some of the sting was taken out of it.

The commission published three reports, in 1925, 1928 and 1929.[7] The main recommendations were enacted in a series of statutes. First came the Local Government (County Boroughs and Adjustments) Act of 1926, which was aimed at slowing down the process of creating and extending the county boroughs. From then on, no county borough could be created, except by the expensive and cumbersome procedure of a local Act, and no such Bill could be promoted by a borough unless it had a population of at least 75,000. Boundary extensions also had to be made by Act of Parliament, unless they were unopposed. The effect of this was just what was intended; it acted as a dam to keep back the flood of proposals for boundary extensions and new creations of county boroughs, but, of course, it did not affect the springs that fed that flood. The populations of the county boroughs continued to grow; the suburbs spread more widely into the counties; the demand grew stronger that the whole town, central core and suburbs alike, should be under one administration, with one police force, one education system, one organisation for planning, and for refuse removal.

The second problem – that of the balance of urban and rural authorities at the second level, and of the large number of very small authorities – was dealt with in the Local Government Act of 1929. This Act, introduced by Neville Chamberlain, carried out several of his major proposals; it abolished the guardians, transferring their functions to the county and county borough councils; it reorganised the system of grants in aid; it gave extensive rate relief to industry and agriculture;[8] but, most relevant to the problem of areas, it provided for each county council to carry out every ten years a review of the boundaries of its county districts, and to submit a scheme of reorganisation to the minister. Though the county councils could propose the amalgamation, creation or abolition of urban and rural district councils, boroughs were regarded as sacrosanct, as being created by Royal Charter, and so not appropriate for suppression by administrative action of a county council or a minister.

The outcome of the first reviews, carried out between 1929 and 1938, was that the urban districts were reduced by 159, and the rural districts by 169, and some 1,300 boundaries were altered. Some county councils carried out their reviews with reforming zeal; others did little about it, and there still remained 249 districts with under 5,000 inhabitants.[9] In Oxfordshire, for example, the number of urban and rural districts was reduced from sixteen to nine, but in the neighbouring county of Berkshire there were no very small authorities, and so there was no change apart from minor boundary adjustments. The survival of so many small authorities became increasingly difficult to justify as transport and other technical changes made the market towns and villages less islands in themselves and more part of a wider community.

Meanwhile, the administration of the metropolis presented its own peculiar difficulties; the urban development of London had completely outgrown the boundaries of the County of London; the City remained, a historical relic and anomaly, like the bull's-eye of a target, of which the next ring was the LCC and the outer ring, reaching to the edge of the built-up area, was a hotch-potch of county boroughs, non-county boroughs, urban districts and rural districts. Separate boundaries, defining areas much larger than the county, were used for such functions as the Metropolitan Police, the Metropolitan Water Board, for purposes of transport, traffic control, main drainage and electricity. Furthermore, these services were each provided by separate, appointed bodies, unco-ordinated with the county council, and the great differences in wealth between Westminster and Kensington in West London, and Poplar and Bethnal Green in the East End, were exacerbated by much higher rates in the poorer boroughs.

So, in 1921, a powerful commission was appointed, under Lord Ullswater, a former Speaker of the House of Commons. Unfortunately, the county council was reluctant to propose changes to the existing structure, and the commission was hesitant to consider them. The result was a completely negative report,[10] and a failure of the government to take any effective action to remedy the obvious defects in the government of London.

Any hope of rapid reform was excluded by the approach and the outbreak of war. This also meant that the proposed second round of country reviews of district boundaries outside London never took place. This had the effect, inevitably, of putting a stop to immediate reorganisation, but also strengthened the demand for reform when peace returned.

Post-War Reconstruction
From 1941 onwards there developed widespread public discussion on the need for change in post-war Britain. What started as a stimulant to wartime morale became a powerful movement anticipating post-war improvements. As the end of the war approached a feeling of optimism developed about the brave new world of the future. Local government could not stand aside from this surge of opinion. As early as 1942 the government had invited the local authority associations to submit their views on reconstruction. Apart from a general dislike of the wartime regional commissioners, the replies were predictable. The Association of Municipal Corporations argued for a single-tier system over nearly all the country; the County Councils Association opposed this policy and argued for a drastic reduction in the number of county boroughs; the district councils wanted to be left alone.

Other organisations took a wider view of the problem. A report from the Labour Party favoured a two-tier structure with regional and area authorities. However, as the number of regional authorities proposed was as many as forty, it is clear that smaller units were intended than the word 'regional' would now convey. A report from NALGO sympathised with the concept of all-purpose authorities but it urged that many services need to be planned over wide areas. So the NALGO scheme envisaged provincial councils, indirectly elected by all-purpose authorities, which would plan while their constituent authorities would administer. A Fabian Society pamphlet also advocated planning by regions.[11]

In 1945 the Coalition Government issued a White Paper on the problems of reorganisation.[12] This proposed the establishment of a permanent commission to survey the whole question of local government boundaries outside the County of London[13] and to make such adjustments as might be desirable. Thus it was hoped to avoid the delays and expenses of private Bill procedure, and also to avoid some of the ill-will between counties and county boroughs which this procedure generated. So the Local Government Boundary Commission was established[14] with power to adjust the boundaries of all local authorities, to unite or divide, but not to create or abolish boroughs, for that would encroach upon the Royal Prerogative. The parent Act gave no power to introduce new types of authority. The terms of reference of the commission did not allow them to change the broad pattern of local government; only to push the boundaries this way or that, without altering the basis of the system.

While the commission was at work, the situation was changing. Professor Cole produced a vigorous plea for regional government,[15] but this was the one policy that united conflicting opinions in town halls and county halls – they agreed to oppose it. Meanwhile other legislation was changing local administration. Boundaries were unaltered but the functions of existing authorities changed substantially. The Education Act 1944 had removed education powers from non-county boroughs and urban districts; the new device of delegation gave the counties full financial responsibility and control over major policy decisions. The National Health Service Act 1946 removed a miscellany of personal health service functions from the boroughs and the districts and passed them over to the county. The Police Act 1946 secured the absorption of almost all non-county borough police forces into the county constabularies. The Town and Country Planning Act 1947 transferred planning powers from the boroughs and districts to the counties. The fire service in pre-war days had belonged to the boroughs and the districts; when it was returned to local authorities in 1947 it was handed back to the counties. Thus, while the Local Government Boundary Commission pondered, a very substantial change had taken place, with the second-tier councils, especially those in the larger towns, losing a considerable proportion of their duties.

The commission ultimately came to the conclusion that it

could not make sense of its job by merely pushing boundaries about; it must also be able to deal with the powers and functions of local government. So, after two years, during which it had moved no boundary a single yard in any direction, it submitted to the minister, Aneurin Bevan, a remarkable report.[16] This stated:

'We have definitely reached the conclusion that, in many areas – and these cover the great bulk of the population – our present powers and instructions do not permit the formation of local government units as effective and convenient as in our opinion they should be . . . Our experience also confirms the statement made recently in Parliament by the Minister of Health (Aneurin Bevan): "Everyone who knows about local government feels that it is nonsense to talk about functions and boundaries separately. They have to be taken together . . ." We have no jurisdiction over functions.'

The commission then went on to sketch the outline of the pattern they would have recommended, had they wider power. In short, they proposed that only the largest of the county boroughs should retain their status as single-tier authorities. The rest of the county boroughs, and the larger non-county boroughs, should be formed into a new category of 'most purpose authorities', known as 'new county boroughs'. The larger counties should be divided, and the smaller united with their neighbours.

The language of the report suggested that everyone was either to be left alone or promoted, and nobody demoted. The probable objections to the merger of counties were forestalled by the promises that these proposals would have no effect whatever 'on the name of a geographical county, on county institutions, on diocesan and other religious organisations, and on all the social, sporting and other activities – for example, qualification for a county cricket team[17] – usually associated with a county'.

It was, however, these proposals – to merge county councils, particularly Hereford and Worcester[18] – that aroused the deepest hostility and the profoundest distaste. Perhaps the strongest political pressure came, however, from the county boroughs, many of which would, in fact, if not in name, lose their status, and many of which, like the central government, were Labour-controlled.

The commission had not pleased the minister by quoting his own words back at him; in the country at large they had stirred up a hornets' nest of resentment. For a year, Mr Bevan took no action; then he met the commission with its chairman, Sir Malcolm Trustram Eve.[19] In a heated discussion, he announced his decision to abolish the commission. So it ended, without having moved any boundaries at all. The minister assured the House of Commons that 'the review of the structure and functions of Local Government is a constant preoccupation of the Government'.[20]

There were two central reasons for the inaction of the Labour Government. Ministers were not prepared to face the almost united hostility of local councils. With the next general election approaching, local government reform could not be other than politically damaging. Yet there were other long-term considerations which dampened interest in the subject. Throughout its history the Labour Party had drawn on the Fabian Society for intellectual stimulus and, at least since 1920, the Fabians had become doubtful about the value of local government as a vehicle for socialist policies.[21] It was a daunting task to try to promote fundamental change through a multitude of independent local councils. Socialism would be achieved more readily through 'democratic centralism'. Local councils would be forced to follow desirable policies through receiving instructions from socialist ministers, and the task of enforcing ministerial wishes might be easier if there were fewer councils to persuade or perhaps coerce. It was this policy that the Labour Government had followed between 1945 and 1948 by moving functions from lower-tier to upper-tier authorities. For this purpose, boundaries were largely irrelevant and the Boundary Commission could be ignored.

The conflict between counties and county boroughs, however, was as acute as ever. Several of the larger boroughs, including Ealing, Poole and Luton, were trying to win county borough status, but the government regularly opposed and defeated their private Bills, on the grounds that general reorganisation was coming soon, and should not be prejudiced. The years went by, and still no policy of general reorganisation was promulgated. Minister quickly succeeded minister[22] and still no policy was announced. In some areas (particularly in Middlesex), relations between local authorities were becoming unduly and embarrassingly strained.[23] The rival local authority associations engaged in a pamphlet war, proposing, each in turn, the total or general extinction of one- or two-tier government.[24]

When Duncan Sandys was the minister, he became impatient with being asked by his civil servants again and again to oppose proposals for the creation of new county boroughs, lest he thereby prejudice the general policy which the government would propose. At the same time, he was assured that a general policy was impossible because the local authorities, and their associations, would never agree. So he called the parties together to see what measure of agreement could be achieved.

Out of this emerged a concordat. The general balance between counties and county boroughs should not be disturbed but, within those limits, the system should be tidied up and improved by two new commissions – one for England and one for Wales. They should have no power to alter the functions or powers of councils, except in the great urban areas, or 'conurbations', where they could work out new schemes. Their authority would not run beyond the top level of counties and county boroughs except in the conurbations, or 'special review areas', where they could work out a new pattern of authorities. Below that, each county (after its boundaries had been settled by the commission) should carry out a review of the districts within the county. Whereas the previous commission had had no jurisdiction over boroughs, this limitation was now lifted. However, if a small borough was merged into the surrounding rural district, it was proposed that it should survive as a separate entity – a parish council, with the trappings of a borough and the title of 'rural borough'. All these suggestions were embodied in a series of White Papers[25] which formed the basis of the Local Government Act 1958.

London and Middlesex
Middlesex presented a unique problem; it contained a number of boroughs which, if judged in terms of population, could expect to gain the county borough status for which they were clamouring. But to grant their demands would have made gaping holes in the county, so that Middlesex County Council would have been left with an oddly shaped residue to administer. As virtually the whole of Middlesex had become an extension of the London conurbation, there was every reason to treat it as part of the metropolis.

In opening the debate on the White Papers in the House of Commons on 29 July 1957, Mr Henry Brooke, the Minister of Housing and Local Government, announced the government's intention to appoint a Royal Commission on the problems of Greater London, including the whole of Middlesex. So later that year, a commission was appointed, with Sir Edwin Herbert[26] as chairman.

Though the most acute part of the problem was the virtual

breakdown of relations between Middlesex County Council and the district councils in its area, there were other difficulties too. The boundaries of the County of London had been fixed in 1888, and had then been taken from those of the old Metropolitan Board of Works established in 1855. Since then, no change had been made, although the urban area and the population had expanded enormously. It had become apparent that a new metropolitan authority was needed, to cover not only the County of London, but also the County of Middlesex and parts of Kent, Surrey and Essex. The Clement Davies Report in 1949[27] had stressed the immediate urgency of establishing an authority which could co-ordinate the planning of Greater London in the post-war period of expansion. Nine county councils and three county borough councils were failing to achieve any plausible plan for the growth of London. Furthermore, the proposed Local Government Commission for England had to know what the area of Greater London was to be, before it could get to work on the Home Counties.

The evidence given to the Royal Commission by the local authorities was negative. Most of them concentrated on defending their existing status and boundaries; the LCC 'refused to discuss any question which did not relate directly to the Administrative County of London – an area which they insisted was still coterminous with London'.[28] Much of the evidence of Middlesex County Council was devoted to polemics against the larger boroughs in the county. The London Labour Party (which controlled the LCC) argued strongly for the retention of the existing arrangements. The Conservatives, on the other hand, had long disliked the LCC (control of which seemed to be permanently in the hands of the Labour Party) and argued for the transfer of functions to the boroughs, and the replacement of the LCC by an indirectly elected co-ordinating body.

The Labour attitude was partly dictated by a fear that the extension of the boundaries to include the middle-class suburbs of Kent and Surrey might tip the electoral balance against them. Herbert Morrison had, however, argued in the past for such an extension,[29] and Professor W. A. Robson's evidence given on behalf of the Greater London Group in favour of such extensions was clearly very influential.

The commission ultimately reached a unanimous recommendation that the area of London government should be extended from 75,000 to 510,000 acres; the population would rise from 3,200,000 to 8,700,000. Middlesex as a local government unit would disappear, and the main burden of local government would be borne by fifty-two 'London boroughs', with a new Greater London Council responsible for education, planning, main roads, fire and ambulance services. The corporation of the City of London was to be left untouched as an anomaly beyond the limits of logic.[30]

Herbert Morrison and the Labour Party attacked the proposals bitterly. But the Conservative Government decided to press ahead with the necessary legislation as quickly as possible, even though it would mean the disruption of many efficiently run services in the County of London – for they did not deny the efficiency of the LCC. Some changes were made to the Royal Commission's proposals. The number of boroughs was reduced to thirty-two so that they would be large enough to be effective education authorities. The Inner London Education Authority (ILEA) was formed to administer this service in the former LCC area: thus, the old LCC Education Department continued in being and the inner London boroughs were differentiated from those on the periphery by having no education powers. In addition, some residential areas[31] on the fringe of the metropolis were excluded from the new Greater London. This change did have some political implications in that it slightly reduced the chance of a Conservative majority on the new GLC.

The Bill was contested vigorously in both Commons and Lords. Herbert Morrison, now Lord Morrison of Lambeth, organised the opposition in the Upper House. His biographers comment that this campaign was 'a personal crusade, fanatically, sadly, almost pathetically, fighting a doomed battle to preserve one of the great symbols of his life's political work'.[32] The Bill was passed without undue difficulty in spite of some protracted debates, and the new régime commenced on 1 April 1965. The Labour view that the measure was a slick manoeuvre to avoid socialist rule in the capital proved groundless when Labour won a handsome victory in the first election for the new authority. Conservatives won control in 1967, but Labour were victorious again in 1973.

The Local Government Commission and the Redcliffe-Maud Commission

Meanwhile, outside London, the Local Government Act 1958 had authorised the appointment of the two commissions, for England and for Wales. So they were appointed, and got to work, the English one under the chairmanship of Sir Henry Hancock, the Welsh under Sir Guildhaume Myrddin-Evans, a retired civil servant.

In England, the Local Government Commission found its task

slower and more difficult than had been expected. The procedure laid down was one which involved a great deal of discussion with everyone concerned, in each area in turn, at each stage. The commissioners first invited local authorities, local and national bodies of all sorts to get in touch with them, explaining their points of view. Then the commission started a series of visits to the area, to discuss matters with the local people. Not only local authorities were heard, but also political parties, Women's Institutes, sports clubs, Boy Scouts, trades councils and old people's clubs. After that, the commission, with the aid of its staff, prepared and published its draft proposals. There then followed another round of written and verbal representations about the draft proposals, after which the commission again withdrew to London to prepare its final report. When this was published, the minister instituted the public inquiry, and so, for a third time, the arguments were deployed.[33] Inevitably, the process took a long time and local authorities became impatient for progress. Furthermore, legal difficulties caused further delays.[34]

The minister, Sir Keith Joseph, found the matter far from simple. One of the first recommendations was that the County of Rutland should be suppressed, its territory being split between two neighbouring counties.[35] Rutland had a population of only 25,000. It had no grammar schools, and no technical college. In education, welfare and other services, it relied on the provision made by the adjoining counties. It was unable to provide itself with all the services that a county should, or that its inhabitants could, reasonably demand. The continued existence of Rutland was indefensible on administrative grounds.

However, the public reaction to these proposals was clear and loud. Led by the chairman of the county council, Sir Kenneth Ruddle, the people of Rutland protested strongly.[36] The services available to them were very good; the rates were low; the scale of operations made democracy a reality; the inhabitants were no less healthy or happy or well-educated than those of other counties.

Though in their final proposals the commission planned to modify the scheme by putting the whole of Rutland into Leicestershire,[37] this did not placate the men of Rutland. To the country as a whole the question presented itself as a conflict between brave little Rutland and overbearing bureaucracy: David and Goliath.

The minister bowed to the storm, and Rutland was reprieved. But other problems were piling up, on Tyneside, in Lancashire and elsewhere; so, by the time the Labour Party came into office in 1964, there was a considerable accumulation of proposals awaiting decisions from the minister.

Richard Crossman was the new Minister of Housing and Local Government – inexperienced, brash and brilliant. He was bored by problems of local government reform, and strangely ignorant about local government. But when he came to look at the pile of accumulated recommendations from the commission, his policy began to take shape.

He came to see clearly two things – that the adjustments recommended by the commission would never avoid the endemic war between county councils and county boroughs, and that extensions of county borough areas involved in many cases the incorporation of 'residential' (and so Conservative) suburbs, which would, when translated into terms of parliamentary constituencies, mean endangering the Labour majority in up to forty seats. So he recorded in his diary,

'I've also had to deal during these first five weeks with the whole question of the Local Government Boundary Commission.[38] I mentioned this subject since discussing this at length with the Dame[39] some days ago, I've talked to my colleagues about it, and I've got them to agree after a great deal of humming and hawing that I can't delay my decisions on the recommendations of the Commission any further, and that I am bound to make and announce these decisions in the near future. They are my personal decisions. Not even the Prime Minister can influence me in them. My colleagues know this, and this gives me an odd detached power in dealing with them. After all, I can make or mar George Brown at Belper, Bert Bowden in Leicester, Bill Wilson in Coventry, Ted Short in Newcastle; each of them knows that as Minister of Housing the decision I make may be life or death for them in terms of representation at Westminster.'[40]

So, with these two considerations influencing his mind, he searched mentally for a solution. Dame Evelyn Sharp was urging him to leave the commission to get on with its statutory task of adjusting the boundaries of counties and county boroughs, but his mind was moving towards a much more drastic remedy.

In September 1965, he was due to talk to the annual meeting of the Association of Municipal Corporations at Torquay. He had agreed with his civil servants that he would speak about press relations and about the ethics of the councillor.

But Dame Evelyn was on holiday. The coast was clear. After a quick word on the telephone with the Prime Minister, he changed the speech, to be an announcement of a decision to appoint a powerful commission which would reform local government from top to bottom.

Having done this, the minister had to face his indignant permanent secretary, placate the Cabinet, and deal with the existing Local Government Commission.

The permanent secretary was appalled by what he had done, and by the subterfuge of doing it while she was away. However, she loyally accepted the position. When, in January 1966, the time came to get Cabinet approval, she got busy organising the Cabinet decision through the channels of the permanent secretaries – 'the Cabinet was effectively rigged; and this was a tactic which my Dame operates with more skill than anybody else I have ever seen'.[41]

Meanwhile, the old commission had come to an end, with a strange, inconclusive meeting with the minister, which left them all wondering whether they had resigned, been dismissed or still existed. It had achieved only a modest degree of reorganisation, and even that was not destined to last. Greater Birmingham had been rearranged as five county boroughs: Teeside, Torbay, Luton and Solihull had become county boroughs. The Isle of Ely was amalgamated with Cambridgeshire, and the Soke of Peterborough with Huntingdonshire, but other proposals had been either delayed or rejected.

A chairman had to be found for the new Royal Commission. Sir Alan Bullock was offered the post, but refused; Lord Beeching,[42] Sir Norman Chester, Lord James of Rusholme, Mr Justice Ungoed-Thomas and Lord Widgery were all considered before the minister decided on Sir John Maud.[43] The membership was soon settled; it included Dame Evelyn Sharp (now retired and a peer), Mr T. Dan Smith, and Mr Derek Senior,[44] a journalist of pronounced views, who had just published somewhat dogmatic opinions on local government reform.

The terms of reference were wide:

'to consider the structure of local government in England, outside Greater London, in relation to its existing functions; and to make recommendations for authorities and boundaries, and for functions and their division, having regard to the size and character of areas in which these can be most effectively exercised, and the need to sustain a viable system of local democracy.'

This left obscure the question whether the commission was to deal with local government finance, and it made no mention of the possibility of some sort of regional organisation, which was to be referred later to the Crowther Commission on the Constitution.[45]

The ministries were the first to give evidence, and, not purely by chance, they all advocated a drastic reduction in the number of local authorities to thirty or forty major councils, with or without a second tier of minor authorities. It was made clear that this opinion, while representing the view of the ministries, did not in any way represent the ministerial view.[46] The commission listened also to the ideas of the local authority associations. Each organisation defended its own interest. The County Councils Association advocated a two-tier system. The AMC, dominated by the thinking of the county boroughs, favoured a one-tier pattern under provincial authorities. The rural districts submitted a report of their own but, in general, this supported the county view. The AMC apart, there was substantial agreement between the associations and co-operation behind the scenes. Thus the rural districts and the parish councils agreed informally not to oppose or attack each other's evidence which urged the retention of more and smaller authorities. The idea of extending the parish council concept into the towns was sympathetically received by the commission.[47]

One major factor in the commission's thinking was the report of the Seebohm Committee on Local Authority and Allied Personal Social Services.[48] This committee had urged that the social services should no longer be split up between the various bodies and tiers of local government which then provided them, and asked the Royal Commission to recommend that housing should be in the same hands as the other personal social services.

They also found that the system of delegation of functions by one authority to another had proved unsatisfactory. Though it might have eased relations by introducing a degree of flexibility into an otherwise rigid system, it had in fact resulted in bad relations between authorities, and in the waste of scarce resources. The principal associations of local authorities were opposed to the system, and the ministries disliked it;[49] in Middlesex the system had been part of the cause of the bad relations between the county council and the district councils.

These and other considerations led the commission to the conclusion that, in the new pattern of local government, the control of the social services, housing, education, planning, and all the other major functions should be in the hands of one single set of local authorities. Furthermore, these authorities should no longer be divided into urban and rural councils; that old dichotomy, dating from the Municipal Corporations Act of 1835, should give way to a recognition that town and country were essentially complementary, rather than conflicting, in their interests. In three great urban metropolitan areas based on Liverpool, Manchester and Birmingham, they proposed a two-tier structure, with a metropolitan authority dealing with planning, transport, water supply, police and fire services over the whole metropolis.

Though most of the power would be vested in the fifty-eight primary councils (somewhat awkwardly called 'unitary authorities'), the commission saw also a great need for more intimate bodies, acting as spokesmen for communities, and providing services of any sort ouside the statutory powers of the unitary authorities. These 'local councils' should be free to provide (with that exception) whatever services they saw fit, without reference to the stultifying doctrine of *ultra vires*. They should have power to levy a rate, with no statutory limit of amount.

At the other end of the scale, they proposed indirectly elected provincial councils, working out strategic plans for the economic, educational and social development of the province. These would replace some of the existing regional bodies, such as the arts and sports councils.

A Memorandum of Dissent was submitted by Derek Senior, who refused to accept the commission's recommendations. He stuck rigidly to the doctrine enunciated in his book.[50] He argued for 35 city regions in place of the commission's 58 unitary authorities, and the introduction of an additional tier of 148 district councils.

The public reaction to the report was not enthusiastic. In parts it was positively hostile, although the members of the commission spoke widely at public meetings in favour of their scheme. But they failed to explain adequately the democratic aspects of the proposed pattern, and the role of the local councils.

The County Councils Association was in general favourable to the proposals though it argued that the provincial councils should be only advisory, and it thought that some of the proposed unitary authorities were too small. While the proposal to merge the county boroughs into the counties was welcome, the association regretted the disappearance of the district councils. It joined with the two associations of district councils in what came to be called the 'tripartite agreement' to urge on the government the need for an intermediate level, between unitary authorities and local councils.

The AMC was once more divided within itself. At its annual meeting at Scarborough in September 1969, the non-county boroughs succeeded in carrying a resolution in favour of an intermediate tier. But ultimately the association came down in favour of a system of unitary authorities (but with 130 to 140 such bodies,[51] instead of the commission's proposal for only 58) with an upper tier of provincial authorities. It would, however, be false to see this as a direct conflict of interest between county and non-county boroughs. The larger non-county boroughs tended to align themselves with the county boroughs, whose status they hoped to achieve. It was more a division between the larger and the smaller boroughs.

The National Association of Parish Councils found the proposals for local councils to be very satisfactory – a real recognition of the need for local authorities with wide powers at the lowest level. It welcomed this part of the report enthusiastically, and doggedly refused to be drawn into the arguments and conflicts about the unitary authorities, provincial councils and intermediate tiers of government.[52] It did, however, express fears that, in too many of the suggested unitary authority areas, the rural population would be heavily outnumbered by the townsmen.

The Rural District Councils Association reacted most strongly against the proposals. They alone of the types of authority then existing would have no after-life in the new dispensation. There would be no successors to the rural districts.

At the annual meeting at Blackpool, the association resolved to reject the report entirely, and to devote the sum of £40,000 to a campaign against the proposals.

The campaign was based on the representation of the rural districts as the champions of small-scale and intimate local government, and the proposition that the commission's proposals would create a remote and impersonal system of government – therein almost ignoring the part of the report that related to the 'local councils'. So it started a large-scale campaign on the slogan 'Don't vote for R. E. Mote'[53] – a plea which some people found confusing as there was no opportunity to vote for or against the Royal Commission's proposals, and some uncertainty about who R. E. Mote was: he was represented in the cartoons as a bowler-hatted civil servant.

Wales

The terms of reference of Redcliffe-Maud had not included either Scotland or Wales. A separate commission, under Lord Wheatley, was appointed to consider the special problems of Scottish local government; events in Wales followed a different course. Under the Act of 1958, a separate commission had been appointed for Wales, not to review the whole structure, but to adjust the boundaries within the existing pattern.

The Welsh Commission was faced with the problem of the wealth and population of Wales being concentrated in the industrial South and the 'landlady belt' of the northern seaside towns. In between the two lay the mountains, thinly inhabited, and very Welsh in sentiment and speech. Of the thirteen existing counties, six had populations of less than 60,000. The commission's draft proposals[54] published in May 1961, were based on the conception of reducing the counties to five – Glamorgan, and four new counties, each linking part of the agricultural centre to the wealth of the north or the south. Long, straggling areas would result, in which Welsh-speaking farmers from the mountains of central Wales would be heavily outnumbered by the very different peoples of the north and south. Protest was immediate and strong.

In their Final Report,[55] they changed the pattern. Now they proposed seven counties, instead of five, including one great central county, of the agricultural heart of Wales. The new counties would not be built by amalgamations of existing counties, but would be defined afresh, with new boundaries. Again, there was strong opposition.

But the commission had apparently little faith in its own recommendations. The report explained that it was not possible to make really satisfactory proposals unless the commission had powers to deal with functions as well as boundaries, and work out a new pattern of local government appropriate to Wales:

'Boundaries cannot reasonably be divorced from functions or from finance. We have tried faithfully to carry out the task assigned to us. We venture to believe that, within the limits imposed upon us, our recommendations are deserving of serious consideration. But we cannot help wondering whether, had we been allowed to consider at least the redistribution of functions, we might not have done a better job . . . That we were not permitted to consider the redistribution of functions was, we believe, for reasons we have already stated, a serious mistake, and was, in fact, a disservice to Wales.'[56]

This was tantamount to an invitation to the minister to ignore the report and start again.

Meanwhile, the pressure of Welsh nationalism was growing. The Conservatives had attempted to appease it by nominating a Minister for Welsh Affairs, but this was little more than an additional title for the Minister of Housing and Local Government.

After consultation between the departments, it was agreed that in Wales the procedure through an open, semi-public commission should be abandoned. Instead, there should be a working party within the department, searching for a solution after consultation with the most influential people in Welsh local government.

The working party had nearly completed its proposals when Crossman suddenly announced the appointment of the Royal Commission under Sir John Maud. The Welsh Office was very reluctant to abandon its own exercise, and made this clear at ministerial and official levels. The Ministry of Housing and Local Government, having been privy to the scheme to set up the working party, could scarcely object to its continuation.

So Wales was left out of the purview of the Royal Commission, and the working party continued with its consideration of a scheme which included an elected Council of Wales, with executive power, drawn partly from central and partly from local government. Below this would be a two-tier pattern of local authorities.

The Welsh scheme was not welcomed in Whitehall, as it clearly would be difficult to fit in with the alternatives that were being considered by the Redcliffe-Maud Commission. Apparently the Secretary of State for Wales, Cledwyn Hughes, put the proposals before the cabinet, but they were rejected in part at least because the introduction of an elected assembly for Wales would make it almost impossible to resist the creation of a similar body for Scotland, and this was not at that time acceptable to the government.[57] So, when in July 1967 the White Paper[58] was published, the scheme was much reduced from this devolutionary pattern, and the Welsh Council was to be an appointed body with only advisory functions.

Instead of a firm proposal for an elected Council of Wales with executive power, there was a tentative suggestion of a nominated body with advisory functions. Below that would be a pattern of five counties (Gwynedd, Powys, Dyfed, Glamorgan and Gwent), and three county boroughs (Cardiff, Swansea and Newport). The county districts were to be reduced from 164 to 36. The parish councils were to be strengthened, and similar bodies set up in the towns, if the people wanted them. All these councils were to be called not parish councils but 'common councils' – a proposal which aroused immediate resentment.[59]

In general, the county councils welcomed the proposals, but the boroughs resented them.[60] But they had yet to be fitted into whatever pattern might emerge in England, for there was an obvious case against too great a divergence between the two countries.

Richard Crossman, who had by this time been moved from the Ministry of Housing and Local Government to be Lord President of the Council, regarded the Welsh proposals as reactionary, inadequate and miserable. He tried to get them revised, as part of a major scheme of devolution, involving a Parliament for Wales. He foresaw the growing demand for devolution as the most explosive issue at the next election. But, though he got the matter referred to a small committee of ministers, he was in the end forced to accept the proposals of the Welsh Office for a very weak nominated Welsh regional council with no executive power and a reorganisation of local government which did not fit in completely with the English pattern.[61]

Conclusion

The Labour Government decided to adopt the Royal Commission's scheme for England with minor alterations, including the extension of the metropolitan, two-tier pattern to two more areas – Portsmouth–Southampton and West Yorkshire,[62] and with minor adaptation for Wales. As soon as possible, the ministry started preparing a Bill to implement the proposals, discussing the details with the local authority Associations. Had the government remained in power, the Redcliffe-Maud scheme would no doubt have been duly enacted by Parliament, and brought into being. But, for reasons quite extraneous to local government, the Conservatives won the election of June 1970, and reconsidered the whole question of local government reform.

It was now seventy years since Dr Redlich had expressed his admiration for the system of English local government. Apart from the abolition of the boards of guardians in 1929, there had been no major change in the pattern outside London. County boroughs had multiplied and extended into the counties, but no general policy had been evolved to bring the system up to date; the reforms that had taken place had been piecemeal and inadequate.

It was not for lack of advice that no general reform had been achieved; there had been three major commissions since 1945, and many departmental committees; political parties and academic critics had published proposals, but still very little had happened. This no doubt was partly due to the fact that there was an enormous weight of influence in favour of retaining the existing system. The local authorities were represented by their five associations, the larger of which have been described as the most powerful pressure groups in Britain. All this influence was deployed against any substantial change while, on the other hand, there was no pressure group in favour of a new revised system. Furthermore, the county councils and borough councils had, through their political affiliations, very close contacts with their members of Parliament, many of whom had served on the local councils, and been selected as candidates by party groups consisting greatly of local councillors.[63] There were no such voices in Parliament for reorganisation.

But yet the case for reorganisation was strong, and had been growing stronger ever since the beginning of the century. Above all, the isolation of the village or the small town had broken down since the invention of motor cars.

NOTES

1   *Local Government in England* (1903), vol. II, p. 115.
2   *West Hartlepool Corporation* v. *Durham County Council* [1907], AC 246.
3   V. D. Lipman, *Local Government Areas, 1834–1945* (1949), ch. 5.
4   Royal Commission on *Local Government*, evidence of Sir Arthur Robinson, Appendix CIII, Statement C, p. 1812, (HMSO, 1928).
5   Later Lord Melchett.
6   Final Report of the Royal Commission on *Local Government*, 1928–9, Cmd 3436, xv. The terms of reference quoted above are as extended by Royal Warrant of 4 August 1926. See pp. 183, 186.
7   *Constitution and Extension of County Boroughs*, 1924–5, Cmd 2506, xiv. 2nd Report on *Areas and Functions*, 1928–9, Cmd 3213, viii. Final Report on *Functions and Constitutions of Local Authorities*, 1929–30, Cmd 3436, xv.
8   See pp. 137–40.
9   Lipman, op. cit., ch. V. See also P. G. Richards, 'Local government reform, smaller towns and the countryside', *Urban Studies*, vol. 2, no. 2, November 1965, pp. 147–62.
10 Report of the Royal Commission on *Local Government of Greater London*, 1923, Cmd 1830, xii. See also W. A. Robson, *The Government and Misgovernment of London* (1948), ch. XIV.
11 See Report on the *Future of Local Government* by the Labour Party Central Committee on Reconstruction (1943); the Interim Report of the NALGO Reconstruction Committee on Reconstruction (1943); *Regional Government* by Regionaliter (1942).
12 *Local Government in England and Wales during the Period of Reconstruction*, 1944–5, Cmd 6579, x.
13 A separate committee, under Lord Reading, was considering the boundaries within the County of London. It never reported.

14　Local Government (Boundary Commission) Act 1945.

15　G. D. H. Cole, *Local and Regional Government* (1947).

16　Report of the Local Government Boundary Commission for the year 1947, 1947–8, (86), xiii.

17　In those days, cricketers could only play for a county in which they had qualification by birth or residence.

18　e.g. Lionel Curtis in *The Times*, 19 January 1948: 'Between the home where I was born in Herefordshire and the Worcestershire boundary which runs along the ridge of the Malvern Hills, is the parish of Colwall . . . In the bottom of the valley is the farm where William Langland, born in Ledbury, worked as a serf. Overlooking the valley is a glen between the Herefordshire Beacon and the Malvern Hills where Piers Plowman lay down to sleep by the primewell and saw in a vision the English society of his time (Edward III), the King, bishops, nobles, squires, freemen and serfs . . . Is the birthplace of English poetry now to be wiped from the map?'

19　Created Lord Silsoe in 1968.

20　466 HC Deb., 27 June 1949, col. 759.

21　A. Sancton, 'British socialist theory of the division of power by area', *Political Studies*, vol. 24, 1976, pp. 158–70.

22　Aneurin Bevan, 1945–50; H. Dalton, 1950–1; Harold Macmillan, 1951–4; D. Sandys, 1954–7; H. Brooke, 1957–60.

23　See Dame Evelyn Sharp, *The Ministry of Housing and Local Government* (1969), ch. III.

24　*Reorganisation of Local Government* (Association of Municipal Corporations, 1954); *Reorganisation of Local Government in England and Wales* (County Councils Association, Urban District Councils Association, Rural District Councils Association and National Association of Parish Councils, 1954); *Local Government Organisation* (Association of Municipal Corporations, 1954).

25　*Areas and Status of Local Authorities in England and Wales*, 1956, Cmd 9831; *The Functions of County Councils and County District Councils in England and Wales*, 1957, Cmnd 161; and *Local Government Finance*, 1957, Cmnd 209.

26　Created Lord Tangley in 1964.

27　Report of the *London Planning Administration Committee* (HMSO, 1949).

28　Report of the Royal Commission on *Local Government in Greater London*, p. 44, 1959–60, Cmnd 1164, xviii.

29　H. Morrison, *How Greater London is Governed* (1935), ch. XV.

30　Report of the Royal Commission on *Local Government in Greater London, 1957–60*, 1957–60, Cmnd 1164, xviii.

31　Banstead, Caterham and Warlingham, Cheshunt, Esher, Staines, Sunbury-on-Thames, Walton and Weybridge and parts of Chigwell and Epsom and Ewell. See G. Rhodes, *The Government of London: The Struggle for Reform* (1970), chs 10 and 11.

32　B. Donoughue and G. W. Jones, *Herbert Morrison* (1973), p. 559.

33　See, e.g., Report No. 9, *Report and Proposals for the Lincolnshire and East Anglia General Review*, appendices 2–5, (HMSO, 1965).

34　*Wednesbury Corporation and Others* v. *Minister of Housing and Local Government* [1965], 1 All. ER 186. Five local authorities in the West Midlands area challenged the validity of the public inquiry into the proposals of the commission, on the grounds that the inspectors failed to make recommendations to the minister, and that they were unwilling to consider alternative proposals. Their argument was rejected.

35 *Draft Proposals,* published 29 February 1960. Most of the county would have been joined to Leicestershire, but the borough of Stamford and Ketton Rural District would have been incorporated into a new county composed of Cambridgeshire, the Isle of Ely, the Soke of Peterborough and Huntingdonshire.
36 See *The Case for Rutland* (1960), published by Rutland County Council.
37 Report No. 3, *Report and Proposals for the East Midlands General Review Area* (HMSO, 1961).
38 Throughout the diary he calls the Local Government Commission for England by the wrong name.
39 Dame Evelyn Sharp, Permanent Secretary 1955–66, created Baroness Sharp in 1966.
40 R. H. S. Crossman, *The Diaries of a Cabinet Minister,* vol. I (1975), pp. 87, 88 (6 December 1964). Crossman seems to have over-estimated the probable consequences of the suggested boundary changes.
41 R. H. S. Crossman, op. cit., vol. I, p. 441.
42 Cecil King, *The Cecil King Diary,* 1972, p. 59.
43 Created Lord Redcliffe-Maud in 1967.
44 Former local government and planning correspondent for the *Guardian.* His views were expressed in a chapter of D. Senior (ed.), *The Regional City* (1966).
45 729 HC Deb., 24 May 1966, col. 291. George Brown, First Secretary of State, was proposing that his Regional Planning Councils should take over physical as well as economic planning. Richard Crossman defeated this idea. (R. H. S. Crossman, op. cit., vol. I, p. 89).
46 739 HC Deb., 23 January 1967, col. 201.
47 For the evolution of the commission's scheme, see B. Wood, *The Process of Local Government Reform, 1966–74* (1976).
48 1967–8, Cmnd 3703, xxxii.
49 See P. G. Richards, *Delegation in Local Government* (1956), and Report of the Royal Commission on *Local Government in England,* vol. I, pp. 41–2, 1968–9, Cmnd 4040, xxxviii.
50 D. Senior (ed.), op. cit.
51 *Municipal Review Supplement,* November 1969.
52 National Association of Parish Councils, *Statement on Redcliffe-Maud Report,* October 1969.
53 See Rural District Councils Association, *Local Not Remote* (1969).
54 Local Government Commission for Wales, *Draft Proposals,* 1961.
55 Local Government Commission for Wales, *Report and Proposals for Wales,* (HMSO, 1963).
56 ibid., paras. 14 and 16.
57 Bruce Wood, *The Process of Local Government Reform,* p. 121, and J. P. Mackintosh, *The Devolution of Power* (1968), p. 147.
58 *Local Government in Wales,* Cmnd 3340.
59 See National Association of Parish Councils, Memorandum to the Secretary of State, 21 November 1967.
60 County Councils Association, Memorandum on the White Paper on Local Government in Wales, *Municipal Review Supplement,* March 1969, pp. 46–50.
61 *Diaries of a Cabinet Minister,* vol. II (1976), pp. 344 and 401.
62 *Reform of Local Government in England,* 1969–70, Cmnd 4276, xviii.
63 See W. J. M. Mackenzie, 'The conventions of local government',

Public Administration, 29, 1951, pp. 345–56; D. E. Butler, 'Local government in Parliament', *Public Administration*, 31, 1953, pp. 46–7; W. J. M. Mackenzie, 'Local government in Parliament', *Public Administration*, 32, 1954, pp. 409–23; B. Keith-Lucas, 'Local government in Parliament', *Public Administration*, 33, 1955, pp. 207–10.

Chapter XI

THE 1972 ACT

The Construction of a New System
Although the Labour Government accepted the broad outline of
the 1969 Report of the Royal Commission, little popular enthusiasm for its proposals was apparent. There was rather more
evidence of support for Mr Derek Senior's Memorandum of
Dissent, not for its detailed proposals, but because it required
the maintenance of a two-tier system of councils. In the Commons debate on the Report, Mr Peter Walker, the Conservative
'shadow' minister for local government was critical of the concept
of unitary authorities.[1]

The Conservative election manifesto for the 1970 campaign
promised: 'We will bring forward a sensible measure of local
government reform which will involve a genuine devolution of
power from the central government and will provide for the
existence of a two-tier structure.' This statement reflected the
widespread criticism that unitary authorities would be remote.
A two-tier scheme necessarily entailed more local authorities,
some smaller units, and more elected councillors. It was popular
because it seemed more approachable. There was also the prospect that when details of a two-tier scheme emerged, they would
look much more like the existing structure – except in the county
boroughs. The element of change would be less drastic than
under the unitary authority concept. So fewer councillors and
local officials would be seriously disturbed. Traditional units
could remain, especially counties. County-wide social and sporting organisations could continue without appearing anachronistic.
The Conservative manifesto quietly reflected the state of public
opinion.

Conservative policy can be viewed also in terms of party loyalties and advantage. Most of the counties regularly elected councils
that were broadly conservative in sympathy even if they were not
formally controlled by a Conservative caucus. The political
complexion of the councils proposed by the Royal Commission
must be a matter for speculation, but some Conservatives in
rural areas felt that the mixture of town and countryside would

react to their disadvantage. In 1970 the pattern of opinion was also influenced by the local election results of the previous three years in which the Conservatives had fared exceptionally well. Almost any change at that time seemed to them a possible political disadvantage. (In fact, such a conclusion was mistaken. The county borough system which separated the larger towns from their surroundings was ideally suited to maximise Labour influence in local government: in the long run, the destruction of county boroughs was certain to be to the detriment of the Labour Party.) The reorganisation of local boundaries also has a subsequent effect on the pattern of parliamentary constituencies. The effect of the Royal Commission's plan on the results of parliamentary elections is even more uncertain, for it would depend on how parliamentary boundaries were drawn within the larger unitary areas. But some Conservative MPs, no doubt, looked over the boundaries of their present constituencies and saw the council estates on the edge of the neighbouring town. They may have reflected that if county boroughs could be retained intact as second-tier districts, then their own parliamentary careers might be less disturbed.

The local government map of England and Wales was, in broad outline, determined by the outcome of the 1970 General Election. But the issue of local government reform went unnoticed in the election campaign itself. There is no reference to the subject in the exhaustive index to the Nuffield study of the election.[2] For Labour the subject could only cause political damage. The Conservatives had not fully worked out their policy. Indeed, the incoming Conservative Government had been provided with a perfect excuse for further delay. Early in 1969 the Commission on the Constitution had been established by the Labour Government to consider the relations between the central government and the several countries, nations and regions of the United Kingdom. Clearly, the main purpose was to survey the problems of devolution to Scotland and Wales, but this would obviously lead on to the question of regional administration in England. It would have been easy for Conservative Ministers to proclaim that the reform of local government must wait until the regional issue was ripe for decision.

Instead, the new government grasped the nettle of reform with vigour. The Ministry of Housing and Local Government was reshaped and became part of the Department of the Environment, a new name stressing a wider view of its responsibilities to promote good conditions for living. After eight months in office, the new Secretary of State, Peter Walker, produced a White

Paper, *Local Government in England*,[3] which asserted that regions would be too big for services provided by local authorities, so reorganisation need not wait upon possible changes at the regional level.

The White Paper was brief. A new system for local government was set out in a dozen pages. The central message of the White Paper was that a fair balance had to be struck between the claims of functional efficiency, which demanded bigger units of organisation, and the claims of representation, which required smaller units. In cases of doubt, the latter consideration should prevail. 'The Government obviously must seek efficiency, but where the arguments are evenly balanced their judgement will be given in favour of responsibility being exercised at the lower level.'[4] The simplest solution, and the one most readily intelligible to the public, would be to have the same system of local administration throughout the country. Unfortunately, this was impossible. Densely populated areas and sparsely populated areas could not be organised in the same way. So the White Paper outlined a plan for county and district authorities to cover the whole of the country, but the distribution of functions between the two levels would vary. The crux of the distinction was the allocation of responsibility for education, including libraries, and the social services. These services could not be provided efficiently for a population of less than about 250,000. So while these functions could be allocated to the lower-tier district authorities in the main conurbations, elsewhere it was necessary for them to be given to the upper-tier counties. This variation in the allocation of duties is of great importance, because education is by far the most expensive local service. It follows that in the six metropolitan counties, which embrace the main industrial areas, the districts spend far more than the counties. In the non-metropolitan counties, the balance falls the other way. Of course, the problem is not simply which council spends most money: greater expenditure, especially on personal services, increases the extent to which an authority impinges on the lives of citizens.

The White Paper nominated six areas to become metropolitan counties, the West Midlands, Merseyside, the Manchester area, South and West Yorkshire and the Tyne and Wear area. Otherwise the detailed geographical application of the principles of the White Paper was relegated to a separate document, Circular 8/71. This circular made detailed proposals for the boundaries of new English counties and metropolitan districts: the boundaries of non-metropolitan districts would be worked out later by a boundary commission. It is notable that the population range of the new metropolitan districts fell as low as 182,000, a figure much below that of many county boroughs which were due to lose their responsibility for education and personal social services. Clearly, the status of a local authority was to depend not merely on its size but upon the nature of the area and its surroundings. The White Paper had suggested that the population range for education and social service authorities should be from 250,000 to 1,000,000: however, four of the non-metropolitan counties substantially exceed the million limit and are still growing. It is arguable that Hampshire, Kent, Essex and Lancashire are too large and remote to organise services which are essentially personal. In fact, this theme was never taken up in public discussion of the White Paper and the subsequent Bill because of the broad agreement to preserve, wherever possible, the traditional counties.

Rural areas had enjoyed the benefit of more intimate local representation through the medium of parish councils. The White Paper recognised the value of these bodies, which were to continue. But what was to be done for the boroughs and urban districts due to lose their separate identities in the reorganisation of second-tier authorities? Two possible solutions were offered. Parish councils could be established in essentially urban areas. Alternatively, local communities might achieve some form of local representation through non-statutory bodies which might be recognised and financially assisted by district councils. Subsequently it was agreed that third-tier councils, known as town councils, should be established for many of these former authorities, subject to a population limit of about 20,000 or not more than one fifth of the population of the district. A total of 382 such councils was established.

A separate document was issued setting out proposals for Wales.[5] They followed the same pattern as the proposals for England. A two-tier system would cover the whole Principality. There were to be seven counties and thirty-six districts. Substantial amalgamations of the existing counties were needed to produce top-tier authorities of adequate size. Even so, Powys, which consists of the rural areas of Mid-Wales, was to have a much smaller population, of around 100,000, than any English county.[6] To English ears, the new form of local government sounded strange because the new counties were given new names: Clwyd, Dyfed, Gwynedd and Powys. Monmouthshire became Gwent. The Local Government Bill contained one major change which increased the number of counties to eight. A fresh county of South Glamorgan was created, which contains only two districts

based on Barry and Cardiff. In effect, Cardiff dominates this
authority and is virtually a county on its own, a situation without
parallel elsewhere. At third-tier level, the use of the word 'parish'
was ended and the authorities were re-styled as 'communities'.

The practical effects of these changes varied greatly. A few
counties survived with their boundaries intact; here the only
alteration was at district level. Many new counties included one
or more of the county boroughs which, inevitably, resented their
demotion. Some unfamiliar counties emerged, notably Avon,
Cleveland and Humberside, based respectively on Bristol,
Middlesbrough and Hull which were joined with their adjacent
areas. Elsewhere, smaller counties were merged together.
Counties adjacent to the new metropolitan authorities often lost
some territory; this affected Lancashire, Cheshire and Warwickshire.

The proposals in the White Paper and the related circular
stimulated a great deal of local lobbying of MPs and ministers.
Indeed, this was no more than a continuation of a behaviour
pattern which had emerged intermittently during the long arguments about local government reorganisation. Some of this
pressure was quiet and effective. The text of the Local Government Bill showed some alterations in the boundaries proposed in
Circular 8/71, and the general effect was to minimise changes in
the *status quo*. The areas of the new metropolitan counties were
trimmed back, and they lost population totalling about 150,000.
There were also some adjustments to the proposed boundaries of
the non-metropolitan counties, which again had the general effect
of permitting areas to remain within their present county. One
important exception to this rule was the treatment of north
Lincolnshire, which the Bill decreed should be moved to the new
county of Humberside. This decision was made in anticipation of
the completion of the new Humber bridge. So Humberside gained
substantial additional population and resources: it also acquired
serious extra problems, for until the bridge was completed the
communications between the opposite sides of the river were
atrocious.

Some authorities failed in their efforts to change government
policy even though their activities gained much publicity. The
parading of a Hereford bull down Whitehall did not prevent the
amalgamation of that county with Worcestershire. Nor did the
beating of Drake's drum stop Plymouth being merged into Devon.
Such lobbying continued while the Bill was passing through
Parliament. At a late stage in the proceedings, ministers accepted
that the Isle of Wight should stay separate from Hampshire and

so escape the absorption threatened by Circular 8/71. The net effect of the lobbying was thus limited, but not negligible. The final outcome, as compared with the circular, was to increase the number of counties by one, the number of metropolitan districts by two, and to effect many adjustments to county boundaries.

A total of 1,886 amendments were made to the original Bill. Of these, 599 arose from the committee stage in the Commons; a further 654 came on the report stage; the Lords made a further 633 alterations to the text.[7] With very few exceptions, all the amendments were introduced by the government; a few changes were proposed by Opposition members and accepted by ministers. This veritable cataract of change demands explanation. The majority of amendments were entirely trivial in content and were needed merely to tidy up drafting. For an extremely complex measure, which embraced the whole span of local authority administration, the Bill had been drafted in a hurry. As detailed consultations on the original text proceeded, a large number of shortcomings became painfully evident. So the Bill had to be modified to accommodate second thoughts and third thoughts.

Although debates on the Bill were long and tortuous, there was no great drama or political challenge. The major issue raised by the Opposition on the second reading of the Bill was whether the provision for Wales should have been put in a separate measure. A great deal of time was spent debating detail which caused some all-night sittings in the Commons. Ministers suffered only one defeat. By a majority of four it was resolved that non-metropolitan districts, and not the counties, should be responsible for refuse disposal. At a later stage of the Bill, in the Lords, the government managed to reverse this decision. The incident was trivial, but it did demonstrate that a strong lobby from the provincial boroughs could have at least a temporary effect. The lobbying continued throughout the debates on the Bill. Even at the eleventh hour, the government accepted some minor changes proposed in the Lords: Wilmslow was spared the transfer from Cheshire to Greater Manchester and Lymington was allowed to stay in Hampshire.

A general agreement emerged that the Bill should pass. The endless arguments over local government reform petered out in an anti-climax. Why did this occur? There was a consensus that some change was long overdue; that many authorities were too small; that the isolation of county boroughs must end; that the conurbations needed a measure of separate treatment. Granted this degree of harmony, the disagreements move towards details.

Certainly, a degree of weariness surrounded the whole question. The major themes had been discussed for so long. It was obviously impossible to get total agreement; some local interests were certain to be displeased. Then the Conservative scheme was easier to accept than the Royal Commission idea of unitary authorities. The upset would be less drastic. The new local government map would still have some resemblance to the old. Local authority associations were broadly content, except the Association of Municipal Corporations. The major complaints came from county boroughs due to be merged into adjacent counties. Where these were presented by a Labour MP, the government could safely ignore the protest. Where the borough council was controlled by Conservatives, and many were, because of Tory successes in local elections between 1967 and 1970, the protest was often muted out of a sense of party loyalty. Similarly, the AMC had a Conservative majority and so were reluctant to oppose government policy. The Bill was also helped by the fact that both government and Opposition backbenchers were far more concerned about other matters, including policy towards Europe, industrial relations and the national economic situation.

Boundaries of districts in the non-metropolitan counties were decided outside the parliamentary arena. The Local Government Boundary Commission made local surveys and consulted local opinion and then produced draft proposals. These were subjected to further local comment, and ultimately the commission made firm proposals which were confirmed by ministerial order. Once more, the effect of local pressure was to reduce the amount of change and produce rather more authorities. The initial plan of the commission was for 274 non-metropolitan districts, of which none had a population below 40,000. Sparsely populated areas, in particular, complained that the new authorities would be too large geographically, and so would be inconvenient for both councillors and the public. The ultimate solution provided for 296 districts, of which fourteen had a population below 40,000. Indeed, the commission moved a long way from its original objective, which had been a 'preferred population range of 75,000 to 100,000'. No fewer than 111 of the 296 districts fell below the 75,000 preferred minimum. Another feature of this reorganisation was that, with few exceptions, the commission did not divide existing authorities. The reform generally consisted of simple amalgamations. As a result, many boundaries were perpetuated that had long ceased to have any justification.

The Administrative Problems of Reorganisation

The task of bringing into operation the Local Government Act 1972 involved the biggest local administrative reorganisation that England and Wales have ever experienced. Naturally, the extent of the upheaval varied from place to place. Some areas were greatly affected by the geographical changes; some areas suffered from the reallocation of functions; the most severe disturbance was experienced where both areas and functions were altered. In the metropolitan areas, an entirely new system of local government was created and the new county authorities had to build up new organisations. Three of the non-metropolitan counties, Avon, Cleveland and Humberside, were in a similar situation. Other new authorities faced rather less serious difficulties. Where a new council was based on an amalgamation of former authorities, it inherited buildings, staff, equipment and other resources.

In some cases, boundaries were unaltered. Five counties stayed the same: Cornwall, Hertfordshire, Isle of Wight, Salop and Wiltshire. Many of the larger districts, the former county boroughs, kept an unchanged shape. Here the problems were restricted to the reallocation of functions. Non-metropolitan counties had to make arrangements for their new responsibility for refuse disposal. Non-metropolitan districts demoted from county borough status had to adjust to the loss of their major duties, education and the social services. The sense of deprivation was acute, for the town hall ceased to be the centre for all local administration.

The metropolitan districts also had a variety of experience. Only two, Liverpool and Wolverhampton, retained exactly the same boundaries, but the change at Manchester was trivial. Most of them were based on a former county borough which provided the basis for the new institution. However, three of the metropolitan districts, Knowsley, Tameside and Trafford, did not include an ex-county borough, so they were faced with the urgent task of building up a new organisation to administer education and the social services.

Local resistance to the reorganisation seriously aggravated the task of getting some of the new authorities off to a smooth start. The resentment felt in Herefordshire to the enforced marriage with a larger neighbour greatly increased the tensions in the new Hereford and Worcester authority. One cause of dispute was the location of the new headquarters. A similar issue arose in South Yorkshire, which decided to operate from Barnsley and not Sheffield, which was a much larger commercial and industrial centre. In contrast, the creation of the new Lincolnshire authority proceeded with harmony because there was no popular protest bringing together what had been the three separate 'parts' of the historic shire. The new metropolitan county of Greater Manchester started with the unusual advantage of a ready-made team of chief officers, for most of the chief officials of the Manchester county borough transferred to the new authority. A few counties suffered very considerable loss of territory and population. Lancashire lost 47 per cent of its population, Northumberland 45 per cent, Somerset 36 per cent, Warwickshire 29 per cent, Durham 26 per cent and Cheshire 23 per cent. This entailed some diminution of staff and scale of operations which could be damaging to morale.

The task of preparation for the change to the new system was facilitated by the nomination of joint committees of existing authorities for each of the new areas. The basic tasks of these bodies was to make arrangements for the election of the new councils, make recommendations about their future organisation and bring together officials to collect information which would assist with the harmonisation of policies and procedures. A general willingness to co-operate in the business of these joint committees indicated a general acceptance of the forthcoming reorganisation. In a few cases co-operation was not forthcoming: the Isle of Wight refused to take part in the joint committee preparing the way for a new Hampshire, a policy that later achieved justification when it was agreed that the autonomy of the island should be preserved. The detailed work of the joint committees was carried out by senior officials who formed a series of working groups to review the details of each of the major services to come under the control of the new council.

Elections for the new councils were held during 1973. County elections were held on 15 March, metropolitan districts went to the polls on 12 April and other districts on 7 June. The transfer date was 1 April 1974, so the counties and metropolitan districts had approximately a year to prepare themselves, and non-metropolitan districts were given a little more than nine months. During this interim period, the newly elected 'shadow' councils worked in association with the authorities they were about to supplant.

The new councils were relatively inexperienced. Many members of the dying authorities did not try to continue under the reformed régime. Individuals' decisions to withdraw were made on grounds of age, of ill health, of growing lack of interest or because the new authorities were larger, more remote and threatened to demand the sacrifice of even more time. The elimination of aldermen also increased the turnover of councillors. Aldermen tended to be elderly and unaccustomed to standing for public election: the change to a new system provided an ideal opportunity for dignified retirement. Further changes of personnel were caused by movements of political opinion, both as between parties and because some rural authorities became dominated by party organisation for the first time.

The shadow councils were in a strange situation. They were not concerned with the normal local government routine of dealing with the contemporary problems of continuing executive responsibilities. Instead, their task was to plan and prepare. They had to frame management structures, agree on standing orders, appoint senior staff, find and allocate accommodation, agree staffing establishments and try to make satisfactory arrangements with other 'shadow' councils in relation to responsibilities that would be shared. Much of this work was abstract, even academic. Even to experienced councillors it was unusual. All this helps to explain why the joint committees formed by the outgoing authorities were often extremely influential. Many of them had prepared schemes for committee structures and departmental structures for the new authority. These plans were based squarely on the Bains Report and the philosophy of corporate management. The shadow councils tended to accept this detailed advice with gratitude. They had to build up a new administrative structure in a hurry; they were often presented with a detailed blueprint of how to do it; unless objections emerged, the simplest solution was to put the blueprint into practice. Since the Bains ideas were not politically controversial, since the local authority associations and chief officers supported the report's general approach, the plans were often accepted with little demur.

Central government departments took an active part in guiding the transition from the older order to the new. A steady flow of circulars and memoranda gave detailed advice or instruction on how various problems should be met. Where necessary, details of the legislation were provided by statutory instruments but their contents were explained in circulars which became the effective working documents. This central direction had the merit of securing uniformity of treatment throughout the country: in the case of staffing matters, such uniformity was essential if serious trouble with trade unions was to be avoided. The high level of central supervision aroused little local resentment. Officials, in particular, were grateful for advice and instructions. Faced with unprecedented problems and a relatively short time to solve them, local government needed to be given a clear framework within which the essential changes could be made.

Rules were required to govern the transfer of assets from the former authorities to their successors. The basic criterion was that property should follow the use to which it had been put. A school building should continue to provide education for children in the neighbourhood: the building should therefore belong to the authority responsible for education in that area. If an office was used to administer social services, it should continue to be used for that purpose. Unfortunately, these simple propositions did not cover all possible situations. Difficulties arose where the area of a former authority was split, especially in relation to property which provided a specialised service for a wide area. Again, there were difficulties in relation to buildings with a variety of uses embodying functions that may have passed on to different authorities. Here the building was allocated to the authority which could lay claim to the majority of the floor-space. There could also be arguments about the use to which a property was put. Thus if a county borough redesignated school playing fields as land for building council houses, it could claim to retain ownership of the site after 1 April 1974. To prevent 'cheating' of this kind, any fresh designations of use after 9 November 1973 were impermissible and the Secretary of State had power to over-rule unreasonable designations made before that date.

The most important aspect of the transfer related to staff. When it became clear that reorganisation was certain to take place, there was some alarm among office staffs. It had been widely argued that the new structure would be more economical. Accordingly, there were fears of redundancy. NALGO became very active in defending the interests of its members. Indeed, reorganisation provided a stimulus to NALGO and helped to make it a more active and militant organisation. In many areas, NALGO sought and obtained guarantees of 'no redundancy'. At national level, complex schemes were agreed to compensate officers for hardship and loss of office due to reorganisation. Appeals machinery was created to deal with individuals who were dissatisfied. In the event, the fears of redundancy proved groundless. The number of office jobs increased rather than diminished, and the economies were not achieved.

Chief officers, their deputies and middle management levels of the professional staff faced varied prospects. They might be promoted, be demoted, or they might find it necessary or advantageous to move. For chief officers and their deputies over the age of 50, there was a possibility of early retirement on highly advantageous terms in relation to pension rights. This provision

234 A HISTORY OF LOCAL GOVERNMENT

was introduced in order to avoid too many chief officers and their deputies applying for the reduced number of top jobs under the new authorities. (A surplus of chief officials staying in post had been one of the major problems experienced in the reorganisation of London local government in 1965.) The encouragement to retire was so successful that considerable opportunities for promotion opened up for relatively young officials immediately below the level of deputy chief officer.

A Local Government Staff Commission was appointed by the government to give both advice and some directions to local councils in relation to establishment matters. The directions were justified in the context of providing uniformity of treatment throughout the country, and also by an attempt to minimise the disturbance caused by mass migration of staff. It was accepted that all senior positions should be open to competition: there was to be no automatic transfer of top officials from an old authority to the new. This produced an element of uncertainty that may have helped to persuade some chief officials to retire. Another consequence was that some competitions tended to be farcical because it was abundantly clear who would be appointed. Where the boundary of a county or a district was unchanged, or virtually so, then it was common practice to appoint the local incumbents to senior positions. Restrictions were also placed on who could apply for particular jobs. Had this not been done, then officials from all over the country could have applied for jobs throughout the country. The result could have been chaotic. Accordingly, the Local Government Staff Commission advised local authorities to observe the following limits. Counties and metropolitan districts could invite applications for the post of chief executive from any local government officer in England and Wales, except from London. Non-metropolitan districts were restricted to applicants from their new county for these posts. Other chief officers had to be recruited from within the new county boundary. For other posts, the authority had to recruit from within its own geographical area. A complete ban was imposed on applications from local government staff in London as it was feared that staff in the metropolis might rush for provincial jobs, attracted by the prospect of rural life and lower living costs. The result could have been a serious shortage of experienced staff in the capital. If an authority claimed it could not make satisfactory appointments because of the geographical limitation, it could ask the Staff Commission for permission to advertise on a countrywide basis. This procedure was often invoked in the case of a category of professional staff in short supply, such as planning officers.

There had been a general expectation that the reorganisation of local government would allow economies in staff. This benefit failed to materialise. Instead, staff increased by nearly 5 per cent. One reason was that the Local Government Act made some aspects of administration more cumbersome. Environmental and physical planning were divided between county and district councils, and the districts had to recruit staff to enable them to carry out their new responsibilities. Another reason was that the initial establishments accepted by the new authorities were over-generous. No doubt there was a natural, humanitarian desire to avoid redundancy, and the newly appointed chief officers were keen to build up strong departments which could provide a good standard of service. The newly elected councillors also wanted to get their authorities off to a new start, and were not perhaps as cost-conscious in the initial stages as they might have been. So local staff increased, and because of the rising salaries due to union pressure and inflation, there was a substantial increase in the administrative costs.

Relations Between Counties and Districts
Although the Conservative Government had rejected the idea of all-embracing unitary authority proposed by the Redcliffe-Maud Commission, it was highly conscious that the success of a two-tier system would depend upon good relations between counties and districts. The basic difficulty surrounding a two-tier arrangement is the possibility of friction and rivalry between the two levels. Decisions have to be made about who is responsible for what. The drawing of demarcation lines offers a powerful cause of trouble. Opportunities for overlapping and mutual frustration have to be reduced to a minimum. Opportunities for co-operation have to be encouraged. The 1972 Act made specific provision for local authorities to use each other's staff or equipment in return for payment. Joint use of computers is a common arrangement. Joint purchasing schemes to obtain price advantages from bulk orders received much central encouragement. It was also recognised that if counties and districts were to work well together, there is a need for flexibility so that local administrative patterns can match local wishes and local conditions.

Against this background, the concept of agency was introduced into the Local Government Act 1972. The idea, quite simply, was that one authority should allow another authority to carry out some part of its functions, subject always to a financial control being imposed on the agent. In practice, agency almost always worked downwards: the district acted as agent for the county. Clearly, this technique has some similarity to the delegation permitted under the Education Act 1944, the Town and Country Planning Act 1947, and in the health and welfare sections of the Local Government Act 1958. But the agency allowed in 1972 was more limited in character, both in relation to the amount of discretion allowed to recipients and in relation to the functions concerned. Both education and the social services were specifically excluded from agency in 1972. If agency were extended to these functions, the former county boroughs might have tried to use it as a means to claw back the duties which they had lost to the counties. It was not to be used as a device to subvert the intention of the 1972 reform to transfer these major services to the counties.

Why, then, was agency introduced at all? It made local administration more complicated. The earlier delegation provisions had come under criticism for causing confusion, delay and divided responsibility. Agency seemed likely to have similar consequences. However, it could be convenient in particular circumstances. In the case of libraries, some counties accepted agency as a means of promoting wider local participation in the running of branch libraries. The task of refuse disposal was transferred by the 1972 Act from boroughs and districts to the counties, but the counties had no experience or technical staff in this field. So it was useful for the counties to arrange for second-tier councils to continue this duty, at least for a limited period. The districts need outdoor staff for a variety of purposes: this staff can be stronger if additional work becomes available through the maintenance of county highways. Thus many districts tried to get county acceptance of agency agreements over roads. Where county and district could not agree over agency, the dispute was referred to the appropriate government department for decision. Except occasionally in relation to highways, the government rulings were always in favour of the counties, and agency was refused.

Other functions were shared between counties and districts as a direct result of statutory provisions. Planning is the most important example. Counties became responsible for broad long-term planning strategy. Districts were made responsible for development control, for applying broad policies to individual situations. Such a division of duty required a high level of co-operation for it to work effectively. Regular consultations developed between county and district planning staff to try to ensure that full co-ordination of policies and decisions was achieved.

Some of the larger counties took considerable trouble over attempting to decentralise their services so that they should be more accessible to the public and more responsive to local opinion. Decentralisation took a variety of forms. The provision of local offices, e.g. for social services, did nothing to involve district councils. But the creation of advisory committees on which the districts were represented gave district opinion a limited voice in county policy. Devon created one of the most extensive decentralisation schemes – a consequence both of its larger physical size and the growth of county responsibilities through taking over wide responsibilities from the county boroughs. The county was divided into four sectors with local headquarters based on Exeter, Plymouth, Torbay and Barnstaple. A parallel set of area committees was established, containing district council representatives; these bodies were given some delegated powers. County area officers were appointed for the main functions with the status of deputy chief officers. Thus Devon attempted to offset the disadvantage of size by forming four separate, subordinate administrative organisations.

Some optional duties of local authorities were made concurrent between the two tiers. Thus they may be performed at either level, or both, or possibly neither. Included in this category are museums, art galleries, the acquisition and disposal of land for planning purposes, caravan sites, aerodromes and recreational provision including country parks, swimming baths and entertainments. It follows that these functions can be organised quite differently in various parts of the country. While this arrangement allows full scope for local initiative it can also cause inaction or duplication.

Thus a variety of measures has been taken to try to co-ordinate county and district local government. Some have a specific statutory origin; some have not. It is perhaps unlikely that even in combination these measures will solve the difficulties of a two-tier system. A pressing need for local authorities is to ease the distress caused by the shortage of housing accommodation. Yet here there is a basic division of duty. Counties provide relief for homeless families, yet the districts are the housing authorities. Subsequently, in 1974, the government encouraged the non-metropolitan counties to delegate their responsibilities for the homeless to the district councils.[8]

The 1972 Act – How Much of a Change?
The Local Government Act 1972 ended the form of local administration which had commenced with the legislation of 1888 and

1894. The later Victorians had produced a system which, outside county boroughs, provided for two-tier, multi-purpose elected authorities which had varied local powers. Urban areas were thought to require more facilities than rural areas. Long before 1972, it was felt that urban and rural areas should have similar services. The distinction made in 1972 between metropolitan and non-metropolitan areas was not based on the idea that different places required more or less local government, but rather that services need to be organised differently where population is highly concentrated.

It is easy to over-estimate the extent of the 1972 reform. The authorities created by the 1972 Act were brand-new legal entities. However, many of the alterations that followed merely continued tendencies that had been present for many years. Furthermore, two major issues were ignored altogether: on both regionalism and finance, nothing of significance took place.

The Redcliffe-Maud Royal Commission had proposed the creation of eight provincial councils. The section of the Report which described the functions of these bodies was somewhat hesitant.[9] The provinces would engage in strategic planning and co-ordination, but were to have few executive powers. The existing local authorities were hostile to the idea of a regional tier which they felt would further challenge their independence. Meanwhile, the appointment of the Crowther Commission on the Constitution enabled ministers to put the regional issue on ice. Curiously enough, there was also a tendency to argue that the concerns of the commission would not affect local government, at least in England. When presenting the Labour Government's White Paper, *Reform of Local Government in England*, to Parliament in February 1970, the Secretary of State commented, 'The Crowther Commission was set up to consider functions which might be transferred, not from local government to provincial government, but from central Government to provincial government.'[10] Thus Crowther was to be thought of in the context of devolution, not as a means to promote regional local government. Such an assurance avoided immediate political difficulty, but local authorities remained suspicious. They found it hard to believe, at least in an English context, that Whitehall departments would surrender important decisions. One of the ideas behind the Local Government Act 1888 had been that it would provide a framework within which some central government powers could be handed down to the newly formed local councils. That idea never bore fruit. Meanwhile, the 1972 legislation did nothing to bring regional government or regional devolution any closer. But the question remained unsolved.

The 1972 Act was also silent on the question of finance. One reason was that a supplementary measure to deal with financial matters was promised for the following session. However, there was further delay and the measure did not appear until the autumn of 1973 and reached the Statute Book immediately before the dissolution of Parliament in February 1974. It made some alterations in the system of distribution of central grants, extended the rate rebate scheme for people with low incomes, but made only negligible changes in the law of rating. Thus the central financial issue – the unsatisfactory nature of local rating – was avoided. A Green Paper issued in 1971 entitled *The Future Shape of Local Government Finance*[11] had seemed mainly concerned to list objections to any fundamental reform of local taxation. No doubt the issues were awkward, both in terms of politics and administration. The work associated with the preparation of the 1972 Act gave ministers and their civil service advisers more than enough to do – so the topic of rating was put aside.

There is a quite separate reason why the Local Government Act 1972 avoided finance. It is quite clear that the economic consequences of the reform were under-estimated. The financial memorandum which was published together with the Bill in 1971 stated that the measure 'will have little direct effect upon local authority finance or expenditure overall'. Presumably this statement was based on a theory that much of the cost of putting new authorities to work, sometimes from new premises, would be offset by the economies achieved from the creation of fewer and larger local councils. In the event, the economies of scale failed to materialise. Or, if they did, they were swamped by the expense of founding new organisations. Some of the reasons for higher costs were noted above,[12] but the political and administrative causes of higher expenditure were greatly reinforced by monetary inflation. The inflation did not of itself increase the claim of local government for real resources, but, since rateable values are fixed, the inflation helped to cause dramatic rises in the poundage. So the public reaction was to condemn the new system as costly and wasteful.

Directly and indirectly, the 1972 legislation did make a major impact on the style of local government. The units became larger; the political element increased; central control was facilitated by reducing the number of authorities; the practice of corporate management tended to strengthen the influence of senior officials; the need to secure the co-operation of staff to carry through reorganisation smoothly added to the importance of the trade unions. All these tendencies were of great import- ance. Yet all of them were manifest long before the legislation appeared. The effect of the Act was not to prescribe new direc- tions for local government, but rather to give it a shove along a road it was already travelling.

None of this should be surprising. Local government is so much a part of the life of the community that, quite inevitably, it must reflect contemporary social pressures. Thus national economic difficulties force the central government to exert more deter- mined control over the economy; stiff competition between the political parties requires them to pay attention to public demands and to intervene in local affairs; in all branches of life, the complexity of affairs gives greater weight to expert opinion. The early 1970s was a peak time for union militancy as the leaders of organised labour sought to challenge the Conservative Govern- ment. Also at this time there was a strong belief that 'big was beautiful'; that larger units could provide better and more economical services. All these ideas and pressures affected both the content of the 1972 Act and the way it worked.

One other general trend was a powerful force on local admini- stration. Throughout the post-war period, and particularly since the 1960s, the public became increasingly articulate in their claims for better services. A great variety of local pressure groups emerged, urging improvements of many kinds. Prominent bodies included the Campaign for the Advancement of State Education, Shelter and local tenants' associations and amenity societies. To satisfy the demands of these bodies necessarily cost money. And local authorities were constantly urged from other quarters to keep down the amount of rate increases. Sometimes this pres- sure came from the central government as part of an anti- inflation policy. Always it would come from ratepayers who objected to paying higher rates.

So local authorities were faced with the situation that more demands were made upon them, but there was a general unwil- lingness locally to foot the bill. Exactly the same tendencies beset the central government. But, for local government, there was one possible way through the dilemma – to try to persuade mini- sters that the Exchequer should meet a higher percentage of local financial burdens. This tactic proved remarkably successful, so that the amount of national grant aid approached twice the revenue obtained from the local rate. The penalty was that local financial independence was undermined. Again the 1972 Act strengthened these tendencies, both by raising expectations about the ability of the new system to provide better services and by adding to administrative costs.

There can be little doubt that the 1972 Act damaged the image of local government in the public mind. Perhaps this is because of confusion about the objectives of the Act. The disagreement over objectives never became clear because the issues were never squarely debated.

Over the years a number of academic writers, particularly Professor W. A. Robson, had urged the need for local government reform in the context that change was essential if local councils were to make a broader and more positive contribution to the welfare of the community. The 1967 Report of the Maud Committee on *Management of Local Government* clearly envisaged that local authorities should be encouraged to raise their horizons; it recommended that local councils should be given a general competence power which would have largely eliminated the application of *ultra vires* to local government.[13] The Royal Commission on Local Government, reported in 1969, hoped that a reformed system would have wider powers covering functions then the responsibility of *ad hoc* nominated bodies.[14] Many of the newly elected councillors in 1973 felt that the new authorities had opportunities to improve the quality of life, opportunities which should not be missed. Many local officials felt the same. Taken together, all this expresses a mood of optimism, a claim for expansion and, inevitably, more expenditure.

However, those responsible for the legislation did not view its purpose in this way. The attitude of the Heath Cabinet towards public administration had been set out in a White Paper, *The Reorganisation of Central Government*, which suggested that some of the failings of public authorities were caused by 'attempting to do too much'.[15] Conservative philosophy demands encouragement for private enterprise and limitations on the role of the state. Accordingly, the drive for local government reform under Conservative auspices was not aimed at expansion of opportunities for local councils: rather was it concerned with seeking economy, and better standards of management.[16] The Conservatives saw the Bains Report as an essential part of the reform. Local authorities should think more carefully about their priorities and take more care to assess the results of their policies. The Conservative White Paper on local government reform emphasised that decisions should be taken locally and with due regard for economy. No mention was made of the desirability of expanding local services.

So there was a clear clash of objectives. Many of those who had advocated reform and many who had the task of working within the new system saw it as providing opportunities for the growth of local services. The Ministers responsible for the legislation were seeking rationalisation and economy. Against this background of uncertainty and divided opinion, the new era of local goverment commenced.

NOTES

1 796 HC Deb., 18 February 1970, cols. 444–56.
2 D. Butler and M. Pinto-Duschinsky, *The British General Election of 1970* (1971).
3 1970–1, Cmnd 4584, xxxii.
4 ibid., para. 13.
5 *The Reform of Local Government in Wales*, Consultative Document, (HMSO, 1971).
6 At this stage it had not been agreed that the Isle of Wight should remain separate from Hampshire.
7 B. Wood, *The Process of Local Government Reform, 1966–74*, p. 149.
8 DoE Circular, 18/74.
9 pp. 109–17, 1968–9, Cmnd 4040, xxxviii.
10 795 HC Deb., 4 February 1970, col. 433.
11 1970–1, Cmnd 4741, xxxii.
12 p. 235.
13 Para. 286.
14 Para 576, 1968–9, Cmnd 4040, xxxviii.
15 Para 2, 1970–1, Cmnd 4506, xx.
16 Paras. 5–9, 1970–1, Cmnd 4584, xxxii.

BIBLIOGRAPHY

Association of Education Committees, *The Threat to Education* (Councils and Education Press, 1957).

Association of Municipal Corporations, 'Reorganisation of local government', *Public Administration* (1953), vol. 31, pp. 285–95, also (1954), vol. 32, pp. 341–9.

Lord Avebury, *On Municipal and National Trading* (Macmillan, 1906).

Sir H. Banwell, 'The new relations between central and local government', *Public Administration* (1959), vol. 37, pp. 201–12.

A. Barker, *The Local Amenity Movement* (The Civic Trust, 1976).

L. P. Barnhouse, *The Impact of Local Authority Associations on Local Government Reorganisation in England, 1966–72* (1972), unpublished MA thesis, University of West Virginia.

J. M. Beck, *A History of Parish Councils and their Representative Associations* (1971), unpublished PhD thesis, University of Kent.

A. H. Birch, *Small Town Politics*, (OUP, 1959).

J. G. Bulpitt, *Party Policies in English Local Government* (Longman, 1967).

D. E. Butler, 'Local government in Parliament', *Public Administration* (1953), vol. 31, pp. 46–8.

D. N. Chester, *Central and Local Government* (Macmillan, 1951).

R. V. Clements, *Local Notables and the City Council* (Macmillan, 1969).

R. V. Clements, 'Political leadership in Bristol and Avon', *Local Government Studies* (1976), vol. 2, pp. 39–52.

G. D. H. Cole, *Local and Regional Government* (Cassell, 1947).

J. Collings, *Land Reform* (Longman, 1906).

J. Collings and J. L. Green, *Life of Jesse Collings,* (Longman, 1920).

County Councils Association, 'Reorganisation of Local Government in England and Wales', *Public Administration* (1953), vol. 31, pp. 176–87; also (1954), vol. 32, pp. 331–49.

County Councils Association, *Memorandum on the White Paper on Local Government in Wales* (CCA, 1968).

C. A. Cross, *Principles of Local Government Law* (Sweet & Maxwell, 1959).

R. H. S. Crossman, *The Diaries of a Cabinet Minister*, 2 vols., (Hamilton: Cape, 1975 and 1976).

J. B. Cullingworth, *Housing and Local Government* (Allen & Unwin, 1966).

L. Darwin, *Municipal Trade* (Murray, 1903).

B. Donoughue and G. W. Jones, *Herbert Morrison* (Weidenfeld & Nicolson, 1973).

J. M. Drummond, *The Finance of Local Government* (Allen & Unwin, 1952).

E. Eaglesham, *From School Board to Local Authority* (Routledge & Kegan Paul, 1956).

J. Elliott, 'The Harris experiment in Newcastle upon Tyne', *Public Administration* (1971), vol. 49, pp. 149–62.

J. Elliott, 'Political leadership in local government: T. Dan Smith in Newcastle-upon-Tyne', in *Local Government Studies*, (1975), vol. 1, pp. 33–44.

K. Feiling, *Life of Neville Chamberlain* (Macmillan, 1946).

H. Finer, *English Local Government* (Methuen, 1933).

H. Finer, *Municipal Trading* (Allen & Unwin, 1941).

M. Foot, *Aneurin Bevan* (MacGibbon & Kee, 2 vols., 1962–73).

J. F. Garner, 'London government and its reform', *Public Law* (1961), pp. 256–70.

Sir Gwilym Gibbon and R. W. Bell, *History of the London County Council* (Macmillan, 1939).

E. W. Gilbert, 'The boundaries of local government areas', *Geographical Journal* (1948), pp. 172–206.

J. Gyford, *Local Politics in Britain* (Croom Helm, 1976).

J. S. Harris, *British Government Inspection* (Stevens, 1955).

O. A. Hartley, 'The relationship between central and local authorities', *Public Administration* (1971), vol. 49, pp. 439–62.

T. Headrick, *The Town Clerk in English Local Government* (Allen & Unwin, 1962).

L. M. Helmore, *The District Auditor* (Macdonald & Evans, 1961).

E. P. Hennock, *Fit and Proper Persons* (Arnold, 1973).

J. Hicks, U. K. Hicks and C. Lever, *The Problem of Valuation for Rating* (CUP, 1944).

U. K. Hicks, 'The Valuation Tangle', *Public Administration* (1954), vol. 32, pp. 229–35.

C. Hill, *Both Sides of the Hill* (Heinemann, 1964).

J. D. Hoffman, *The Conservative Party in Opposition* (MacGibbon & Kee, 1964).

C. R. H. Hurle-Hobbs, *The Law Relating to District Audit* (Knight, 1955).

K. Isaac-Henry, 'Local authority associations and local government reform', *Local Government Studies* (1975), vol. 1, no. 3, pp. 1–12.

Institute of Municipal Treasurer and Accountants, *The Rating of Dwellings: History and General Survey* (IMTA, 1958).

G. W. Jones, 'The Local Government Commission and county borough extensions', *Public Administration* (1963), vol. 41, pp. 173–87.

G. W. Jones, 'A forgotten right discovered', *Parliamentary Affairs*, (1966), vol. 19, pp. 363–72.

G. W. Jones, *Borough Politics* (Macmillan, 1969).

G. W. Jones, 'Herbert Morrison and Poplarism', *Public Law* (1973), pp. 11–31.

G. W. Jones, 'Political leadership in local government: how Herbert Morrison governed London, 1934–1940, *Local Government Studies* (1973), No. 5, pp. 1–12.

B. Keith-Lucas, 'Municipal boroughs and *ultra vires*', *Public Administration*, (1949), vol xxvii, pp. 87–90.

B. Keith-Lucas, *The English Local Government Franchise* (Blackwell, 1952).

B. Keith-Lucas, 'The training of town clerks', *Public Administration* (1953), vol. 31, pp. 13–17.

B. Keith-Lucas, 'County meetings', *Law Quarterly Review* (1954), pp. 109–14.

B. Keith-Lucas, 'Local government in Parliament', *Public Administration* (1955), vol. 33, pp. 207–10.

B. Keith-Lucas, 'The independence of chief constables', *Public Administration* (1960), vol. 38, pp. 1–15.

B. Keith-Lucas, *The Mayor, Aldermen and Councillors* (Unservile State Papers, 1961).

B. Keith-Lucas, *The Councils, the Press and the People* (Conservative Central Office, 1962).

B. Keith-Lucas, 'The Dilemma of Local Government in Africa', *Essays in Imperial Government* (Blackwell, 1963).

C. W. Key, *Red Poplar* (Labour Publishing Co., 1925).

Sir Sidney Kimber, *Thirty-eight Years of Public Life in Southampton* (Kimber, 1949).

C. King, *The Cecil King Diary* (Cape, 1972).

Labour Party, *Report on Future of Local Government* (Labour Party, 1943).

G. Lansbury, *My Life* (Constable, 1928).

H. J. Laski, W. I. Jennings and W. A. Robson (eds.), *Century of Municipal Progress,* (Allen & Unwin, 1935).

J. M. Lee, *Social Leaders and Public Persons* (OUP, 1963).

V. D. Lipman, *Local Government Areas* (Blackwell, 1949).

J. E. MacColl, 'The party system in English local government', *Public Administration* (1949), vol. 27, pp. 69–75.

W. J. M. Mackenzie, 'The conventions of local government', *Public Administration* (1951), vol. 29, pp. 345–56.

W. J. M. Mackenzie, 'Local government in Parliament', *Public Administration,* (1954), vol. 32, pp. 409–23.

R. M. Macleod, 'Law Medicine and public opinion: the resistance to compulsory health legislation', *Public Law* (1967), pp. 107–28 and 189–211.

H. Macmillan, *Tides of Fortune* (Macmillan, 1969).

H. Maddick and E. P. Pritchard, 'The conventions of local authorities in the West Midlands', *Public Administration* (1958), vol. 36, pp. 145–55; and (1959), vol. 37, pp. 135–43.

A. H. Marshall, *Financial Administration in Local Government* (Allen & Unwin, 1960).

G. Marshall, *Police and Government* (Methuen, 1965).

E. Melling, *History of the Kent County Council* (Kent County Council, 1974).

C. Mellors, 'Local government in Parliament – 20 years later', *Public*

Administration (1974), vol. 52, pp. 223–9.

R. J. Minney, *Viscount Addison* (Odhams, 1958).

H. Morrison, *How Greater London is Governed* (Lovat Dickson, 1935).

NALGO, Interim Report on the Reform of Local Government Structure, (NALGO, 1943).

National Association of Parish Councils, *Statement on the Redcliffe-Maud Report* (NAPC, 1969).

K. Newton, *Second City Politics* (OUP, 1976).

T. H. O'Brien, *History of the Second World War, Civil Defence* (HMSO, 1955).

Lord Onslow, *63 Years* (Hutchinson, 1944).

Julia Parker, *Local Health and Welfare Services* (Allen & Unwin, 1965).

RIPA, *New Sources of Local Revenue* (Allen & Unwin, 1956).

D. Read, *The English Provinces* (Arnold, 1964).

J. Redlich and F. W. Hirst, *Local Government in England*, 2 vols (Macmillan, 1903); abridged version ed. by B. Keith-Lucas (Macmillan, 1958).

A. M. Rees and T. Smith, *Town Councillors: a Study of Barking* (Acton Society, 1964).

D. E. Regan, 'The Police Service: An Extreme Example of Central Control over Local Authority Staff', *Public Law* (1966), pp. 13–34.

Regionaliter, 'The Regional Commissioners', *Political Quarterly*, (1941), vol. 12, pp. 148–53.

G. Rhodes, *The Government of London: the Struggle for Reform* (Allen & Unwin, 1970).

P. G. Richards, *Delegation in Local Government* (Allen & Unwin, 1956).

P. G. Richards, 'Local government reform: smaller towns and the countryside', in *Urban Studies* (1965), pp. 147–62.

P. G. Richards, *The Local Government Act 1972: Problems of Implementation* (Allen & Unwin, 1975).

W. A. Robson, *The Law Relating to Local Government Audit* (Sweet & Maxwell, 1930).

W. A. Robson, *The Development of Local Government* (Allen & Unwin, 1931).

W. A. Robson, 'The reform of London government', *Public Administration* (1961), vol. 39, pp. 59–71.

W. A. Robson, *Local Government in Crisis* (Allen & Unwin, 1966).

W. A. Ross, 'Local Government Board and after: Retrospect', *Public Administration* (1956), vol. 34, pp. 17–25.

Rural District Councils Association, *Local not Remote* (RDCA, 1969).

Rural District Councils Association, *The New District Councils, a Blueprint for the Future* (RDCA, 1970).

Rutland County Council, *The Case for Rutland* (Rutland CC, 1960).

S. Salvidge, *Salvidge of Liverpool* (Hodder & Stoughton, 1934).

A. Sancton, 'British socialist theory of the division of power by area',

Political Studies (1976), vol. 24, pp. 158–70.

C. J. Schneider, 'The revival of Whitleyism in British government', in *Public Administration Review* (1953), vol. 13, pp. 97–105.

Sir L. A. Selby-Bigge, *The Board of Education* (Putnam, 1927).

P. Self, 'The Herbert Commission Report and the values of local government', *Political Studies* (1962), vol. 10, pp. 146–62.

D. Senior, 'The city region as an administrative unit' (1965), in *Political Quarerly*, vol. 36, pp. 82–91.

D. Senior (ed.), *The Regional City* (Longman, 1966).

Dame Evelyn Sharp, 'The future of local government', *Public Administration*, (1962), vol. 40, pp. 375–86.

Dame Evelyn Sharp, *The Ministry of Housing and Local Government*, (Allen & Unwin, 1969).

L. J. Sharpe, 'The Report of the Royal Commission on Local Government in Greater London', *Public Administration* (1961), vol. 39, pp. 73–92.

L. J. Sharpe (ed.), *Voting in Cities* (Macmillan, 1967).

A. Shaw, *Municipal Government in Great Britain* (T. Fisher Unwin, 1895).

E. D. Simon, *A City Council from Within* (Longman, 1926).

S. D. Simon, *A Century of City Government* (Allen & Unwin, 1938).

K. B. Smellie, *History of Local Government* (Allen & Unwin, 1946).

A. Spoor, *White Collar Unions* (Heinemann, 1967).

J. D. Stewart, *Management in Local Government* (Knight, 1971).

Mary Stewart, *Unpaid Public Service* (Fabian Society, 1964).

H. Tracey (ed.), *The British Labour Party* (Caxton Publishing Co., 1948).

Sir A. M. Trustram Eve, *The Future of Local Government* (Athlone Press, 1951).

Urban District Councils Association, Report on the Reorganisation of Local Government (UDCA, 1947).

J. H. Warren, 'The party system in local government', *Parliamentary Affairs* (1951–2), vol. 5, pp. 179–94.

J. H. Warren, *The Local Government Service* (Allen & Unwin, 1952).

Beatrice Webb, *Our Partnership* (Longman, 1948).

S. and B. Webb, *English Poor Law Policy* (Longman, 1910).

S. and B. Webb, *Statutory Authorities for Special Purposes* (Longman, 1922).

West Midland Group, *Local Government and Central Control* (Routledge & Kegan Paul, 1956).

K. C. Wheare, *Government by Committee* (OUP, 1955).

B. D. White, *A History of the Corporation of Liverpool* (Liverpool University Press, 1951).

P. Wilding, 'The administrative aspects of the 1919 housing scheme' *Public Administration* (1973), vol. 51, pp. 307–26.

F. M. G. Willson, *The Organisation of British Central Government, 1914–1956* (Allen & Unwin, 1957).

C. H. Wilson (ed.), *Essays in Local Government* (Blackwell, 1948).

N. Wilson, *The Municipal Health Services* (Allen & Unwin, 1946).
N. Wilson, 'The local government service since the war', *Public Administration* (1952), vol. 30, pp. 131–8.
H. V. Wiseman, 'The Leeds Private Bill, 1956', in *Public Administration* (1957), vol. 35, pp. 25–44.
H. V. Wiseman, 'Local government in Leeds', *Public Administration* (1963), vol. 41, pp. 51–69 and 137–56.
B. Wood, *The Process of Local Government Reform, 1966–74* (Allen & Unwin, 1976).
R. Wraith, *Local Government in West Africa* (Allen & Unwin, 1964).
K. Young, *Local Politics and the Rise of Party* (Leicester University Press, 1975).

Government Publications

1901: *Local taxation.* Final Report of the Royal Commission, 1901, Cd 638, xxiv.
1902: *Repayment of loans by local authorities.* Report of the Select Committee, 1902 (239) viii.
1906: *Poplar Union.* Report by J. S. Davy and TS of the shorthand notes, 1906, Cd 3240, Cd 3274, civ.
1909: *Poor laws and relief of distress.* Report of the Royal Commission, 1909, Cd 4499, xxxvii.
1910: *Electoral systems.* Report of the Royal Commission, 1910, Cd 5163, Cd 5352, xxvi.
1914: *Local taxation.* Final Report of the Departmental Committee, 1914, Cd 7315, xi.
1914: *Local Government Board.* Annual reports to 1919, subsequently annual reports of the Ministry of Health.
1920: *Procedure governing Bills which involve charges.* Report of the Select Committee, 1920 (257), viii.
1922: *National expenditure.* 1st Interim Report of the Committee, 1922, Cmd 1581, ix.
1922: *Parish of Poplar Borough. Expenditure of the Guardians.* Report of Special Inquiry, 1922 Non-Parl. Ministry of Health.
1923: *Local government.* Minutes of evidence taken before the Royal Commission. Pt I, evidence of Mr I. G. Gibbon, Ministry of Health. HMSO, 1923.
1923: *Local government of Greater London.* Report of the Royal Commision, 1923, Cmd 1830, xii, Pt. I.
1924: *Rescission of the Poplar Order.* Memorandum, 1924, Cmd 2052, xix.
1925: *Local government.* 1st Report of the Royal Commission, 1924–5, Cmd 2506, xiv.
1926: *Cross-river traffic in London.* Report of the Royal Commission, 1926, Cmd 2772, xiii.
1928: *Local government.* 2nd Report of the Royal Commission, 1928–9 Cmd 3213, viii.
1929: *Local government.* Final Report of the Royal Commission,

1929–30, Cmd 3436, xv.

1933: *Local government and public health consolidation.* Interim Report of the Committee, 1932–33, Cmd 4272, xiii.

1934: *Qualifications, recruitment, training and promotion of local government officers.* Report of the Departmental Committee, 1934, Non-Parl. Ministry of Health.

1936: *Local government and public health consolidation.* 2nd Interim Report of the Committee, 1935–6, Cmd 5059, xi.

1940: *Distribution of the industrial population.* Report of the Royal Commission, 1939–40, Cmd 6153, iv.

1942: *Social insurance and allied services.* Report of the Inter-Departmental Committee (Beveridge Report), 1942–3 Cmd 6404, vi.

1944: *Valuation for rates.* Report of the Departmental Committee, 1944, Non-Parl. Ministry of Health.

1945: *Local government in England and Wales during the period of reconstruction.* White Paper, 1944–5, Cmd 6579, x.

1946: *Care of children.* Report of the Inter-Departmental Committee, 1945–6, Cmd 6922, x.

1946: *New towns.* Interim Report of the Committee, 1945–6, Cmd 6759, xiv. 2nd Interim Report, 1945–6, Cmd 6794, xiv. Final Report, 1945–6, Cmd 6876, xiv.

1947: *Expenses of members of local authorities.* Report of the Inter-Departmental Committee, 1946–7, Cmd 7126, xiii.

1948: *Local Government Boundary Commission Report for 1947,* 1947–8 (86), xiii.

1949: *London planning administration.* Report of the Committee, 1949 Non-Parl. Ministry of Town and Country Planning.

1950: *Local government manpower.* 1st Report of the Committee, 1950, Cmd 7870, xiii.

1951: *Local government manpower.* 2nd Report of the Committee, 1951–2, Cmd 8421, xvi.

1956: *Areas and status of local authorities in England and Wales.* White Paper, 1955–6, Cmd 9831, xxxvi.

1956: *Cost of the National Health Service.* Report of the Committee, 1955–6, Cmd 9663, xx.

1956: *Health visiting.* Report of a Working Party, 1956, Non-Parl. Ministry of Health.

1957: *Functions of County Councils and County District Councils in England and Wales,* 1956–7, Cmnd 161, xxvi.

1957: *Law relating to mental illness and mental deficiency.* Report of the Royal Commission, 1956–7, Cmnd 169, xvi.

1957: *Local government finance. England and Wales.* White Paper, 1956–7, Cmnd 209, xxvi.

1959: *Report of the Ministry of Housing and Local Government 1958.* 1958–9, Cmnd 737, xv.

1959: *Socal workers in the local authority health and welfare services.* Report of the Working Party, 1959, Non-Parl. Ministry of Health.

1959: *Structure of the public library service in England and Wales.*

Report of the Committee, 1958–9, Cmnd 660, xvi.

1959: *Working of the monetary system.* Report of the Committee, 1958–9, Cmnd 827, xvii.

1960: *Children and young persons.* Report of the Committee, 1959–60, Cmnd 1191, ix.

1960: *Local government in Greater London.* Report of the Royal Commission, 1959–60, Cmnd 1164, xviii.

1960: *Youth service in England and Wales.* Report of the Committee, 1959–60, Cmnd 929, xxi.

1961: *Local Government Commission for Wales.* Draft proposals.

1961: *School building.* 8th Report from the Estimates Committee, 1960–61 (284), vi.

1962: *Police.* Final Report of the Royal Commission, 1961–2, Cmnd 1728, xx.

1963: *Local Government Commission for Wales.* Report and proposals for Wales, 1963, Non-Parl. Ministry of Housing and Local Government.

1963: *Traffic in towns.* Reports, 1963, Non-Parl. Ministry of Transport.

1965: *Impact of rates on households.* Report of the Committee, 1964–5, Cmnd 2582, xxii.

1965: *Bognor Regis Inquiry.* Report, HMSO, 1965.

1967: *Local government in Wales.* White Paper, 1966–67, Cmnd 3340, lix.

1967: *Management of local government.* Report of the Committee, 1967, Non-Parl. Ministry of Housing and Local Government.

1967: *Staffing of local government.* Report of the Committee, 1967, Non-Parl., Ministry of Housing and Local Government.

1968: *Local authority and allied personal social services.* Report of the Committee, 1967–8, Cmnd 3703, xxxii.

1969: *Local government in England.* Report of the Royal Commission, 1968–69, Cmnd 4040, xxxviii.

1969: *People and planning.* Report of the Committee, 1969, Non-Parl. Ministry of Housing and Local Government.

1970: *Reform of local government in England.* White Paper, 1969–70, Cmnd 4276, xviii.

1970: *Reorganisation of central government.* White Paper, 1970–1, Cmnd 4506, xx.

1971: *Future shape of local government finance.* Green Paper, 1970–1, Cmnd 4741, xxxii.

1971: *Local government in England.* Government proposals for re-organisation, 1970–1, Cmnd 4584, xxxii.

1971: *Reform of local government in Wales.* Consultative document, 1971, Non-Parl., Welsh Office.

1972: *New local authorities. Management and structure* (The Bains Report). 1972, Non-Parl. Department of the Environment.

1973: *Constitution.* Report of the Royal Commission, 1973–4, Cmnd 5460, xi.

GENERAL INDEX

Abercrombie, Sir Patrick 63
ad hoc authorities 35, 53, 202–3, 241
Adams, Sir Ryland 197
Addington Committee 34
Addison, 1st Viscount 163
aerodromes 39, 237
agency arrangements 235–6
Air Raid Precautions 33, 45–7, 164
Albemarle Committee 63
aldermen 23–4, 32, 98, 105–6, 107, 112, 120, 232
Aldridge, L. G. M. 197
Alexander, William P. (baron Alexander of Potterhill) 183, 187, 191
Allen Committee 141, 150, 151
allotments 37, 162
amenity societies 60, 240
animals, contagious diseases of 13, 35
areas, *see* boundaries
Areas and status of local authorities in England and Wales, White Paper 207
Armstrong, William (baron Armstrong of Sanderstead) 190
Arnold-Baker, Charles 187
art galleries 237
Ashton, Sir Hubert 97
Asquith, H. H. (1st Earl of Oxford and Asquith) 200
Association of County Councils 196
Association of District Councils 196
Association of Education Committees 158, 183, 187, 189, 191, 197, 243
Association of Mayors and ex-Mayors of Metropolitan Boroughs 180
Association of Metropolitan Authorities 196
Association of Municipal Corporations 23, 24, 31, 42, 55, 180, 181–2, 191, 211, 243; composition of 181–2; consitution of 185–6; government departments and 182, 185, 189, 190; reorganisation and 194–6, 203, 213, 214–5, 220, 229

associations of local authorities 20, 45, 60, 97, 106, 119, 170, 180–98, 213; as negotiating bodies 164, 176, 182, 184–5, 188–9; collaboration 193; conflicts amongst 183–4, 191–6, 203; government departments and 182, 184–5, 187–90; nomination to public bodies by 187–8; parliamentary activity 31, 55, 182, 185–8, 194; party politics and 185–6, 196; re-organisation and 191–6, 203, 206–7, 213, 214–15, 218, 219, 229, 232; unification attempts 194–6; *see also* under names of associations
asylums 13, 35, 69
Atkin, Lord Justice 81–2
Attlee, C. R., 1st Earl 169
Attorney-General v. De Winton 33
Attorney General v. Fulham Corporation 61
Attorney General v. Leeds Corporation 34
Attorney General v. Leicester Corporation 34, 178
Attorney General v. Manchester Corporation 39
Attorney General v. New South Wales Perpetual Trustee Co 33
Attorney General and the Board of Education v. the County Council of the West Riding 125
audit 153–7, 160; borough 153, 154–5; district 39, 153–7, 162; Poplar and 80–5; internal 156; professional 39, 155, 156, 157
Avebury, 1st Baron 61, 243

Bains Report 59, 107, 232, 241; *see also* management structures
Baker, C. E. and Lees, A. J. 182
Bankes, Lord Justice 81–2
banking services 36, 40
Banwell, Sir Harold 23, 181, 185, 187, 188, 243
Baring, Sir Godfrey 99
Barker, Anthony 64, 243
Barlow Commission 49

INDEX OF LEGISLATION